CHOICES in DEAFNESS

A Parents' Guide to Communication Options

Edited by Sue Schwartz, Ph.D.

WOODBINE HOUSE ▪ 1996

Second Edition

 Published in the United States of America by Woodbine House, Inc., 6510 Bells Mill Rd., Bethesda, MD 20817. 800-843-7323.

Cover Illustration by: Loel Barr

Library of Congress Cataloging-in-Publication Data

Schwartz, Sue
Choices in deafness : a parents' guide to communication options / edited by Sue Schwartz. — 2nd ed.
p. cm.
Includes bibliographical references and index.
ISBN 0-933149-85-9 (paper)
1. Deaf—Means of communication—United States—Case studies. 2. Children, Deaf—United States—Language—Case studies. 3. Children, Deaf—Services for—United States—Directories. 4. Hearing impaired children—Services for—United States—Directories. I. Schwartz, Sue.
HV2471.C46 1996
362.4'2'088054—dc20 96-19692
CIP

Manufactured in the United States of America

10 9 8 7 6 5 4 3 2 1

Dedication

To the parents of children who are deaf or hard of hearing.

To my colleagues in this exceptional field of deafness.

To the children who are deaf and hard of hearing who continue everyday to show us how outstanding and wonderful they are.

To all of you, I give my heartfelt love for being a part of my life for over thirty years.

Table of Contents

Acknowledgements

To the staff at Woodbine House, who have supported and encouraged the publication of this updated edition of *Choices.*

To my colleagues, who have shown me new and different ways to look at communication options.

To all of the contributors to this work, who have written and rewritten their work to meet the quality of excellence this book portrays.

To Jenny Isaman, who spent endless hours typing to help me complete this manuscript in a timely fashion.

To my friends, who have supported me in times of crisis and joy.

To my incredible family, who has endured more than any family should have to.

My deepest love to Sid, Debra, Jeff, and Barry.

Foreword

Sheila Doctors, M.A.

When *Choices in Deafness* was first published in 1987, it was a rare book in the field of education of deaf children. It was almost unheard of to find a book that did not represent one camp or another in the war between the manualists and the oralists. I was especially proud to write the foreword to the original *Choices* because of that.

It was exciting and refreshing to see in print an honest effort to present information about all three methodologies—total communication, oralism, and cued speech. *Choices* was willing to present the pros and cons of these important approaches, without bias, which trusted its readers to make their own decisions. And even rarer in this controversial field of deaf education, *Choices* trusted parents to tell their own stories. I have always felt that the great strength of *Choices* lay in the power of the parents' own voices, as they described their own personal choices for their children.

Much has happened in the years since *Choices* was first published. Many new developments have taken place, making the challenge of parent choice an even greater challenge in 1996 than it was in 1987. The Deaf Revolution took place on the Gallaudet University campus, bringing the excitement of the first Deaf president to that institution. Soon after, came a tremendous push for bilingual-bicultural education, emphasizing American Sign Language (ASL) and Deaf culture.

During the same decade, and just as revolutionary, we have seen remarkable developments in technology—especially the advent of multi-channel cochlear implants and FDA approval for cochlear implants in children as young as two. We have seen the introduction of behind-the-ear FM auditory trainers and digital hearing aids. With such technology, has come a resurgence of interest in auditory-verbal education.

It is clearly time for an update of *Choices in Deafness* and I am again proud to write the foreword for the updated version. I believe readers will find that the many new developments and new options in deafness are presented and explored just as thoroughly and just as objectively.

Perhaps the most exciting aspect of this updated version, however, is that the students profiled in the first edition have grown up. Now they tell their own stories. Because, as supervisor of their public school program for the deaf, I have known all of these wonderful young people personally, reading their stories has been an immeasurable joy for me. But you do not need to know them personally to be instantly swept up in their lives, in their successes, and in their own challenges and choices. Nothing could be more compelling or inspiring.

With the first edition of *Choices,* we anticipated that parents who were actually confronting decisions about how to educate their own deaf children would be the main readership. That has certainly proved true. Many, many parents have told us that *Choices* was the first book they read upon learning that their child was deaf. That will probably continue to be the readership for the new, updated *Choices,* too. Therefore, a word of caution: with choices, come headaches.

We know that it is always hard for parents to decide among the very disparate approaches for educating deaf children. Parents typically begin this process with little or no background in deaf education. Yet they, and they alone, must make this important choice. Today, with even more choices, the challenge will be even more daunting. And, unfortunately, there are many strident voices in this field who will also be advising parents.

Some will strongly emphasize the rightness of this, or the wrongness of that approach. Some will probably make the headache worse. It is my deepest hope that amidst the clatter, *Choices* will continue to provide a voice of reason, of balance, and above all, of hope. As you read the students' stories, you will see that, although their parents may have made different choices, the one choice they all made was to support their deaf child, unequivocally. The students' stories will convince you that with support, and love, and commitment from their parents and educators, children who are deaf really can do anything!

INTRODUCTION

SUE SCHWARTZ, PH.D.

When you first realize that you are going to become parents, you begin to fashion dreams about your new child. Your friends and family celebrate with you and contribute their own fantasies. Will he be as tall as Dad? Will she be as smart as Mom? Should we enroll him or her in law school, medical school, or business school?

As the waiting months go by, the two of you prepare for your newest family member by decorating the nursery, buying toys, and reading books. And everything is done with an eye to stimulating your baby's young and open mind. You discuss the advantages and disadvantages of home birth, birthing center, and hospital birth as avidly as you once debated political policies. At last your infant is born and you wait for your dreams to become reality.

Slowly, however, another reality begins to creep in. Comparisons with your friends' babies show some differences in your baby. What a sound sleeper he is! How noisy she is when she is awake! If your baby has brothers or sisters, you compare this new addition with your previous babies and there is a difference. But you aren't sure just what the difference is.

Fear becomes a part of your daily routine. There are the unspoken fears between husband and wife. Your defensive reactions to your family's well-meaning comments. As the fear grows, you finally begin to voice it. First you whisper your suspicions to each other, then you ask out loud. Does our baby hear? What is the matter? What do we do with our suspicions and fears? What do we do now?

Choices in Deafness gives you the facts you need and the explanations you must have in order to answer your questions, settle your fears, and start down the road to refashioning your dreams and building new expectations for your child. Many other parents have gone through what you are going through, and in this book they will tell you how they did it and what happened. They will also reassure you that your new reality can be as bright as the one you are leaving behind. One of the new additions to this edition of *Choices in Deafness* is an update from the students themselves as to what they have been doing during the years since their stories were told in the first edition of *Choices* published in 1987.

The book begins with a medical chapter describing what deafness is and how it is diagnosed. The next chapter discusses the audiological testing your child will undergo and how that relates to your child's educational program. A new chapter brings you the latest information on cochlear implants and explains how this procedure might be an option for your child. The book then discusses communication options that may be available in your area: Auditory Verbal Therapy, Bilingual Bicultural Education, Cued Speech, Oral, and Total Communication. These options are presented in alphabetical order, so as not to imply a preference toward one or the other.

New to this edition is the chapter on Auditory Verbal Therapy. Although this therapeutic approach has been in existence for many years, the new developments in hearing aid technology and the increased use of cochlear implants have made this approach more practical than it was before, since it is highly dependent on a strong auditory component.

The chapter on Bilingual-Bicultural education is also new to this edition. The use of American Sign Language (ASL) in the education of individuals who are deaf has been discussed for years and years. However, the impetus for this new movement was the student protest at Gallaudet University in March of 1988. At that time, the board of directors of the University was comprised predominantly of hearing people. The opportunity arose to elect a new president of the University. There were three candidates, all highly qualified and two of whom were deaf. The board chose the only hearing candidate among the three. The students rose up in protest, closed the campus for a week, got full-scale media attention, and eventually were successful in obtaining a deaf president for the University. This gave deaf individuals a power that was unprecedented and led to a renewed interest in deaf culture and the language of the deaf, American Sign Language. Since 1988, nine programs across the nation have adopted a Bilingual-Bicultural approach to the education of students who are Deaf, so the method has been included here. (In the past, deaf students typically learned to communicate using one of the other methods described in this book, and only later learned to use ASL. ASL was not generally used as the first communication method for young children.)

Cued Speech, Oral, and Total Communication were presented in the first edition of *Choices* and remain viable options today. These systems are discussed from a professional perspective, as well as from the viewpoints of parents and the students themselves.

A very important addition to this edition is the viewpoint from a deaf adult, Jack R. Gannon, who can speak clearly about Deaf Culture as it is today. We feel this is a valuable contribution from a well-respected member of the Deaf Community.

At the end of the book there is a reading list so that you can find other books to help you, a directory of organizations that serve the deaf, and an index to help you find information within this book. An appendix, new to this edition, briefly describes the various types of sign systems that are in use today.

A STEP–BY–STEP OUTLINE OF WHAT TO DO

Once you have decided to check out your suspicions that your child has a hearing loss, the very first step is to take her to visit your pediatrician.

VISITING THE PEDIATRICIAN

At this visit, you should explain clearly what your concerns are and what you have seen with your child. Try to make up a list of times that you have noticed that she doesn't respond to sound and bring this list with you. As difficult as it may be, try to share all of the information that you have about your child. You are the one who knows the most about her normal behavior. Your pediatrician should listen carefully to you and ask some specific questions. "When did she crawl, sit up, walk, etc.?" Then he needs to thoroughly examine your child to see if all of her developmental milestones are being met. He may even try to do some general testing of your daughter's hearing. However, most pediatricians do not have the sophisticated equipment needed to do this accurately.

At this point, your pediatrician should acknowledge your concerns and may suggest an evaluation by an ear specialist. If he does not, and you are still concerned, ask for the name of an otolaryngologist (ear-nose-throat doctor) in your area. If your doctor doesn't know of one or does not feel it is necessary, call a local hospital and ask for the name of an ear, nose, and throat specialist.

Visiting the Ear, Nose, and Throat Specialist

When you visit this specialist you should, once again, have your list of concerns with you. Update this list as necessary. The otolaryngologist will examine your child's outer ear structure and middle ear structure to determine if there is a problem that he is able to see. In most cases, he will not see anything wrong with the structure of the ear and will ask you to go for a complete hearing evaluation. He should be able to recommend a hearing testing facility in your area. If he is not familiar with a facility in your area that tests hearing, you can call a local hospital, the health department for your county or district, or a local university. These places often have special equipment for testing hearing or can refer you to a place that does.

■ Visiting the Hearing Testing Facility

At the hearing testing facility, you and your child will go into a soundproof room. This is usually a very small room and you may feel a bit uncomfortable. It is important that you try to relax as much as you can so that your child does not sense your feelings and become tense. An audiologist—the professional who will test your child's hearing—will first talk to you for a few minutes to find out some of your child's history. By now, you are an old hand at the history-taking session and have your notes and lists with you. As tiresome as it may seem, each professional will need to ask you many of the same questions and if you are prepared, the interview will go much more quickly.

After the interview, the audiologist may leave you and go into another section of the soundproof room. You may or may not be able to see her through a mirror. In any case, she can see you through her side of the mirror. She has a machine in her room called an audiometer which will produce many sounds of different tones and different loudnesses. She will make these sounds and watch to see if your child reacts in any way to them. She can control how loud and soft these sounds are. It is important that you realize that she will only keep making the sounds louder if your child does *not* respond at the softer tones. Therefore, even though the sounds may seem especially loud to you, they will not be that loud to your child. If your child is able to tolerate wearing earphones, each ear may be tested separately. If not, a lot of information can be obtained by seeing how your child responds using both ears.

After testing all of the different tones, the audiologist may use some familiar conversation to see if your child responds to speech sounds. She may say, "Hi, baby," "Where's Mommy?" or other phrases familiar to children who are able to hear.

If your child is an infant or for other reasons is unable to respond to these sounds, a special testing session will be scheduled so that a Brainstem Evoked Response test can be administered. This test and other common hearing tests are explained in more detail in Chapter Two.

At the end of the testing session, the audiologist will explain the findings of her testing. It is a good idea to take your spouse or a friend with you because if you are going to hear unpleasant news, it is best to have someone who may be able to ask some of the questions you forget in the stress of the moment.

If the testing has confirmed that your child has a hearing loss, the audiologist will suggest that you contact an educational program in your area. She will also suggest that you make another appointment so that different hearing aids can be tried with your child to see which one gives her the most amplification. Try to do this on a different day because by now both you and your child will probably be very tired and have already had to absorb a lot in one day. If the audiologist is not aware of educational programs for deaf children in your area, you can call the local school system and they will tell you what is available. If they do not have a program for children your child's age, you can call the national organizations for the deaf. A list of these is in the resource section at the end of this book. These organizations will be able to help you find a program close to you.

The Hearing Aid

The audiologist at the hearing center will be able to suggest the kind of hearing aid that your child should wear. (See Chapter Two for a detailed explanation of what types of hearing aids there are and how they work.) She can refer you to a hearing aid dealer who will sell you the hearing aid or she may be able to sell you the aid herself. Often when a young child is diagnosed with a hearing loss, it is advisable to wait several months, and sometimes longer, before buying your own hearing aids. Sometimes, it is not clear in the beginning exactly what kind of amplification your child will need. Ask your center about the possibility of loaner aids while you are still evaluating the exact nature of your child's loss. In the meantime, you can call around and check on the prices of the hearing aids you are considering to see where you can get a good price. Prices can vary a great deal.

By now you are probably wondering where you will get the money to pay for the devices your child will need. The first thing to do is to check your health insurance policy. Then ask the hearing aid dealer about financial assistance plans that they may offer. Remember to include the cost of a warranty and repair costs in your calculations.

Once you have the hearing aid, make sure the hearing aid dealer or audiologist explains to you how the aid works and how to take care of it. It is also important for you to understand that once you have purchased a hearing aid for your child, your expenses do not end. For your child to wear the hearing aid, she must have a custom-fitted earmold made especially for her. The price of earmolds also varies and you will want to ask about the price while you are with the dealer. It is also important for you to know that your child will need new earmolds as she grows. As the rest of her body grows, so will her ear canal and if the earmold does not fit properly, it will give off a squealing noise caused by feedback from the hearing aid. It is also important for you to realize that hearing aids run on batteries and this is an additional ongoing expense. How often you change the batteries depends on how long your child wears the aid. In general, full-time users of hearing aids change their batteries about every two weeks. Some audiologists and school systems have plans to help you buy batteries in bulk and thereby save some money.

It is often very difficult for people to understand how a hearing aid works. We are very familiar with corrective glasses. We know that when we put on glasses, we are usually able to see clearly. This is not the case with a hearing aid, particularly if your child has a sensorineural hearing loss. The hearing aid will make the sound louder for your child but not clearer. (There is more discussion about this in Chapter 2.)

Once you own a hearing aid, you should plan to report back to the testing facility at least once a year for regular checks of how the aid is working and how it is helping your child. Some educational programs for the deaf have an Educational Audiologist on the staff. Have this professional regularly check on how well the aid is working for your child.

Your child may not like wearing the hearing aids in the beginning. Naturally they feel a little strange in her ears. First, the fit of the earmold will feel different and second, she will be hearing sounds for the first time and not be aware of what they are. Be patient. She will get used to them in time. If you're lucky, your child will take to the aids readily and never have a minute of trouble wearing them. If, however, you do run into problems, try this plan. First and most importantly, decide for yourself that these hearing aids are important. Treat them as if they are medicine that she must take for an illness. You would not allow her to control whether she takes that medicine or not. So, first your attitude must be to accept this as part of her normal, everyday routine. Try introducing this addition to her daily routine in just that matter-of-fact manner. She gets up, gets dressed, and puts on her hearing aid.

If this little routine doesn't go quite so smoothly, try a different approach. Start with mealtime or a favorite story time. The time you pick should be a time when you can give your child your undivided attention. Put the hearing aid into her ear and immediately feed her, play with a toy with her, or read her a story. After one or two minutes when she has kept her hearing aid in, *you* take it out. Do this three or four times in the next half hour, each time telling her how proud you are that she is wearing the aid. Speak to her even if you don't think she understands your words. You can show her by your expression and actions that you are pleased with her. Repeat this activity as many times during the day as you are able. Remember, you must be able to give her your undivided attention at these times. By the end of a week, if you are consistent and positive, your child should be wearing her hearing aids all the time. Soon it will be an established part of her routine and neither of you will give it another thought!

THE EDUCATIONAL PROGRAM

While you and your child are adjusting to her hearing aid, you will need to look into enrolling her in an educational program. A hearing loss that is greater than 25 decibels (dB) will seriously affect the learning of language and speech. (See Chapter 2 for a discussion of how hearing losses are measured.) This is why it is imperative that you enroll in a program that specializes in working with students who are deaf.

As a parent, you should know that there is a federal law entitled IDEA or Individuals with Disabilities Education Act which guarantees a free and appropriate education for all students with disabilities, including deaf students. The word "free" means just that: all components of your child's educational program must be provided at no cost to the families of students who qualify. The term "appropriate" is generally interpreted to mean that the education provided is individually designed to meet the needs of the child. Unfortunately, it does not necessarily mean that it is the best possible program, or even comparable to the education provided students who do not have disabilities. Understandably, the term "appropriate" has come under much discussion, particularly as it applies to students who are deaf. For some programs, the term "appropriate" is interpreted as "adequate," so that if a child who is deaf is earning "Cs" in class, the program is considered adequate.

There has been much debate over these issues and many lawsuits have been filed regarding the provisions of IDEA. For help understanding these issues, you may want to find the excellent book entitled *Federal Disability Law in a Nutshell* by Bonnie Tucker, which is listed in the Reading List. If you have further questions, the National Association of the Deaf operates a Deaf Law Center. Contact information can be found in Appendix C.

To qualify for special educational services, your child must be determined to have an "educationally significant hearing loss." Each program defines what an educationally significant hearing loss is, so you will want to check with the programs you are considering having your child attend. The audiologist will be able to help you find programs that might be suitable.

If your child qualifies, she will be given instruction individually designed for her unique learning strengths and needs. By law, she must also receive any "related services" (such as speech therapy or counseling) that are needed for her to benefit from her educational program.

As a parent, you have a right to meet with school personnel to discuss the services you feel your child needs, as well as to discuss the goals you want her to be working on. For example, you may want her to learn fifty new words and to begin using three-word sentences. To help her meet those goals, you may ask the school to provide a variety of special services.

By law, these services must be provided in the *least restrictive environment*. Generally speaking, the "least restrictive environment" is interpreted as being the classroom that gives a child maximum freedom while still allowing her to reach her learning goals. Where it comes to the education of deaf students, the term is defined in many ways by different people. Some people feel that the child's neighborhood school provides the least restrictive environment, while others feel that a school only for deaf children provides the least restrictive environment. In many communities, there are other options as well, such as center programs for deaf children that are provided in the environment of regular education schools. Some programs are residential and some are day programs. There are many options in most areas of the country and you will have to decide which is the best for your deaf child and your family.

In Kathryn Meadow's book, *Deafness and Child Development,* a comparison is made between residential and day class settings for deaf students. She writes that day classes allow the deaf student to live at home with her family and enjoy the benefits that implies. Having your child in a day program close to home gives you the opportunity to be more closely involved in her education. However, a deaf student is a minority in a day setting. Often age range and academic levels in this program vary widely. Many of the teachers in day classes are hearing; therefore deaf role models are not readily available.

In a school for the deaf, your child might live in a dormitory with other deaf students. Some residential programs accept students as young as three years of age and there is some discussion about lowering that age to two. If you live close enough to the school, your child could also be a day student there. There are pros and cons of living at school and living at home, so you will want to consider the options carefully. If your child is a residential student, she will be separated from her family, which can create a sense of isolation. On the other hand, she will have an opportunity to create a place for herself in the deaf community. There are usually many deaf teachers, counselors, and administrators who give the students adult role models to emulate. With more deaf students of similar ages, it may be possible to have more homogeneous academic placements. That is, your child will not be placed with much older or younger students with widely varying abilities just because they are the only deaf students in the school.

The trend seems to be toward fewer residential schools and more day schools and classes. Some programs may offer choices within the same community and assist you in making these choices, while others may refer you to other programs. One source of information is the April issue of the *American Annals of the Deaf* which annually lists many programs for the deaf in the United States and Canada. Other sources are listed in the Resource Guide at the end of this book.

Before you make a decision, see what is available in your area. You may live in an area that has only one or two programs. You need to visit each program and see how it actually runs. As emphasized in the chapters about the different communication methods, programs vary and staff training varies. You must see for yourself. You will be able to "feel" whether the program is right for you. Go with those feelings until you begin to "feel" a need to change for any reason. Trust your feelings. Ask for support from your child's educational team. Remember, you know your child best and you will be coordinating the decisions on her future growth.

Once you and the school personnel agree on goals for your child, the services needed to help her reach those goals, and the setting where your child should receive her instruction, this information will be recorded in a written document. If your child is birth to age two, the document will be called an Individualized Family Service Plan (IFSP); if she is between three and twenty-one, the document will be called an Individualized Education Program (IEP). Under IDEA, the school system is required to follow your child's IEP or IFSP in providing her educational services.

When you enroll in a program, keep in mind that it will take a while for your youngster to begin to be able to use her hearing or understand the signs, cues, or lipreading. Remember that a hearing child does not begin to talk until close to one year of age. Your deaf child will need at least that long to listen once she has her hearing aids. Often it will take longer than that before you notice that she is understanding what you are saying.

Once your child is enrolled in an educational program and has appropriate hearing aids, you may think you can sit back and rest. Not so! When you have read the parents' and students' stories in this book, you will know that each of you has a lot of hard work ahead. Whatever communication method you decide on, you will have to become involved in the school program to know what to work on and how to help your child. Most school staff will welcome your involvement. Get to know them. Use them as resources. If you can volunteer your time, the rewards for both you and your child will be enormous.

SPEECH AND LANGUAGE

Critical language learning takes place during a child's first three years. When your child has a hearing loss, it significantly affects the way in which she will acquire language and subsequently, speech. As your child's first, and most important, teacher, you will need support during this crucial time to help you know how to maximize language learning. Fortunately, more and more professionals are recognizing and responding to this need. In 1994, most early intervention programs that served deaf children reported having parent infant programming that was both home- and school-based. That is, school personnel visited the families of deaf children in their homes, in addition to providing instruction within a school setting.

In fact, the need for parent support continues beyond the infant years. Crucial decisions need to be made as deaf students advance in school. Perhaps other learning needs may become apparent as your child gets older and starts learning academic information. Perhaps there may be a fluctuation in her hearing loss which requires different amplification. Perhaps you may feel there is a need to change the communication option you originally chose. You will need support to make these decisions, as well as to cope with other concerns that having a deaf child brings all through the school years. Some educational programs even have parent support personnel on staff.

It is very hard to know exactly how to judge your child's progress in the development of speech and language. Each child is a unique individual with her own special skills. I urge you to look only at your child. Avoid the temptation to compare her to her brothers, sisters, cousins, or other children in the program. Keep a list of words *she* learns. Notice that she seems to understand more this week than last week. Notice that her behavior is a lot calmer now than it used to be. See her for the child *she* is. She is not like anyone else. She will develop language and speech just as quickly as her own system will allow.

Conclusion

You have just begun the very challenging job of raising and helping to educate your deaf child. You will find many moments of despair and many more moments of joy when your child learns a word or concept. One of the best presents you can give yourself is to join a local or national parents' group that can give you the support and guidance that you need for the valleys and mountains of your life with your deaf child. The educational program that you are in will be able to help you find such a parent group. Some national parent organizations are listed in the Resource Guide at the end of this book. Some programs have a professional on staff who is available to help you, just as there are professionals on staff to help your child. Reach out and become involved. Both you and your child will benefit.

1

A Medical Approach to Hearing Loss

Stephen Epstein, M.D.

Introduction

The more you know about your child's hearing loss, the better you will be able to contribute to his growth. You, as parents, are the ones who create the basic foundation for your child's acceptance of his hearing loss and his motivation for achievement. This chapter will therefore acquaint you with the possible causes of hearing loss in children and the medical approach that can be used to diagnose a hearing loss. This is the same basic information that enables your physician to diagnose a hearing loss as *early as possible,* so that *early* intervention and treatment can be started to allow your child's thinking skills, speech and language, and educational abilities to develop.

Were you aware that deafness in children still occurs in significant numbers today? Approximately one tenth of one percent of all newborns, or about 4,000 children, are born profoundly deaf each year in the United States alone. This means that they can't hear even the loudest sounds without amplification. Another 10-15 percent of newborns demonstrate a partial hearing loss that is also educationally significant.

When a child has an undetected or untreated hearing loss, it interferes with thinking skills and speech and language development. As a result, his progress in school will be delayed. What is most surprising is that even today, with all the modern medical and audiological techniques available, an educationally significant hearing loss may still go undiagnosed in a child as late as six years of age! It is important to obtain the diagnosis as early as possible so that intervention and treatment can begin right away.

FIGURE 1. THE ANATOMY OF THE EAR AND CRITERIA BY WHICH HEARING LOSS IS CLASSIFIED

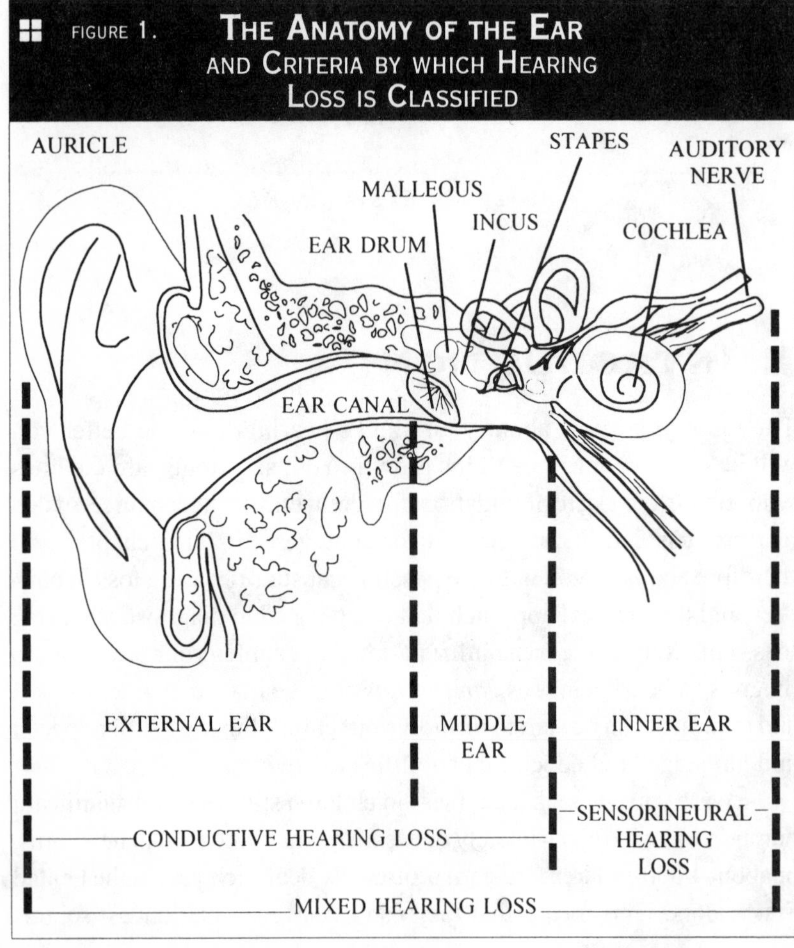

How We Hear

Sound travels through the air in the form of waves of varying frequencies (speed of vibration). The frequencies of these waves determine the pitches of the sounds that we hear. The sound waves are channelled into the external ear canal, where they are then transmitted to the middle ear. (See Figure 1.) The middle ear, consisting of the eardrum and the three small bones in the middle ear cavity, serves primarily as an amplifying system. This is essential to compensate for the loss of the intensity of sound as it travels from the air medium of the middle ear to a fluid medium within the inner ear or cochlea.

In the inner ear or cochlea, sound travels as waves of fluid to a specific area depending on the frequency of the sound. The fluid movement then causes a tiny, flexible structure called the tectorial membrane (see Figure 2, p. 4) to vibrate against the hair cells. This stimulates the auditory nerve, which transmits the sound stimuli to the auditory center in the brain. Here the components that make up the sound and speech we hear are coordinated and sent to higher centers of the brain for interpretation.

How Hearing Losses Are Classified

Hearing loss can be classified three different ways: 1) based on location of the disease within the ear; 2) based on the onset of the hearing loss in relation to speech and language development; 3) based on the cause of the disease within the ear. Table 1 on page 5 shows these classifications in outline form; the next sections explain them in more detail.

Classification Based on the Location of Disease within the Ear

Your child's hearing loss can be classified into three basic types depending on the location of the disease within the ear.

Conductive Hearing Loss. A conductive hearing loss results when a problem that originates with the outer ear or middle ear prevents or impedes sound from being *conducted* to the inner ear. Figure 1 shows that the external ear consists of the auricle (the outer portion of the ear) and the ear canal. The middle ear consists of the ear drum, the middle ear cavity and the three bones: the malleus, incus, and stapes. A conductive hearing loss can stem from an abnormality of development, such as the absence or incomplete

FIGURE 2.

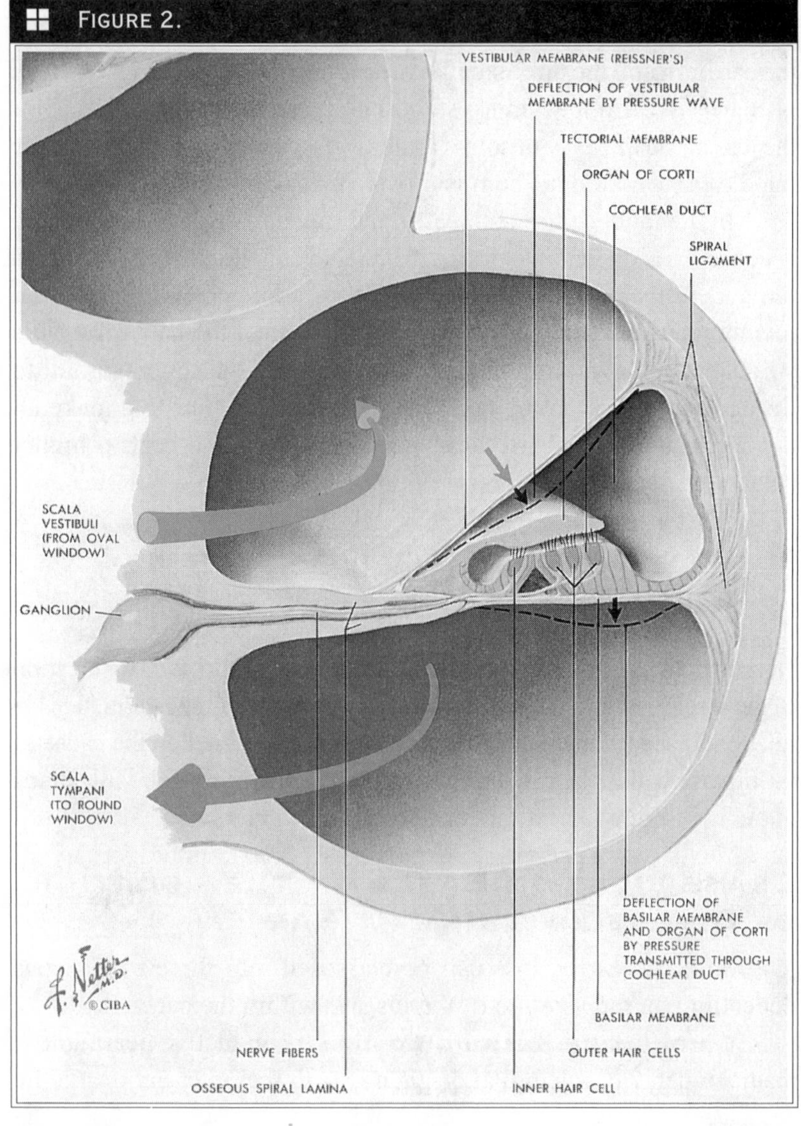

TABLE 1. SIMPLIFIED CLASSIFICATION OF HEARING LOSS

1. BASED ON THE LOCATION OF THE DISEASE WITHIN EAR
   - A. Conductive Hearing Loss
   - B. Sensorineural Hearing Loss
   - C. Mixed Hearing Loss
2. BASED ON THE ONSET OF HEARING LOSS IN RELATIONSHIP TO SPEECH DEVELOPMENT
   - A. Prelingual
   - B. Postlingual
3. BASED ON THE CAUSE OF THE HEARING LOSS
   - A. Genetic Hearing Loss
   - B. Nongenetic Hearing Loss

formation of a part of the external or middle ear system (for example, the ear canal or one of the bones in the middle ear). The problem can also be caused by disease within the external ear or the middle ear such as severe and continuous otitis media (inflammation of the middle ear often accompanied by fluid buildup). This type of hearing loss can generally be corrected by medical or surgical means so that hearing is permanently restored.

SENSORINEURAL HEARING LOSS. A sensorineural hearing loss results from an abnormality of development or disease affecting the cochlea—the organ that converts sound waves to electrical energy—or the auditory nerve—which transmits the sound stimuli in the form of electrical impulses to the auditory center of the brain. In general, sensorineural hearing loss cannot be treated by current medical or surgical techniques because there is permanent damage to the inner ear or auditory nerve. There are, however, several causes of sensorineural hearing losses that can be treated. These include sudden onset of blockage of circulation or infection within the inner ear, auto-immune disease (the body's reaction to its own tissue), a perilymphatic fistula (a leak of inner ear fluid), Meniere's Syndrome (a buildup of inner ear fluid), and tumors of the auditory nerve (acoustic neuroma). In these conditions, sensorineural hearing loss may improve *if* medical or surgical treatment is begun *before* permanent damage occurs.

Mixed Hearing Loss. A mixed hearing loss involves both a sensorineural and conductive component. The conductive part of a mixed loss may be treated by medical or surgical means, depending on the type of disease present and the percentage of the total hearing loss it may represent.

The doctor who diagnoses your child's hearing loss should be able to tell you whether your child has a conductive hearing loss or a sensorineural hearing loss that may be treatable, based on his medical examination and a complete evaluation of your child's hearing.

Classification Based on the Onset of the Hearing Loss in Relation to Speech and Language Development

A prelingual hearing loss is one which is present prior to speech and language development. A postlingual hearing loss develops after speech and language development has begun or has been completed, which could be between the second and sixth year. In general, the longer a child has had normal hearing, the more chance he has of maintaining that knowledge of the language he has developed.

Classification Based on the Cause of the Disease within the Ear

As illustrated in Table 1, hearing loss in children can be simply classified as genetic or nongenetic.

Genetic Hearing Loss

A genetic hearing loss is one caused by the presence of an abnormal gene within one of our forty-six chromosomes. Genes are the bits of chemical material that determine our physical, intellectual, and other traits—including eye color, body build, and shape and function of ear structures. They are located on the chromosomes, rod-shaped bodies found in the nucleus of the cells in our body. Ordinarily, children have 46 chromosomes in every cell—23 inherited from their mother, and 23 from their father.

A genetic hearing loss is one caused by the presence of an abnormal gene within one or more of our chromosomes. This abnormal gene may have been passed on by either one or both of the parents or it may have developed as the result of a spontaneous mutation or change during fetal development. About 30 percent of all children born with or who develop an early onset hearing loss have a genetic type of hearing loss.

About 70 percent of children born with a genetic hearing loss have developed the hearing loss because they inherited the same abnormal gene from each parent. These are the *autosomal recessive* conditions. The abnormal gene does not affect the child's hearing unless he inherits it from both parents. If he inherits the abnormal gene from one parent and the normal gene from the other, the normal gene will override the abnormal gene and his hearing will not be affected. He can, however, pass the abnormal gene on to her own children.

Parents of children with autosomal recessive types of hearing loss may both have normal hearing. This would be the case if they each had one normal and one abnormal gene. But each of their children would usually have a 25 percent chance of having a hearing loss. This is because each child has the possibility of inheriting either 1) one normal gene from each parent (and so would have normal hearing), 2) a normal gene from the mother and an abnormal one from the father (and so would have normal hearing but could pass the abnormal gene on), 3) an abnormal gene from the mother and a normal one from the father, or 4) an abnormal gene from each parent (and so would have a hearing loss). This type of hearing loss may be absent in several generations within a family, as it only shows up when two people with the same abnormal recessive gene marry and have children.

About 30 percent of children born with a genetic hearing loss have developed the hearing loss as the result of an *autosomal dominant* gene. In contrast to recessive genes, dominant genes override normal genes. If a child inherits a normal gene from one parent and an abnormal gene from the other, she *will* be affected by the abnormal gene. With the presence of an autosomal dominant gene, usually one parent has a hearing loss, and there is over a 50 percent chance that their children will have a hearing loss. This type of hearing loss is usually present in more than one family member and is usually present in most generations.

It is also possible that a mutation or defect in a gene may occur within a family so that their children may be the first members of an extended family to develop a hearing loss, with or without other organ system abnormalities. This explains why there are certain families with more than one child with a hearing loss and no other family history of hearing loss going back several generations.

In about two-thirds of children with genetic type hearing losses, the hearing loss is the only problem (Non Syndromic Hearing Loss). In about one-third of children, there are also problems in other parts of the body (Syndromic Hearing Loss). See Table 2 on pages 13–16 for examples of Syndromic and Non Syndromic Conditions.

Nongenetic Hearing Loss

A nongenetic hearing loss is one caused by an event resulting in incomplete or abnormal development of the ear structures prior to birth or producing damage to the fully developed ear structures during the immediate birth period or sometime after birth. There are no abnormal genes present, and, therefore, there is no chance of transmitting a nongenetic hearing loss to future generations. This type of hearing loss occurs in about 70 percent of children born with a hearing loss.

The classification in Table 2 on pages 13–16 has been simplified to include only the most common conditions related to hearing loss in children. It does not include x-linked or sex gene related hearing loss, which occurs in about 2 percent of children born with a genetic type of hearing loss. These types of hearing loss occur as the result of an abnormal gene on the sex chromosomes—the pair of chromosomes that determine whether a child is male or female. (All other genetic conditions are carried in the *autosomes*—the chromosomes that determine traits other than gender.)

■ The Medical Evaluation

Right from birth, there are medical and audiological evaluations you can ask for that will help you decide whether your baby has a hearing loss. Some are listed here as a guide for you, but check with your pediatrician to make sure that your child is getting a complete evaluation. Explain your concern to him and enlist his help. If you feel that your worries are not being taken into consideration, ask for another opinion, especially with a physician who specializes in disorders of the ear and hearing.

INDICATORS FOR HEARING LOSS IN CHILDREN

If your child is a newborn, you should become familiar with the list of indicators for hearing loss in children. These include the most common factors that can place a baby "at risk" for a hearing loss and should be a red flag to you and your child's doctor. It has been demonstrated that newborns with one or more of these factors have a higher than normal incidence of hearing loss. If your child has a history of one or more of the following factors, insist that your pediatrician evaluate him as early as possible.

1. **FAMILY HISTORY OF A HEARING LOSS**—This is usually a genetic type hearing loss which is usually present in parents, siblings, or close relatives. It is important to stress that a family history is important in order to diagnose a genetic hearing loss since testing for the presence of abnormal genes is not currently available. It is important when evaluating a family history for hearing loss that you go back at least three generations since, as it has been illustrated, an autosomal recessive hearing loss may not be present in all generations.

2. **HISTORY OF MATERNAL ILLNESS OR MATERNAL OTOTOXIC DRUG INTAKE**—as illustrated in Table 2.

3. **LOW BIRTH WEIGHT**—under 3.3 pounds or 1500 grams.

4. **PRESENCE OF OTHER HEAD, FACIAL, OR EXTERNAL EAR ABNORMALITIES**—as illustrated in Table 2.

5. **PROLONGED NEONATAL JAUNDICE**—especially when the newborn requires *exchange transfusion* (its blood must be completely replaced due to a reaction of the mother's blood and the baby's blood because of a different blood type). For example, the mother is Rh(+) and the baby is Rh(-) or the mother is Type A and the baby is Type B.

6. Poor APGAR Rating—as illustrated in Table 2.

7. Admission to Newborn Intensive Care Unit—because of items 3 and 6 associated with insufficient functioning of major organ systems such as the heart and lungs and requiring ventilation for more than five days.

8. Parental or Caregiver Concern about Hearing and Speech Development—Only 50 percent of children born with a hearing loss have any of the indicators listed above. Therefore, if you are concerned, that is sufficient grounds for requesting that your child's hearing be tested even though no indicators are present.

It is important to stress at this point that you should suspect a hearing loss if: 1) your child demonstrated, at birth, one or more factors from the List of Indicators; or 2) as your child gets older, he demonstrates poor speech and language development, poor behavior and personality characteristics, and poor school performance. Any time you, or anyone who knows your child well, express concern about your child's hearing, this alone is an indication for further evaluation.

Steps in Evaluating a Possible Hearing Loss

The first step in evaluating a possible hearing loss is the medical examination. During the first part of this examination, the doctor will ask you questions so that he can put together a complete history.

Taking a History

The doctor will begin by gathering information about your family's history. As mentioned earlier, the family history should go back at least three generations and involve as many members of your family, including adults and siblings, as possible.

Next, the doctor will ask questions about the mother's overall health and record of pregnancy and delivery. He will want to know whether there were any medical problems during pregnancy, such as diabetes, hypothyroidism, or syphilis. A thorough investigation of any illness or ototoxic drug intake during pregnancy is also important. I want to stress again that the absence of any external signs and symptoms of illness during pregnancy does not entirely rule out the possibility of an illness. It is also essential for the doctor to ask questions about the actual delivery and birth, since fetal distress, poor fetal oxygenation, and poor vital signs at birth (low APGAR rating) can all cause hearing loss. The doctor will also need to know your child's birth weight.

As part of the evaluation, be sure to mention whether your baby had prolonged jaundice after birth, especially requiring exchange transfusion because of blood incompatibility. Remember, a hearing loss can result if there are high levels of bilirubin—the byproduct of the breakdown of red blood cells—causing jaundice in a newborn.

All of the above conditions have the potential to produce damage to the inner ear hair cells with resulting sensorineural hearing loss.

Physical Exam

After the history is completed, the doctor will give your child a complete physical. During the physical, the doctor should examine different parts of your child's body to check for various syndromes associated with hearing loss.

Make sure your physician completely examines your child for the following:

1. **Facial and external ear abnormalities**—special X-rays, including CAT scanning of the ears, may be necessary to evaluate the middle and inner ear.

2. **Craniofacial anomalies**—X-rays of the head, face, and neck should be made to rule out craniofacial defects.

3. **Thyroid gland**—your child should be examined for an enlarged thyroid gland, which is associated with hearing loss in Pendred syndrome.

4. **Cardiovascular system**—an electrocardiogram should be administered to determine whether there are certain abnormalities of the heartbeat which are associated with hearing loss in Jervell-Lange Nielsen Syndrome.

5. **Kidney and genitourinary system abnormalities**—kidney and urinary function studies should be performed, as abnormalities may be a sign of Alport syndrome or Bronchio-Oto-Renal syndrome.

LABORATORY TESTS

Blood tests and urine tests of both the mother and the newborn should be completed. These tests can confirm whether the mother had an illness during pregnancy that could lead to a hearing loss in her child. The illnesses that will be tested for include rubella, toxoplasmosis, syphilis, herpes, and cytomegalovirus. Blood and urine testing in the newborn is especially reliable in identifying cytomegalovirus infection.

CONCLUSION

As this chapter has emphasized, an *early* diagnosis of a hearing loss is vital so that your infant or child can begin receiving the help he needs as soon as possible. If your child has any of the factors on The List of Indicators for Hearing Loss, you should request a medical workup to determine whether he has a hearing loss. Remember, however, that only 50 percent of children born with a hearing loss have any indicators. Therefore, if you, another family member, or anyone associated with your child suspects that your child may not be hearing well, *insist* that his hearing be tested no matter how many different steps you have to take. If you talk to parents or caretakers of children who were born with a hearing loss, their early suspicion of the hearing loss was usually the single most reliable indicator.

REFERENCES

"Advances in the Genetics of Deafness." (1995) *Boys Town National Research Hospital Bulletin of HHIRR.* Vol. 1, No. 2. Spring.

Gorlin, R.S., Toriello, H.V., Cohen, M.M. (1995) *Hereditary Hearing Loss and Its Syndromes.* New York: Oxford University Press.

Grundfast, K.M. (1993) "Hereditary Hearing Impairment in Children." *Advances in Otolaryngology - Head and Neck Surgery.* Vol. 7. Mosby Yearbook, Inc.

Joint Committee on Infant Hearing. (1994) "Position Statement." *Bulletin American Academy of Otolaryngology - Head and Neck Surgery.* Vol. 13, No. 12. December.

Netter, F. (1970) *Clinical Symposium.* Vol. 22. November 2. Ciba Pharmaceutical Company. Plate IV.

TABLE 2. CAUSES OF HEARING LOSS

I. GENETIC HEARING LOSS—caused by the presence of an abnormal gene; present in approximately 30 percent of all children who are born with a hearing loss or develop early onset hearing loss

A. SYNDROMIC HEARING LOSS—associated with other organ system abnormalities—present in approximately 1/3 of children born with genetic hearing loss

1. AUTOSOMAL DOMINANT HEARING LOSS—at least one parent has a hearing loss, and there is a 50% chance the offspring will acquire a hearing loss. Hearing loss usually present in most generations

ASSOCIATED WITH SENSORINEURAL HEARING LOSS
(A more detailed description of these syndromes can be found in reference 2 at the end of the chapter.)

A) WAARDENBURG SYNDROME—associated with pigmentary changes of the hair and eyes (i.e. white forelock and two different colored irises) and wide space between eyes

B) ALPORT SYNDROME—associated with abnormal function of the kidneys (may also be the result of an abnormal x chromosome)

C) NEUROFIBROMATOSIS II—associated with bilateral tumors of the auditory nerve and nodular growths on the skin

ASSOCIATED WITH A CONDUCTIVE OR MIXED TYPE (CONDUCTIVE AND SENSORINEURAL) HEARING LOSS

A) TREACHER COLLINS SYNDROME—hearing loss associated with differences of the mid–facial area and external ears

B) CROUZON SYNDROME—hearing loss associated with bulging eyes, underdevelopment of midface, and recessed jaws

C) BRONCHIO–OTO–RENAL SYNDROME—hearing loss associated with pit formations in front of ears, a cyst under the skin along the side of the neck, which is a residual of embryonic development, and poor development of the kidneys

D) OSTEOGENESIS IMPERFECTA—hearing loss associated with thin bone formation all over body and stapes fixation

2) AUTOSOMAL RECESSIVE HEARING LOSS—both parents may have normal hearing, and there is a 25% chance that the offspring will develop a hearing loss. Hearing loss may not be present in all generations

ASSOCIATED WITH SENSORINEURAL HEARING LOSS

A) USHER SYNDROME—hearing loss associated with pigmentary changes in the retina of the eye and visual abnormalities, including blindness. There are five types of Usher Syndrome—refer to reference number 2 on page 12 for more detail

B) JERVELL-LANGE NIELSEN SYNDROME—hearing loss associated with cardiac abnormalities

C) PENDRED SYNDROME—hearing loss associated with enlarged thyroid

B. NON SYNDROMIC HEARING LOSS—hearing loss with no other organ system abnormalities–present in 2/3 of children born with genetic hearing loss

1. AUTOSOMAL DOMINANT HEARING LOSS—at least one parent has a hearing loss, and there is a 50% chance that the offspring will acquire a hearing loss

ASSOCIATED WITH SENSORINEURAL HEARING LOSS

A) FAMILIAL DELAYED ONSET PROGRESSIVE SENSORINEURAL HEARING LOSS—hearing loss may be absent or minimal at birth but usually becomes progressive as child becomes older

ASSOCIATED WITH CONDUCTIVE HEARING LOSS

A) CONGENITAL OTOSCLEROSIS—hearing loss associated with congenital fixation of stapes

II. NONGENETIC HEARING LOSS—caused by an event resulting in incomplete development of ear structures prior to birth or damage to the fully developed ear structures during the immediate birth period or sometime after birth. There are no abnormal genes present, and there is no transmission to future generations. Occurs in 70% of all children born with a hearing loss. The majority of cases involve hearing loss alone. Other organ systems may be involved depending on the nature and severity of precipitating event.

A. PRENATAL HEARING LOSS—caused by an event occurring prior to birth

1. **INFECTION INVOLVING THE WHOLE BODY OF THE MOTHER DURING PREGNANCY**—due to cytomegalovirus (CMV), syphilis, herpes, or toxoplasmosis. Maternal rubella infection is now rare due to vaccine
2. **MATERNAL DRUG INTAKE DURING PREGNANCY**—due to intake of drugs that are damaging to the inner ear structures, (neomycin, gentamicin, streptomycin) and/or narcotic drugs

B. PERINATAL HEARING LOSS—caused by an event that occurs during the immediate birth period

1. **LOW BIRTH WEIGHT**—below 3.3 lbs.
2. **POOR APGAR SCORE**—measures newborn vital signs such as alertness, color, reflexes, heart rate, and respiratory rate with maximum score of 10. Scores of less than 4 after one minute and less than 6 after five minutes are indicators for possible hearing loss

C. POSTNATAL HEARING LOSS—caused by an event that occurs after birth

1. **JAUNDICE AT BIRTH**—requiring replacement of newborn's blood with new blood from a compatible donor
2. **ADMISSION TO NEWBORN INTENSIVE CARE UNIT (NICU)**—requiring prolonged respiratory ventilation for more than five days
3. **OTOTOXIC MEDICATIONS (NEOMYCIN, GENTAMICIN)**—usually in combination with a diuretic such as Lasix given to a newborn–in more than a single dose
4. **MENINGITIS**—usually secondary to H. influenza bacteria–This is becoming rare due to vaccination of all children with HIB vaccine to prevent H. influenza meningitis

III. CONDITIONS ASSOCIATED WITH HEARING LOSS WHERE IT IS UNCERTAIN WHETHER OR NOT THERE IS A GENETIC FACTOR

A. GOLDENHAR SYNDROME (HEMIFACIAL MICROSOMIA)—a conductive or mixed type hearing loss associated with poor development of one side of the face

B. WILDERVANCK SYNDROME—conductive or mixed type hearing loss associated with eye muscle weakness and fusion of the neck spine

C. CHARGE ASSOCIATION—is not considered a syndrome but a random association of different organ systems abnormalities—including a mixed type hearing loss, abnormalities of the eyes, heart, and genitals, and retarded growth and mental development

D. DOWN SYNDROME—hearing loss is common and is primarily conductive in nature due to abnormalities of the middle ear or secondary to otitis media (recurring middle ear infections or persistent fluid in the ears) as a result of poor eustachian tube function. About 20–30% of children with Down syndrome have a sensorineural hearing loss alone or in combination with a conductive hearing loss.

2

The Audiological Assessment

Kathryn S. Copmann, Ph.D.

Introduction

The first step in selecting an educational method for your deaf or hard of hearing child is to have her hearing tested. A complete audiological assessment must be performed to determine which sounds your child is able to hear and how loud these sounds must be for her to hear them. It is particularly important to learn how well your child hears speech. Evaluating hearing in a young child is not always easy. However, with new advances in technology, a number of different tests can be performed to determine what your child is able to hear. Which tests are done will be decided by your audiologist based primarily on your child's age.

This chapter discusses audiological test procedures and related information. It explains the two general types of testing that a young child may need to undergo: 1) objective or physiological/electrophysiological testing, and 2) subjective or behavioral testing. The chapter also reviews the meaning of the test results, some of the effects of hearing loss, and types of amplification that are available to your child.

OBJECTIVE TESTING

PHYSIOLOGICAL TESTING

Physiological tests are objective, since they require no responses on the part of your child. These tests evaluate the function of the ear. There are two physiological tests which your child may have done: 1) impedance testing, and 2) otoacoustic emissions testing. Impedance testing evaluates the function of your child's middle ears, whereas otoacoustic emissions testing evaluates your child's cochlea, the part of the inner ear that is responsible for hearing.

IMPEDANCE TESTING

Impedance testing consists of a battery of objective tests that are routinely given to assess the physiology or function of a child's middle ear. Specifically, these tests evaluate your child's middle ear system, including the ear drum (tympanic membrane) and the bones (the ossicles) contained in the middle ear space. They are very useful in determining whether or not your child's middle ear is functioning normally.

Although impedance testing consists of a number of tests, the one that is most frequently performed is **tympanometry.** This test measures the flexibility and the condition of the middle ear system. The results of the test are plotted on a graph known as a **tympanogram.** If your child has a middle ear infection, then her middle ear will not be functioning normally and the tympanogram will indicate that.

In order to perform tympanometry, a special piece of equipment, an impedance meter or tympanometer, is used. The audiologist places a "probe," which has a rubber tip on its end, a short distance into your child's ear canal. Tympanometry is very quick and painless to your child, and is run automatically by the tympanometer. Because this test does not require your child to make a response, it can be performed on a child of any age, it is reliable, and its results are accurate.

Tympanometry is a valuable tool in determining how well the middle ear is performing its important function—namely, sending the sound to the inner ear. However, although tympanometry tells us how well the sound reaches the inner ear, it does not tell us what the inner ear can do with that sound. Therefore, tympanometry is not a hearing test. Your child can have a **normal** tympanogram and still have a hearing loss in the inner ear. If the tympanogram is **abnormal** though, a problem exists in the middle ear.

Otoacoustic Emissions Testing

Otoacoustic emissions testing assesses the function of your child's cochlea—the portion of the inner ear which transforms sound vibrations into signals that are transmitted to the brain. To perform this test, a "probe" that looks very similar to the probe used for impedance testing is placed a short distance into your child's ear canal. A sound is sent into your child's ear. When the sound reaches the inner ear, the cochlea, an "echo" occurs if your child's hearing is normal or near normal. However, if she has a hearing loss of greater than a mild degree, then this "echo" will not occur. Otoacoustic emissions testing can therefore tell the audiologist whether your child has a hearing loss of more than a mild degree. This test is painless to your child and can be completed in a few minutes.

Electrophysiological Tests

Electrophysiological procedures are also objective, since they do not require a response on the part of your child. These tests measure the response of a person's brain to sound by measuring the electrical activity of the brain. They are especially useful to the audiologist when evaluating infants or young children. A young child cannot raise her hand to indicate she has heard, nor can she repeat words. Therefore, the accuracy of behavioral tests is sometimes questioned, and additional testing must be done to determine your child's ability to hear. So if a hearing loss is suspected or if your audiologist does not feel that she has obtained an accurate behavioral test on your child, then an electrophysiological test may be recommended.

Auditory Brainstem Response (ABR) Testing. The electrophysiological test that is often used with infants and young children is the auditory brainstem response test or ABR. You may also hear it referred to as the BAER (brainstem auditory evoked response) test or the BSER (brainstem evoked response) test. The auditory brainstem response test measures a change in the electrical activity of the brain in response to specific sounds.

To have an ABR, your child may first need to be sedated. Next, wires (electrodes) which are connected to a computer will be attached to her head. Headphones will be placed on or in her ears. A "click," a special sound which sounds like the clicking of a typewriter, will be presented to your child one ear at a time. The computer will measure how your child's brain reacts to these clicks.

The results of this test are depicted in the form of a wave pattern. The audiologist will evaluate the test results to determine: 1) how much time passed between when the "click" was presented and the wave pattern occurred; 2) whether the expected wave pattern is present; and 3) the similarity or difference between the wave pattern obtained from each ear. This information will enable the audiologist to estimate your child's hearing loss.

■ BEHAVIORAL TESTING

Behavioral testing can provide some additional information about your child's ability to hear. This type of testing requires your child to respond in some way and is performed in a sound-treated test booth. Different types of sounds, such as tones, noises, or speech are used. These sounds may be presented through speakers, headphones, or a bone conduction vibrator. Which sounds and tests are used, as well as the responses expected from your child, depend on: 1) your child's age at the time of the test; 2) at what age the hearing loss occurred; and 3) how long your child has had a hearing loss. As your child gets older, more information about her hearing can be obtained.

The overall goal of a behavioral audiological evaluation is to learn how your child hears tones and speech. Ideally, four tests are performed:

1. PURE-TONE AIR CONDUCTION TESTING—In this test, tones are presented to your child through headphones which are placed on her ears.

2. PURE-TONE BONE CONDUCTION TESTING—For this test, tones are presented to your child through a vibrator, which is placed behind her ear or on her forehead.

3. SPEECH RECEPTION THRESHOLD TESTING—This test evaluates how loud speech must be before your child can hear it. The results of this test are expressed in decibels (dB) and should agree with the results of pure-tone air conduction testing.

4. WORD RECOGNITION (ALSO KNOWN AS WORD DISCRIMINATION) TESTING—This test assesses how **clearly** your child can hear speech. The results of this test are expressed in a percentage.

All four of these tests cannot be performed on an infant or very young child. A young child cannot repeat words to the audiologist! However, a number of tests and special procedures can be used which will give the audiologist a great deal of information about what your child is able and unable to hear. First let's talk about what each of the four tests listed above is. Then we will take a look at the type of testing you can expect your child to have.

Pure-Tone Air and Bone Conduction Testing

Pure-tone testing is used to test your child's ability to hear the tones which are necessary for hearing speech. In order to get a complete picture of your child's hearing loss, tones must be presented to your child in two different ways: 1) through headphones (air conduction) which are placed on your child's ears; and 2) through a bone vibrator (bone conduction) which is placed on your child's head. A comparison of your child's ability to hear via air conduction and bone conduction will provide the audiologist with important information about your child's hearing loss. This is discussed further under the section "Classification of Hearing Loss" on page 27.

For both air and bone conduction testing the audiologist tries to determine what the softest tones are that your child is able to hear. The testing method chosen will depend on your child's age. The different methods which may be used will be discussed in the next section. The results of your child's first few behavioral hearing tests may not be completely accurate since your child may be very young and/or may not yet know what sound is. However, as discussed above, electrophysiological and physiological tests, which provide accurate information about your child's hearing, can be performed at any age.

SPEECH AUDIOMETRY

The goal of speech audiometry is to determine how well your child hears speech. How much can be learned depends on many factors. Some of these are: 1) how old your child is at the time of the test; 2) the age when your child's hearing loss occurred; 3) what your child's speech and language skills are; 4) how familiar your child is with the testing procedures; 5) how old your child was when the hearing loss was diagnosed; and 6) how familiar your child is with the audiologist.

There are two pieces of information that the audiologist wants to learn about your child's ability to hear speech. The first is what is the softest speech that your child is just able to hear. The second is how clearly your child can hear speech. The first measure, the softest speech that your child is just able to hear, is known as the **speech reception threshold** or **SRT.** In order to obtain this measure the audiologist will say two-syllable words, such as airplane, baseball, ice cream, and cowboy, to your child using an audiometer. The audiometer permits the audiologist to control the loudness of her voice precisely. Your child may be asked to respond by pointing to a picture of the words or by repeating the words. As the test progresses, the audiologist will make her voice continuously softer until the **softest** level is reached where your child can hear **one half** of the words presented. This level is known as your child's speech reception threshold or SRT and is measured in decibels. (See the section on *The Audiogram* for an explanation of decibels.)

A young deaf or hard of hearing child may not yet have sufficient language to permit the audiologist to obtain a speech reception threshold. Your child may not yet know the words the audiologist will be saying. If this is the case, then the audiologist will try to obtain a **speech detection threshold** or **SDT** (also known as speech awareness threshold or SAT). During speech detection threshold testing, your child need not identify the words the audiologist is saying. Instead, the audiologist will ask your child to indicate when she hears the audiologist, even though your child may not know what the exact words are. Or the audiologist may say words and observe your child to determine whether she heard the words.

The second test performed in speech audiometry is word recognition testing. The goal of this test is to determine how clearly your child can hear speech under two conditions. The first condition is when speech is presented at an average **conversational loudness**. Depending on the amount of hearing loss your child has, she may or may not be able to hear at this loudness. In the second condition, speech is presented at a loudness which is **optimal** for your child. Determining which loudness level is optimal for a child often requires a good deal of trial and error! To determine your child's word recognition ability, the audiologist may ask her to point to a picture, a piece of clothing, a body part, or to repeat a word.

How Will Your Child Be Tested?

Now that we have reviewed the four basic audiological tests, let's discuss the tests your child is likely to have.

Testing Children under the Age of Two

Behavioral Observation Audiometry

If your child is under the age of two years, she will be tested using behavioral observation audiometry or BOA. In this type of test, your child must respond to sound in a way that can be observed by your audiologist. The sounds may be tones, noises, or speech sounds which may be presented to your child through speakers, headphones, or a bone conduction vibrator. Usually, these sounds will be presented beginning at very soft levels. Then the sounds will be made louder until your child makes a response to indicate that she has heard the sound.

In order to test each ear separately, the audiologist will try to place headphones on your child. If your child is an infant or toddler, she may not want to keep the headphones on her head! If that happens, then the audiologist may present noises or speech sounds to your child through a speaker and watch how she responds. Or, the audiologist may stay in the room with your child and use noisemakers, such as a rattle and a horn, to test your child's hearing. The audiologist will probably also present a loud noise to your child to try to startle her. Some responses your child may make which would indicate that she heard are:

- a startle
- an eyeblink or a widening of the eyes
- searching for the sound
- starting to cry
- turning or looking in the direction of the sound

The responses your child makes will depend on her age, how much hearing she has, and the type of sound(s) used.

TESTING TODDLERS AND PRESCHOOLERS

PLAY AUDIOMETRY AND VISUAL REINFORCEMENT AUDIOMETRY

As your child gets older she will be able to make more responses to sound and therefore the tests used will be different. Beginning at about the age of two years, the audiologist will perform pure-tone testing using play audiometry, which may be paired with visual reinforcement audiometry or VRA. In play audiometry, your child will play a "game" with the audiologist. The audiologist will present a series of tones to your child. Each time your child hears a tone, she may be asked to drop a block into a box, or "mail a letter" into a toy mailbox. When your child makes a correct response, she may be shown a mechanical toy (rabbit, elephant, clown) as a "reward" or "reinforcement" for her response. This is called visual reinforcement audiometry. Using toys to "reward" your child helps to keep her attention and makes the test more fun. Usually, your audiologist will begin by trying to obtain responses to the three pitches (frequencies), 500 Hz, 1000 Hz, and 2000 Hz, which are the most important for hearing speech. Depending on how your child responds, additional frequencies may be tested.

SPEECH AUDIOMETRY

In order to evaluate your child's ability to hear speech, the two speech audiometric tests discussed above will be administered. Once your child is able to identify words, speech reception threshold (SRT) testing will be done. To perform this test, the audiologist will show your child pictures or objects, such as a baseball, hot dog, and airplane. Then the audiologist will ask her to point to the pictures, one at a time. As the audiologist is speaking she will make her voice progressively softer until your child is unable to hear the words. In this way, a measure of how loud speech must be before your child can hear it, **the speech reception threshold,** can be obtained.

The second measure of how your child hears speech, **word recognition testing,** will provide information regarding how clearly your child hears speech. Your child may be asked to point to clothing or body parts. By using words such as chin, pants, head, leg, arm, shirt, foot, socks, nose, and eyes, the audiologist can get an idea of how well your child hears a wide range of speech sounds. You can assist your audiologist for both speech reception threshold testing and word recognition testing by letting her know which words are in your child's vocabulary. The age at which these tests will be performed depends primarily on your child's language ability.

TESTING SCHOOL-AGED CHILDREN

CONVENTIONAL AUDIOMETRY

By about age five, your child will be ready for a conventional audiological evaluation. This evaluation consists of the four tests discussed above: 1) pure-tone air conduction testing, 2) pure-tone bone conduction testing, 3) speech reception threshold testing, and 4) word recognition testing.

As was done in play audiometry, the audiologist places headphones on your child's ears and presents a series of tones to your child in order to perform pure-tone air conduction testing. Now that your child is older, she will probably be asked to raise her hand, rather than to drop a block, when she hears a tone. And, now that your child is older, the audiologist will be able to test additional frequencies. Once again the bone conduction vibrator will be used to test your child's ability to hear through bone conduction. Again your child will be asked to raise her hand each time a tone is heard.

Speech reception threshold testing and word recognition testing can yield more precise information as your child becomes older and acquires more language. In order to test your child's speech reception threshold, she may be asked to point to a picture or to repeat a two-syllable word such as mushroom, bathtub, or birthday. The words that are used and the type of response requested of your child will depend largely on her language ability.

Word recognition testing may be performed in a number of ways depending on your child's language ability. As discussed above, the goal of word recognition testing is to determine how clearly your child can hear speech which is presented under two conditions: 1) at an average conversational loudness, and 2) at a loudness which is optimal for your child. In order to administer a word recognition test under each condition, the audiologist may ask your child to repeat a list of one-syllable words or point to pictures of words such as school, ball, or spoon. The percentage of words which your child is able to correctly identify will be calculated.

FIGURE 1. AUDIOGRAM WITH "SPEECH BANANA"

In order for your child to be able to hear speech, her thresholds must be within the "speech banana" or better.

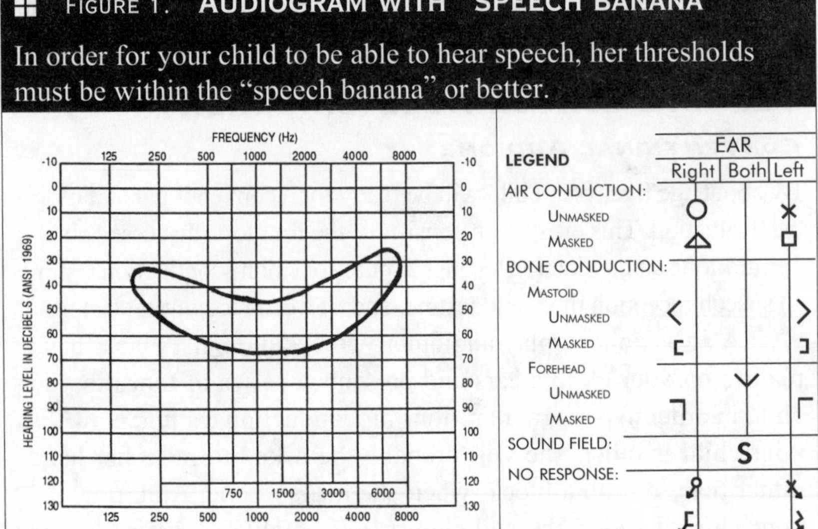

As was true with speech reception testing, your child's language ability at the time of the test will largely determine exactly how the test is administered. If your child is not yet able to repeat words, your audiologist may use a test known as the WIPI, Word Intelligibility by Picture Identification, to evaluate your child's word recognition ability. This test consists of a series of pages with six pictures on each page. All of the pictures on each page have the same vowel, but different consonants—for example, sm_o_ke and c_o_ke. If this test is used, your child will be asked to point to the picture which corresponds to the word the audiologist says. Once again the percentage of words which are correctly identified is calculated. If your child has not yet developed sufficient language, then word recognition testing cannot be performed.

THE AUDIOGRAM

The results of your child's hearing test will be recorded on an audiogram (Figure 1). An audiogram displays your child's hearing in each ear for tones heard through headphones (air conduction), and for tones heard through the bone vibrator (bone conduction). The audiogram is a graph or "picture" of your child's hearing.

Moving from left to right on the audiogram are the various pitches (frequencies) which are tested, ranging from the lowest pitch sound on the left (125 Hz) to the highest pitch sound (8000 Hz) on the far right. The frequency of a sound is expressed in Hertz (Hz), which stands for cycles per second. The higher in frequency a sound is, the higher we perceive its pitch to be. Moving from the top of the audiogram to the bottom are the volumes (intensities) tested, varying from very soft at the top to extremely loud at the bottom. The intensity or loudness of a sound is expressed in decibels (dB). Symbols which represent your child's hearing in the right ear are recorded in red or round circles, and symbols depicting your child's hearing in the left ear are recorded in blue or "Xs." The further down the audiogram the symbols are recorded, the more loudness was needed for your child to hear.

Look at the audiogram on page 26 and the symbols found in the legend. You can see that different symbols are used to show your child's responses for sounds presented through headphones and through the bone conduction vibrator. The results which are recorded on the audiogram are used to classify the hearing loss in terms of:

- Type of Hearing Loss
- Degree of Hearing Loss
- Configuration of Hearing Loss
- Symmetry of Hearing Loss

Classification of Type of Hearing Loss

As explained in Chapter 1, hearing losses can be classified either as conductive, sensorineural, or mixed. A conductive hearing loss results if a problem occurs in the outer or middle ear. If your child's inner ear, the cochlea, is not functioning properly, then a sensorineural hearing loss will exist. It is also possible for problems to exist simultaneously in the outer or middle ear and in the inner ear. For example, if your child's inner ear is not functioning properly and your child is experiencing a temporary ear infection, then a mixed hearing loss will result.

By comparing your child's ability to hear through headphones to her ability to hear through bone conduction, the type of hearing loss your child has can be determined. If your child has a conductive hearing loss, her hearing will be better for bone conduction sounds than for air conduction sounds. In a sensorineural hearing loss the hearing loss is equal for both air and bone conduction sounds. With a mixed hearing loss, there is a hearing loss for both air conduction and bone conduction sounds, but the hearing loss is greater for air conduction sounds.

Conductive hearing losses can often be treated medically or surgically. If your child has a sensorineural hearing loss, there is no medical or surgical treatment that can fully restore hearing. However, a hearing aid may be of help to your child. We will talk more about hearing aids later in this chapter.

FIGURE 2. DEGREES OF HEARING LOSS

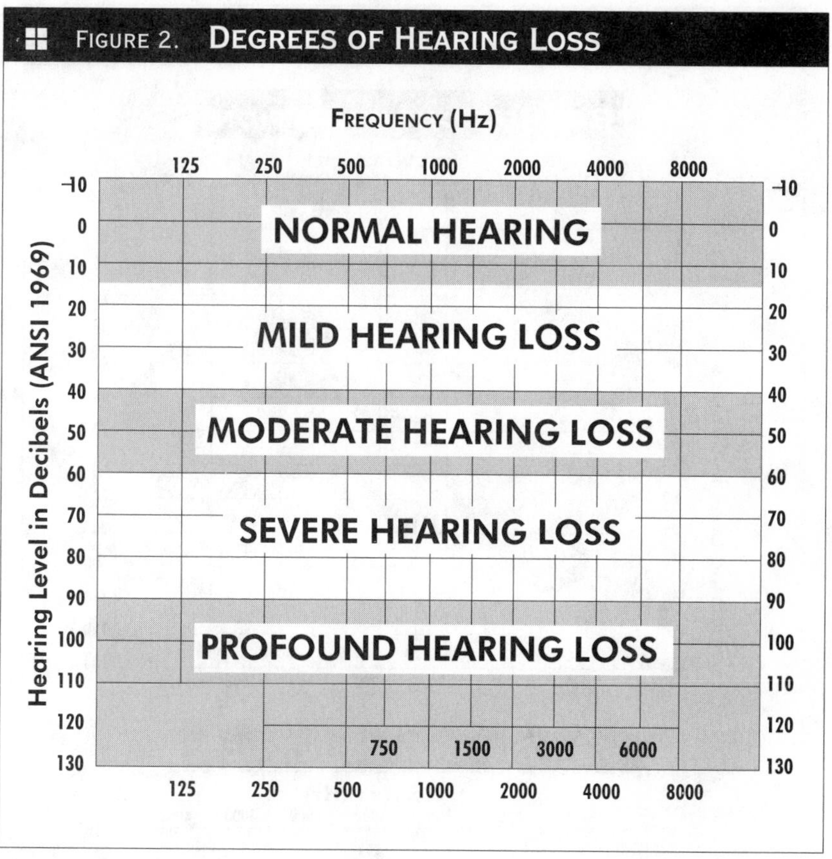

CLASSIFICATION OF DEGREE OF HEARING LOSS

The next important fact about your child's hearing that the audiogram tells us is the amount or degree of hearing loss your child has (Figure 2). There are many different ways of classifying the degree of hearing loss. However, most professionals today agree that even a small amount of hearing loss in a child may result in educational problems. The chart above is one way of classifying the amount of hearing loss a child has. The decibel levels indicated show how loud a sound has to be for an individual to hear it.

The amount of hearing a deaf or hard of hearing child has is referred to as her residual hearing. We will talk more about this later.

FIGURE 3. AUDIOGRAM CONFIGURATIONS

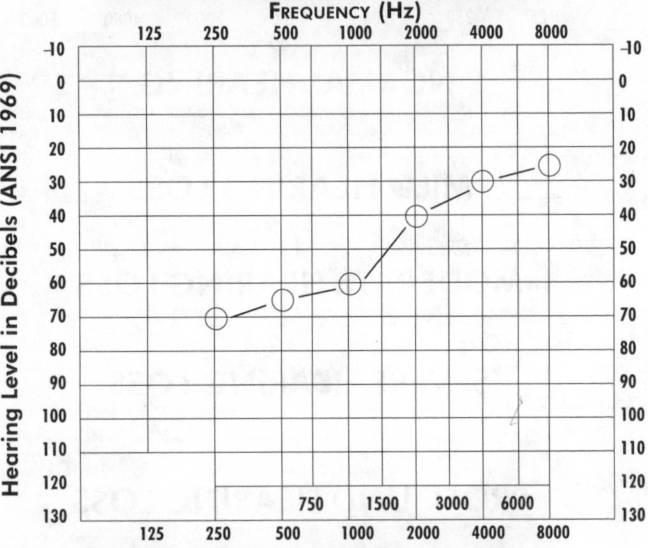

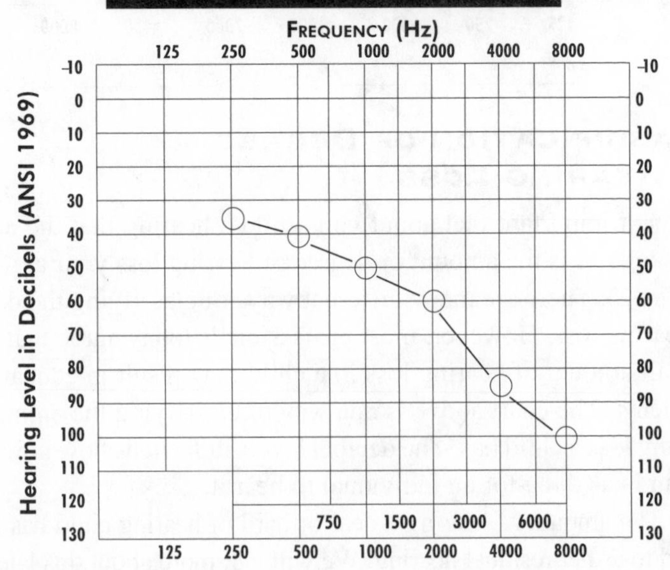

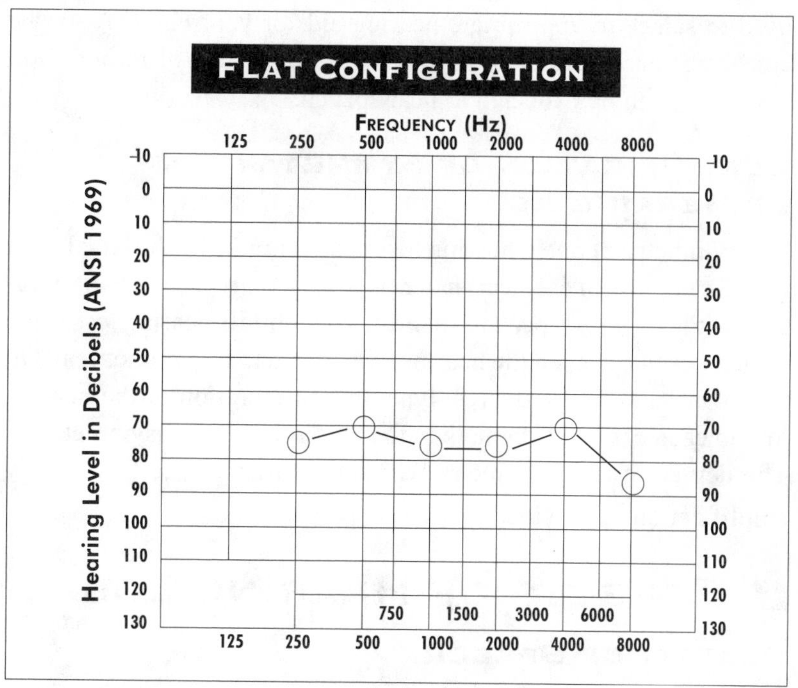

CLASSIFICATION OF CONFIGURATION OF HEARING LOSS

The configuration, or shape, of your child's hearing loss is the next important fact that the audiogram tells us. Can your child hear low pitched sounds but not high pitched sounds? If so, this would be classified as a "sloping" configuration. Does your child have better hearing for sounds which are high pitched than for sounds which are low in pitch? This shape of hearing loss would be classified as a "rising" configuration. Or is the same amount of loudness needed for your child to hear a sound, regardless of the pitch of the sound? This shape of hearing loss would be classified as a "flat" configuration. (See Figure 3 for examples of these three configurations of hearing loss.)

The configuration of the hearing loss yields important information to the audiologist regarding which sounds must be amplified in order for your child to hear speech best. This information is used to select an appropriate hearing aid for your child. Also, the configuration of the hearing loss gives some idea of how clearly your child can be expected to hear speech.

Classification of Symmetry of Hearing Loss

The symmetry of one's hearing loss is determined by the equality of the hearing loss in each ear, in terms of degree, type, and configuration. If the degree, type, and shape of your child's hearing loss is the same in each ear, then the hearing loss is said to be symmetrical. On the other hand, if the degree, type, or configuration of the hearing loss in each ear is different, then the loss is said to be asymmetrical. The degree of the asymmetry will determine the specifics of how amplification is provided.

Effects of Hearing Loss

Clarity of Speech

Perhaps the most important educational effect of a permanent sensorineural hearing loss is its effect on the **clarity** of the speech which your child will hear. The clarity of the speech signal your child receives depends largely on the degree of her hearing loss. That is, it depends on her residual hearing—the amount of hearing that your child has. Residual hearing determines not only which sounds can be heard but also how clearly these sounds are heard. If your child cannot hear speech in a **clear and consistent** manner, then it will be more difficult for her to learn language. The greater your child's hearing loss is and the less clearly she is able to hear speech (the poorer her word recognition ability is), the more important it will be for you to: 1) provide her with consistent language, 2) provide her with meaningful language, and 3) repeat words, phrases, sentences, and stories to her.

One way to help ensure that your child receives consistent language that is as clear as possible, **within the limits of her hearing ability**, is to have her fitted with appropriate amplification. Let's discuss some of the possibilities.

AMPLIFICATION ALTERNATIVES

Unfortunately, no device will restore perfectly normal hearing. It is important to be realistic about the benefits and limitations of hearing aids. However, exciting advances in technology have occurred and continue to occur at a rapid pace! Today, devices and technology that did not exist five or ten years ago are available to your child. These devices fall into three general categories: 1) conventional personal hearing aids, 2) FM Systems, and 3) new technology.

Whichever type of amplification alternative you and your audiologist decide is best for your child, the goals of amplification are the same: 1) to make the best possible use of your child's residual hearing, 2) to make speech audible to your child, and 3) to provide her with the best hearing possible.

As discussed before, decisions about amplification for your child will be made based on symmetry and severity of hearing loss, as well as your child's age. In some cases, your audiologist may recommend fitting only one ear with a hearing aid. However, if your child has a hearing loss in both ears, it will usually be best for her to receive two hearing aids (binaural amplification). Benefits of binaural amplification include:

- better ability to locate a sound (localization);
- better hearing in the presence of noise;
- less amplification needed in each ear;
- more natural sound quality.

TYPES OF AMPLIFICATION

Certain components are common to most types of amplification. They all have:

1. **A MICROPHONE,** which picks up sound from the environment and sends this sound inside the device to an

2. **AMPLIFIER,** which increases the loudness of the sound. This amplified sound is then sent to a

3. **"SPEAKER"** (similar to your stereo speaker but a great deal smaller!), which delivers the sound to one's ear through

4. SOME METHOD OF CONNECTION. The method of connecting the device to the ear could be an earmold or the hearing aid itself.

Let's have a look at each type of amplification alternative.

CONVENTIONAL PERSONAL HEARING AIDS

There are many types of conventional personal hearing aids, which are manufactured by numerous companies. Those which may be appropriate for your child include: 1) behind the ear (BTE), 2) in the ear (ITE), and 3) in the canal (ITC). Which type your audiologist recommends will depend mainly on how severe your child's hearing loss is and your child's age.

With modern advances in hearing aid technology, children with moderate, severe, and profound hearing losses can receive appropriate benefit from behind the ear (BTE) hearing aids. A BTE, as its name implies, fits behind one's ear. It is connected to an earmold, a piece of plastic which is custom made to fit the user's ear. So, if your child is fit with a BTE she will also need an earmold. Since the earmold must fit her ear exactly, the audiologist must take an impression of her ear. In young children, it is common for earmolds to need replacing every six months to one year, as the ears grow. If your child is young and/or active, you may want to use a "huggy"—a plastic device that holds the BTE firmly in place.

Your audiologist will discuss care of the hearing aid and earmold with you as well as safety information (i.e., keeping hearing aid batteries away from your young child). Some BTE hearing aids are equipped with **direct audio input** for use with auditory trainers. We will discuss direct audio input in more detail later in this chapter.

As your child becomes older, and if she has sufficient residual hearing, you may wish to consider an in the ear (ITE) or in the canal (ITC) hearing instrument. With ITE and ITC type hearing aids, the hearing aid itself is molded to fit inside your child's ear. They are not practical for use with younger children, since the entire hearing aid would have to be remade frequently as your child grows. Also, keeping these types of hearing aids inside a young child's ear can be a problem!

FM SYSTEMS

There are two general categories of FM systems: 1) FM auditory trainers, which are traditional FM systems, and 2) FM hearing aids. Both work in essentially the same manner. Both FM auditory trainers and FM hearing aids (such as the "Free Ear" and the "Extend Ear") consist of a microphone, transmitter, and a receiver.

The way these devices work is remarkable. The person who is speaking wears the microphone and the transmitter. This person is a kind of "radio station" sending a "radio signal" to the person wearing the receiver. The deaf or hard of hearing child wears the receiver. This receiver acts like your car radio in that it picks up the radio signal from the person speaking! Since the speaker's voice is being sent by an FM radio signal, the loudness and clarity of the speaker's voice is not diminished by the distance between the speaker (transmitter) and your child (receiver). The transmitter is capable of sending the signal several hundred feet. Therefore, even if the person speaking and your child are far apart, your child will hear with the same loudness and clarity that she would if the speaker were only six inches away!

Two major differences between traditional FM systems (auditory trainers) and FM hearing aids are: 1) the size of the receiver, and 2) the physical convenience of the systems. Let's talk about traditional FM systems or auditory trainers. These devices include a receiver that is approximately the size of a package of cigarettes. The child wears the receiver on her back, chest, or on a belt. Cords connect the receiver to your child's ears. If your child has hearing aids which are equipped with direct audio input, then cords will connect the receiver directly to your child's hearing aid. The major advantage to using direct audio input is the **consistency** of sound, especially speech, that your child will hear. All sounds your child hears while wearing the auditory trainer (which is connected directly to her hearing aid) will pass through her hearing aid before reaching her ears. Therefore, the sounds which she hears while wearing the auditory trainer in school, and while wearing her hearing aids at home, will be very similar.

As is true of FM auditory trainers, FM hearing aids also consist of a microphone, transmitter, and receiver. With FM hearing aids, the receiver portion of the system is small enough to be contained in a behind the ear (BTE) type hearing aid, rather than in a unit worn on the body. Because the receiver is contained in the hearing aid itself, an FM BTE is heavier than a conventional BTE. This increased weight may be a factor when considering FM hearing aids for young children. However, two physical advantages of an FM hearing aid versus an auditory trainer are that: 1) since the aid is worn behind the ear, there are no cords involved, and 2) the receiver is smaller. As with FM auditory trainers, the person speaking to a child using an FM BTE wears a microphone and a transmitter. The need to wear the microphone and the transmitter may present a minor inconvenience. However, the major advantage to having your child wear an FM hearing aid is the consistency of sound which your child will hear in all of her listening situations.

Auditory trainers are typically the property of the school your child attends and therefore are usually worn only at school. If your child has FM hearing aids, however, she could wear them both at school and at home. As mentioned earlier, this use of the same device at home and at school would provide more consistent sound to your child.

New Technology

Many exciting advances have been made in technology for deaf and hard of hearing persons. Advanced electronic devices are now available that present sound in new and different ways. These devices include: 1) transposers, 2) programmable personal hearing aids, and 3) cochlear implants.

Transposers. Transposers are devices that were developed for persons with little or no hearing for high pitch (frequency) sounds. The way transposers work is to change, or transpose, the *high pitched* sounds such as /s/,/sh/,/f/ which the person *cannot* hear, into *low pitched* sounds which the person *can* hear. In this way, sounds which your child would otherwise be unable to hear are made audible to her. Of course, sounds will not sound the same to your child as they do to you. However, with a transposer, she will be able to hear more sounds. If your child has very little or no hearing for high pitched sounds, she may be a candidate for a transposer.

PROGRAMMABLE PERSONAL HEARING AIDS. Recently, personal hearing aids which can be programmed by a computer have become available. These devices are programmed specifically to fit the user's hearing loss. In some programmable hearing aids, the programming is based on how the user hears very soft sounds as well as on how the user hears sounds of many different loudnesses. Very young deaf or hard of hearing children typically do not have enough experience with sound to be able to be fit with programmable hearing aids. However, as your child becomes older and gains sufficient knowledge of sound, a programmable hearing aid may be appropriate.

COCHLEAR IMPLANTS. Cochlear implants (which are discussed further in Chapter Three) are sophisticated devices that are implanted directly into a person's cochlea, the part of the inner ear that is responsible for hearing. Basically, cochlear implants replace the damaged hair cells of the inner ear. These devices consist of both external and internal components. A popular cochlear implant, the Nucleus 22 Channel device, consists of the following major components: 1) a speech processor, 2) a microphone, cable, and transmitter, and 3) the cochlear implant itself. The cochlear implant itself consists of a receiver/stimulator and a group of electrodes known as an electrode array. The microphone picks up sounds from the environment and sends them through a tiny wire to the speech processor. The speech processor changes speech into an electronic code. That code is sent through a tiny wire to the transmitter. The transmitter then sends the coded signal across the skin to the receiver/stimulator portion of the cochlear implant. The receiver/stimulator changes the code into electronic signals. These special signals are sent to the tiny electrodes that have been inserted into the cochlea. These electrodes directly stimulate the nerve fibers in the hearing (auditory) nerve. The nerve fibers send messages to the brain and these messages are interpreted by the brain as sound. It is quite a complex process!

Children who are receiving no benefit from a conventional hearing aid and who meet other criteria established by the Food and

Drug Administration (FDA) are candidates for a cochlear implant. Once a child is implanted, the habilitation process begins. First, the implant must be programmed to deliver appropriate signals to the child's cochlea. Then the child must be taught to interpret and attach meaning to the sounds that are being sent to the brain by the implant. The programming and habilitation procedures take time and patience.

Determining whether your child is a candidate for a cochlear implant is a difficult process. The implantation of very young children is controversial. Should you wish to consider a cochlear implant for your child, contact a cochlear implant center. These centers are located throughout the country and are typically housed in hospitals. Your audiologist will be able to help you locate one. You will receive a great deal of information from the center which will assist you in determining whether a cochlear implant is appropriate for your child.

CONCLUSION

The process of educating your deaf or hard of hearing child begins with the measurement of her hearing ability. Through the various audiological tests described above, you will receive information which will help you decide which educational method to choose for your child. However, this decision is only the beginning! You will have many choices to make along the way. During this process you may sometimes be frustrated by what seems to be a lack of progress, and other times be elated by the growth you see. These emotions are, of course, normal. Work with your child. Accept your child. Although the presence of a hearing loss significantly affects the life of your child, she is a **child first** and a child with a hearing loss second. You will find that, as with any child, her needs will change. Her audiological needs may change over time. In addition, her emotional and educational needs will change. As these changes occur, remember that your audiologist is one of the professionals who can help you. Call on her. Ask her questions and share your concerns. As parents, you are your child's single most valuable resource, but you are not alone!

3

The Cochlear Implant

Stephen Epstein, M.D.

Introduction

The cochlear implant is one of the most significant advances in treating hearing loss since the development of the hearing aid. For some children with a profound sensorineural hearing loss, it offers a relatively new and promising road to improved communication abilities. It has enabled some children with a profound hearing loss to hear without visual aids and to develop speech and language more effectively than with hearing aids and other assistive devices.

History of the Cochlear Implant

For decades, scientists have been working on different models of the cochlear implant—an electronic device designed to compensate for absent or poorly functioning hair cells in the inner ear. Only recently, however, has the cochlear implant become a viable option for many children with a profound hearing loss.

The first model of the cochlear implant, consisting of a single channel electrode, was tested in adults in the early 1980s. It received Food and Drug Administration (FDA) approval for commercial use in adults only in 1984. At the same time, this model of the cochlear implant was first used on a trial basis with children. During testing, it was found to provide an awareness of environmental sounds, improve lipreading or speechreading skills, and help some children modulate their own voices. Because of the limited benefits achieved and the concern for the long-term effect of continuous electrical stimulation on the developing ear and brain in children, the FDA did not approve the single channel cochlear implant for commercial use in children at that time.

In a matter of years, technological advances led to the development of the multichannel cochlear implant. After several years of clinical trials, this new model was proven to provide better speech reception and to result in better speech production. There was also mounting evidence that the cochlear implant is safe for long-term use in children. Consequently, the 22 multichannel cochlear implant was approved for commercial use in children in the United States in 1990. As of this writing, over 5000 children worldwide have received the 22 multichannel cochlear implant. Another model, the 16 multichannel cochlear implant, is undergoing testing prior to receiving FDA approval for commercial use in children. The original model, the single channel cochlear implant, is no longer approved for commercial use for either adults or children as of this writing.

How Does the Cochlear Implant Work?

The cochlear implant is designed to take over the function of an inner ear that does not work properly. This is in contrast to a hearing aid, which simply amplifies sound. To understand how the cochlear implant actually works, it will help to have some background on the physiology of the ear and how we hear.

The sounds that we hear, whether they be spoken words, background noises, or music, consist of invisible multi-frequency waves that travel through the air and are received by the ear. These sound waves cause vibrations of the eardrum and the tiny bones within the middle ear. (See Figure 1 on page 2, which shows a cross section of the components of the ear.) The middle ear serves as an amplifier to compensate for the loss of intensity of the sound as it travels from an air medium outside the ear to the fluid medium of the cochlea or inner ear. The vibrations transmitted from the middle ear produce waves within the inner ear fluid, causing an interaction between the tectorial membrane and the hair cells positioned throughout the cochlea. (See Figure 2 on page 4, which shows the cross section of the inner ear.)

The interaction between the tectorial membrane and the inner ear hair cells creates an electrical stimulus, which is transmitted to the auditory nerve. Finally, the auditory nerve transmits these electrical stimuli to the auditory center within the brain, where they are all coordinated and coded into the sounds we hear.

Most children with a profound hearing loss do not have inner ear hair cells that function normally. In fact, the most common defect associated with genetic or nongenetic hearing loss in children is the reduction or absence of functioning inner ear hair cells. Often, however, there is nothing wrong with these children's auditory nerves. It has been shown that they *can* perceive sound if the nerve is directly stimulated, bypassing the nonfunctioning inner hair cells.

The basic principle of the cochlear implant is to replace the function of the absent or diminished inner ear hair cells. It does so by sorting out the many different frequencies of incoming sounds and coding them into electrical signals that resemble those created by a normally functioning inner ear. These electrical signals are picked up by the auditory nerve and transmitted to the auditory center within the brain, where they are coordinated and coded into the sounds that we hear.

As mentioned earlier, the multichannel cochlear implant can enable some individuals to hear and understand the spoken word without the use of visual systems such as speechreading, cues, or sign language. The cochlear implant can only work, however, if the individual has a normally functioning auditory nerve and auditory center in the brain. This is because the cochlear implant replaces the function of the inner ear hair cells only. For more information, see the section on "Who Can Benefit from Cochlear Implantation," on page 46.

COMPONENTS OF THE COCHLEAR IMPLANT

The cochlear implant has two basic components: an external component consisting of a microphone and sound processor and an internal component consisting of a receiver/stimulator and an electrode. The internal component has to be surgically implanted.

EXTERNAL COMPONENT. The external component consists of a microphone. This microphone is similar to a behind-the-ear hearing aid and functions similarly to a hearing aid by receiving the

TABLE 1. HOW THE COCHLEAR IMPLANT WORKS

1. Sounds are received by the **MICROPHONE** located at the level of the ear.
2. These sounds are then sent by a thin wire to the **SPEECH PROCESSOR.**
3. The **SPEECH PROCESSOR** sorts out these sounds and converts them to special codes.
4. The codes are sent back through the thin wire and relayed to the **TRANSMITTER** attached to the skin just behind the ear.
5. The codes are then sent across the skin to the **RECEIVER STIMULATOR** located just beneath the skin behind the ear.
6. The **RECEIVER STIMULATOR** converts these codes into electrical signals.
7. The electrical signals are then sent to the wire-like **IMPLANT** containing the electrodes located within the first turn of the cochlea.

sound stimuli. In a hearing aid, however, the sound is simply amplified, whereas in the cochlear implant the sound is sent to a speech processor by a thin connecting cord. The speech processor selects and codes those sounds that are useful for understanding speech. These electronic codes are then sent back up the thin cord to the external coil. The external coil is attached to the receiver stimulator, which has been surgically implanted underneath the scalp.

INTERNAL COMPONENT. The internal component consists of the receiver stimulator, which is about three inches long and is implanted beneath the scalp. The receiver stimulator converts the sound codes to electrical signals. These signals are then sent to the electrodes distributed along a wire-like structure that is implanted within the first turn of the cochlea. The number of electrodes im-

8. Within the cochlea, the electrical signals are relayed through the wire-like implant to the appropriate electrodes, where the **NERVE FIBERS** are stimulated.

9. This stimulation is picked up by the **AUDITORY NERVE** and sent to the brain, where it is recognized as sound.

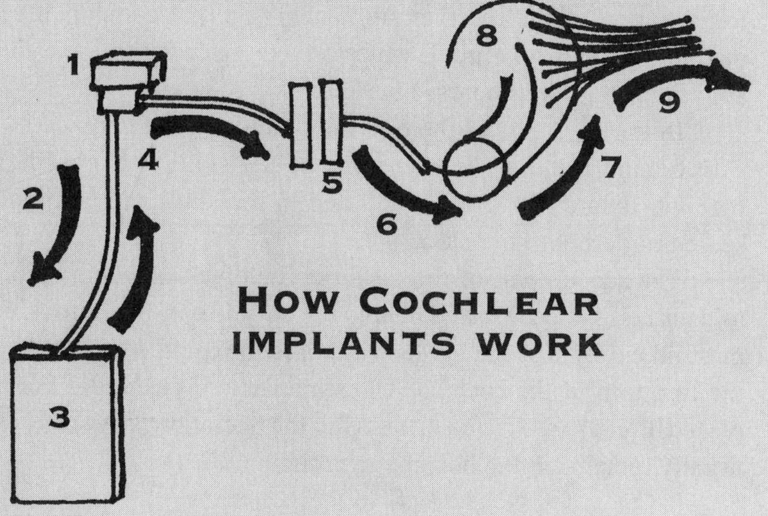

HOW COCHLEAR IMPLANTS WORK

planted within the cochlea depends on the model of cochlear implant. The 22 multichannel cochlear implant has 22 arrangements of electrodes and the 16 multichannel cochlear implant has 16 arrangements of electrodes that can be implanted within the cochlea. These arrangements of multiple electrodes provide a number of independent channels of stimulation. This means they are able to stimulate the cochlea at different frequencies, just as the hair cells in a normally functioning cochlea do. Consequently, these current models of cochlear implants provide more information about the acoustic signals, and, therefore, make better speech recognition possible.

The 22 channel cochlear implant has an external component and internal component that are held together by a magnet. The 16 channel cochlear implant has an external and internal component that are attached directly by a connector that protrudes from the skin. The advantage of this type of connection is that it is more adaptable to change, and because no magnet is present, it is MRI compatible. Other differences between these two devices will be discussed later in this chapter.

■ THE SURGICAL PROCEDURE FOR THE COCHLEAR IMPLANT

Implantation of the receiver stimulator (internal component) is a major surgical procedure. It is performed under general anesthesia and takes about four hours.

In the first part of the operation, an incision is made in the skin behind the ear, and the bone of the skull is exposed. The receiver is laid in a pre-formed bed in the skull and completely sealed underneath the skin.

The second part of the operation involves exposing the mastoid air cell system located behind the middle ear. It is through this mastoid cavity that the surgeon exposes the middle ear cavity and the first turn of the cochlea. The stimulator or electrodes are then placed directly into the cochlea. After the operation is over, the child usually remains in the hospital overnight.

Post-Implantation Procedures

Immediately following the implantation of the internal component, your child will not be able to hear, since the external and internal components will not have been hooked up. About six weeks after surgery, your child will return for what is called the stimulation session or tune-up. At this time, the external component of the cochlear implant is attached to the internal component. In the 22 channel cochlear implant, the external coil of the stimulator and the receiver are attached by a magnet. In the 16 channel cochlear implant, there is a button protruding through the skin for attaching the external coil and internal receiver together.

After the external and internal components are hooked up, the audiologist will program the speech processor for your child's individual hearing needs. To do so, he or she will measure the threshold level and maximum comfort level for each of the electrodes. This first session is generally very exciting, as it will be the first time that your child will "hear" any kind of sound. Sometimes, however, the first session may be disappointing if you expected your child to hear more. This is why it is important to have a realistic expectations about the cochlear implant.

Following the initial tune-up, your child will have several other programming sessions until the cochlear implant itself is fine tuned to your child's individual hearing needs. These programming sessions may be spread over several months. It may take several months before your child becomes acclimated to the cochlear implant and begins to derive any benefit.

Once the cochlear implant is completely programmed and fine tuned, then the most important part of the post implantation process begins. At this time, your child will be trained to listen with the cochlear implant. Your child must learn or relearn to associate the new sound sensations with meaningful speech and other sounds in the real world. Some training sessions will focus on speech reception, and other sessions will focus on speech and language production. A multidisciplinary team composed of audiologists, speech/language pathologists, rehabilitation specialists, and educators familiar with the cochlear implant will be essential to helping your child learn to listen and speak.

In short, the benefits of a cochlear implant do not occur effortlessly and instantaneously. It may take as long as a year before your child has achieved significant benefit. Experience has also shown that many children continue to improve as the years go on.

Who Can Benefit from Cochlear Implantation?

On May 15-17, 1995, a Consensus Development Conference on Cochlear Implants in Children was held on the campus of the National Institutes of Health in Bethesda, Maryland. For one and a half days, a non-biased, non-Federal panel of experts listened to presentations by investigators and clinicians involved with cochlear implants and to questions and statements from conference attendees. The panel then formulated the following recommendations for cochlear implantation in children.

Age of Implantation

As illustrated in Table 2, the ideal age of implantation is 24 months. It is still unclear whether there is an advantage in implanting a child younger than two. This is especially the case if there is impending bony growth within the inner ear in children with a hearing loss secondary to meningitis. There is also a question as to whether there is a significant difference if a child is implanted at two to three years compared to four to five years of age. Regardless of the age of implantation, all children must have tried using hearing aids and other assistive devices for at least six months to one year before implantation is attempted.

In studies, children achieved better results with the cochlear implant if the time elapsed between the onset of the hearing loss and implantation was relatively short. Children with early onset hearing loss who were implanted after age eight or nine or during adolescence did not usually learn to hear as well as children who were implanted at a younger age. There were, however, individual differences in the amount of benefit children of different ages received.

DEGREE OF DEAFNESS

The ideal candidate is a child who:

- has a profound sensorineural hearing loss;
- has had a trial period of appropriate amplification combined with intensive auditory training; and
- has not achieved appropriate speech and language development.

Further investigation will determine whether children with a severe-to-profound sensorineural hearing loss, who have undergone intensive auditory training, may also be good candidates for the cochlear implant.

MEDICAL CRITERIA

The child must otherwise be in good health and be able to benefit from the post-implantation process. The medical workup should

TABLE 2. CRITERIA FOR THE COCHLEAR IMPLANT IN CHILDREN

- Your child must be at least two years of age.
- Your child must have a bilateral profound hearing loss.
- Your child must have had a trial of hearing aids and/or other assistive listening devices along with intensive auditory training for six months to one year.
- You and your child must be interested in developing oral speech and language with or without visual input.
- Your child must be in good health.
- Your child must be free of active ear disease such as infection of the middle ear or mastoid cavity.
- You and your child must be motivated about using the cochlear implant.
- You and your child must have realistic expectations concerning the outcome.

include a CAT scan of the inner ear to rule out any abnormalities of the cochlea which might interfere with the implantation process. As long as a portion of the inner ear appears to be present, it is possible to perform the cochlear implant.

Psychological Criteria

The child and his family must have a positive attitude and must be motivated in regard to the cochlear implant. They must be aware of the complications and must have realistic expectations as to the outcome.

Determining Whether Your Child is a Candidate for a Cochlear Implant

If your child fulfills all of the criteria in Table 2, you should seek consultation at a reputable cochlear implant program. During the pre-implantation evaluation, your child will receive a complete audiological, speech and language, and medical evaluation. This will include a CAT scan (special x-rays) of the inner ears to evaluate the anatomy of the cochlea. There may also be a psychological evaluation to determine underlying motivations and expectations. As discussed below, you should also weigh the potential benefits and drawbacks to cochlear implantation if your child *is* determined to be a candidate.

Factors to Consider

Potential Benefits of the Cochlear Implant

The cochlear implant does not restore normal hearing. It can, however, improve a child's speech perception and speech production. How much improvement there is in a child's hearing, speech, and language acquisition varies widely. Factors such as age of onset of deafness, age of implantation, intensity of rehabilitation, and mode of communication all contribute to this variability. Children implanted at younger ages usually produce consonants, vowels, intonation, and rhythm more accurately. Children with profound deafness who use the cochlear implant usually develop better speech and language than similar children who use hearing aids or vibrotactile devices (devices that transmit sound through the skin) (Geers and Moog, 1994).

There are no reliable factors that can accurately predict which children will benefit most from implantation. In general, though, children whose hearing loss occurred after the development of speech and who have been deaf for a shorter duration (6 months to a year) tend to do better than children whose hearing loss was present prior to the development of speech and who have been deaf for a longer duration (greater than two years). However, it has been shown that all children continue to improve with time, regardless of their hearing background.

COMMON CONCERNS ABOUT THE COCHLEAR IMPLANT

Many parents are reluctant to consider cochlear implantation for their children because they are waiting for the "ideal system." This may not be a realistic approach to take, however. Remember, time is of the essence. As mentioned earlier, the shorter the time between the onset of deafness and the time of implantation, the more successful implantation usually is. Both the 22 and the 16 multichannel cochlear implants are flexible, in that both the speech processors and the internal multichannel electrodes can be changed and upgraded.

Current studies indicate that prolonged electrical stimulation from the cochlear implant produces no long-term ill effect on the developing brain or ear. In addition, changing the internal electrode produces little damage to the inner ear structures. Studies of the inner ears of people who have received the cochlear implant have shown very little reaction to the implanted electrode. There may be some destruction of inner ear cells, but the positive effect of the cochlear implant far outweighs this minimal loss of cells.

INFORMED CONSENT

As parents of a child with a profound hearing loss, it is up to you to decide whether to elect cochlear implantation. Learning as much as you can about the cochlear implant, as well as other options, will empower you in your decision making. Your child should be included in the informed consent process as much as possible, since his active participation is crucial to the (re)habilitative process. As parents, you must understand that the cochlear implant does not restore normal hearing and that improvement in hearing and speech is highly variable. No one will be able to predict beforehand what effects an implant might have on your child's abilities. You must be informed of the advantages and disadvantages and risks associated with cochlear implantation. In addition, you must understand the importance of long-term rehabilitation in receiving maximum benefit from the cochlear implant.

Choosing a Cochlear Implant Design

As explained above, multichannel cochlear implants are much more effective than the earlier single channel implants. It is clear that providing a number of parallel independent channels of stimulation gives the best opportunity to achieve *open set speech perception* (hearing and recognizing the spoken word without the use of a visual system). What is not clear, though, is whether there is an optimal number of channels on the cochlear implant. At least four to six seem to be necessary, however.

If you are considering a cochlear implant for your child, you are probably wondering which model would give your child the most benefit: the 22 multichannel cochlear implant or the 16 multichannel cochlear implant. Each has its pros and cons, which should be carefully considered. The bottom line is that your child will achieve the best performance with the speech processor that best duplicates the sound conversion of the cochlea.

As described earlier, one difference between the 16 and 22 multichannel cochlear implants is how the external and internal components are connected. In the 22 multichannel cochlear implant, a magnet attaches the external and internal components together. In the 16 multichannel cochlear implant, there is a direct connection through the skin between the external and internal component. This provides a more flexible connection to the electrodes in case a change in speech processors is desired. It is also easier to troubleshoot electrode problems. In addition, the 16 multichannel system does not contain a magnet, so it is MRI compatible. Modifications are being made in the 22 channel multichannel implant so that it can be MRI compatible as well.

The other major difference between the two models of cochlear implants is in the number and types of electrodes. The 22 multichannel cochlear implant system has an arrangement of 22 evenly spaced platinum band electrodes. It produces a pulsating electrical stimulation. Of the systems available, this system allows for the greatest number of possible stimulation sites in the inner ear. The 16 multichannel cochlear implant consists of 16 electrodes arranged in pairs. This system permits more than one type of speech coding; that is, the user can select between pulsating or alternating stimulation. Some children may be more receptive to one form of stimulation than another, depending on the number and location of hair cells present within the cochlea.

At present, it is unclear which cochlear implant provides better speech reception for children. One reason is that we still do not fully understand all of the variables that contribute to a successful outcome. After more data is collected, perhaps one model of implant will be determined to be more effective than the other. As of this writing, the speech processors of both multichannel cochlear implants are continuously being modified and improved, and both the 22 channel and the 16 channel implanted electrodes are in the process of being redesigned as well.

How to Select a Cochlear Implant Program

If your child is a potential candidate for a cochlear implant according to the criteria listed earlier, it is extremely important that you select a cochlear implant program that involves a multidisciplinary team of physicians, audiologists, speech/language pathologists, specialists, and educators in the (re)habilitation process. There are many reputable cochlear implant centers throughout the country. These centers offer good access to a multidisciplinary team and have had experience performing a number of cochlear implant procedures in children.

For the name of a reputable cochlear implant center near your home, contact:

- Alexander Graham Bell Association for the Deaf ; (202) 337–5220
- American Academy of Otolaryngology—Head & Neck Surgery; (703) 836–4444
- American Academy of Audiology; (703) 524–2000
- American Speech Language Hearing Association (ASHA); (301) 897–5700.

REFERENCES

Cochlear Implants in Adults and Children. (1995) NIH Consensus Development Conference. May 15-17. National Institutes of Health. Bethesda, MD.

Cohen, N.L., Gordon, M.L. (1994) "Cochlear Implants: Basics, History and Future Possibilities." *SHHH Journal.* January/February.

Geers, A.E., Moog, J.S. (1994) "Effectiveness of Cochlear Implants and Tactile Aids for Deaf Children," *The Volta Review.* Vol. 96, No. 5. November.

Miyamoto, R.T. (1995) "Cochlear Implants." *Otolaryngology Clinics of North America.* Vol. 25, No. 2. April. Philadelphia, PA: W.B. Sanders Company.

4

The Auditory-Verbal Approach

A Professional Point of View

Warren Estabrooks, M.Ed., Cert. AVT

I'm learning to listen
I'm willing to try
Nothing's impossible
Reach for the sky
I may not be perfect
Though I'd like to be
I'm learning to listen
Just being me
(Estabrooks, 1994)

Never before has there been such potential for hearing! With powerful hearing aids and cochlear implants, the majority of children who are deaf or hard of hearing have access to spoken language. Through the

Auditory–Verbal Approach, these children can use their hearing potential to learn to talk through **listening**.

Many children who are deaf or hard of hearing, even those with profound losses, have usable hearing which, when amplified appropriately, enables them to hear spoken language and learn to listen and talk. This is the mission of the Auditory–Verbal Approach.

"When carried out with the necessary thoughtfulness" (Ling, 1993), expertise, guidance, and love, many children who are deaf or hard of hearing learn to communicate through listening and talking. Goals of the Auditory–Verbal Approach include attendance at a regular school and verbal communication with the butcher, the baker, and the candlestick maker, most of whom converse in spoken language. "Our bias is toward communication through spoken language rather than against alternative methods." (Ling, 1990)

AUDITORY–VERBAL THERAPY

Auditory–verbal therapy sessions are on–going, diagnostic evaluations of the child's and the parents' progress. They are conducted jointly by an auditory–verbal therapist (see below) and the parent(s). The children learn to listen to their own voices, the voices of others, and the sounds of their environment in order to communicate effectively through spoken language. By consistent use of appropriate hearing aids or a cochlear implant, auditory–verbal therapy encourages natural communication development in play and active involvement in daily life, including participation in a regular school and in the mainstream community. (Pollack, 1985; Estabrooks & Samson, 1992; Estabrooks, 1994) The Board of Directors of Auditory–Verbal International, Inc. (AVI)[1] adopted the following position statement (1987):

> *THE AUDITORY–VERBAL PHILOSOPHY IS A LOGICAL AND CRITICAL SET OF GUIDING PRINCIPLES. THESE PRINCIPLES OUTLINE THE ESSENTIAL REQUIREMENTS NEEDED TO REALIZE THE EXPECTATION THAT YOUNG CHILDREN WHO ARE DEAF OR HARD OF HEARING CAN BE EDUCATED TO USE EVEN MINIMAL AMOUNTS OF AMPLIFIED RESIDUAL HEARING. USE OF AMPLIFIED RESIDUAL*

1. Auditory–Verbal International, Inc., a non–profit organization, supports the auditory–verbal approach through a worldwide membership of parents, professionals, and persons who are deaf or hard of hearing.

HEARING IN TURN PERMITS CHILDREN WHO ARE DEAF OR HARD OF HEARING, TO LEARN TO LISTEN, PROCESS VERBAL LANGUAGE, AND TO SPEAK.

The goal of auditory–verbal practice is that children who are deaf or hard of hearing can grow up in regular learning and living environments, enabling them to become independent, participating, and contributing citizens in mainstream society. The auditory–verbal philosophy supports the basic human right that children with all degrees of hearing impairment deserve an opportunity to develop the ability to listen and to use verbal communication within their family and community constellations.

PRINCIPLES OF AUDITORY–VERBAL PRACTICE

The Principles of Auditory–Verbal practice are:[2]

- To detect hearing impairment as early as possible through screening programs, ideally in the newborn nursery and throughout childhood.
- To pursue prompt and vigorous medical and audiologic management, including selection, modification, and maintenance of appropriate hearing aids, a cochlear implant, or other sensory aids. (For more information, see "Suggested Procedures for Audiological and Hearing Aid Evaluation" at the end of the chapter.)
- To guide, counsel, and support parents and caregivers as the primary models for spoken language through listening and to help them understand the impact of deafness and impaired hearing on the entire family.
- To help children integrate listening into their development of communication and social skills.
- To support children's auditory-verbal development through one–to–one teaching.
- To help children monitor their own voices and the voices of others in order to enhance the intelligibility of their spoken language.

2. Adapted from Pollack 1985, and printed by permission of AVI.

- To use developmental patterns of listening, language, speech, and cognition to stimulate natural communication.
- To continuously assess and evaluate children's development in the above areas and, through diagnostic intervention, modify the program when needed.
- To provide support services to facilitate children's educational and social inclusion in regular education classes.

In collaboration with professionals, parents learn to create exciting listening and learning environments, where skills in listening (audition), speech, language, cognition, and communication are integrated, following natural developmental sequences. The Auditory-Verbal Approach requires a special partnership among parent, physician, audiologist, and *auditory–verbal therapist.*

AUDITORY–VERBAL THERAPIST. An auditory–verbal therapist is a qualified educator of children who are deaf or hard of hearing, an audiologist, and/or a speech-language pathologist who has chosen to pursue a career supporting the guiding principles of the Auditory–Verbal Approach. Auditory–verbal therapists receive additional specialty instruction and experiences through university courses and/or from certified auditory–verbal master clinicians. They may be certified by Auditory–Verbal International, Inc. (AVI).

Figure 1 illustrates the team model used by the Auditory–Verbal Therapy Program at North York General Hospital (NYGH) in Toronto. The left–hand side of the model shows the primary members of the team, with the child and her family as the primary focus. The right–hand side illustrates other members of the team who play a variety of interactive roles throughout the duration of the program.

THE THERAPY PROCESS

Individualized diagnostic therapy is necessary to determine whether the Auditory–Verbal Approach is appropriate for a particular child and family. It takes six to eighteen months to come to this decision, depending on a number of variables (see page 61). Occasionally, this process may take longer.

FIGURE 1. AUDITORY—VERBAL THERAPY PROGRAM: NYGH TEAM MODEL

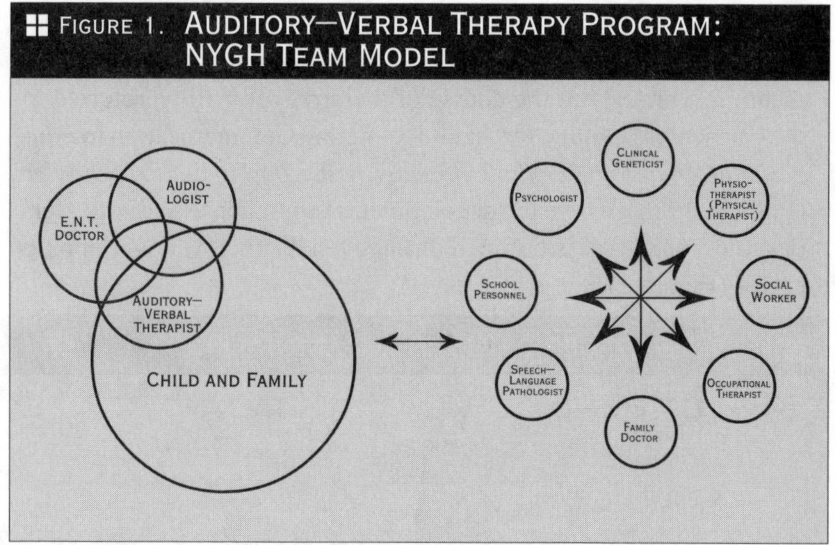

Most auditory–verbal programs offer weekly therapy sessions, lasting for an hour or an hour and a half each. Through motivation and guidance, you will acquire the confidence to use different techniques and strategies to achieve specific goals. The auditory–verbal therapist demonstrates; you practice. Then you and the therapist discuss the interaction.

During the course of therapy sessions, the auditory–verbal therapist suggests specific targets (goals) for you to work on at home. Targets for younger children may include: drawing attention to sounds in the environment, babbling with your child, learning vocabulary, developing prepositions, or beginning small conversations. Targets for older children may include: story-telling, developing speech and auditory skills in the presence of "noise," or learning school-based subject material. These targets are incorporated in play, in "ordinary" daily routines, in "structured" activities, and in song. (Estabrooks, Birkenshaw–Fleming, 1994).

Targets for your child will depend on her developmental stage. Children who are deaf or hard of hearing need the same listening, learning, and language foundations as children who can hear, regardless of their chronological age. During the development of listening, each baby or child needs to progress through a number of stages.

Early on, you will come to understand *The Schedules of Development* (Ling, 1977), in audition, speech, language, and communication. Throughout the course of therapy, you will be referred to the Curriculum Outline for Auditory–Verbal Communication in *Educational Audiology for the Limited Hearing Infant and Preschooler* (Pollack, 1985), where the developmental approach to auditory–verbal communication is outlined through ten distinct, yet overlapping stages (Figure 2).

FIGURE 2. STAGES OF LISTENING AND TALKING*

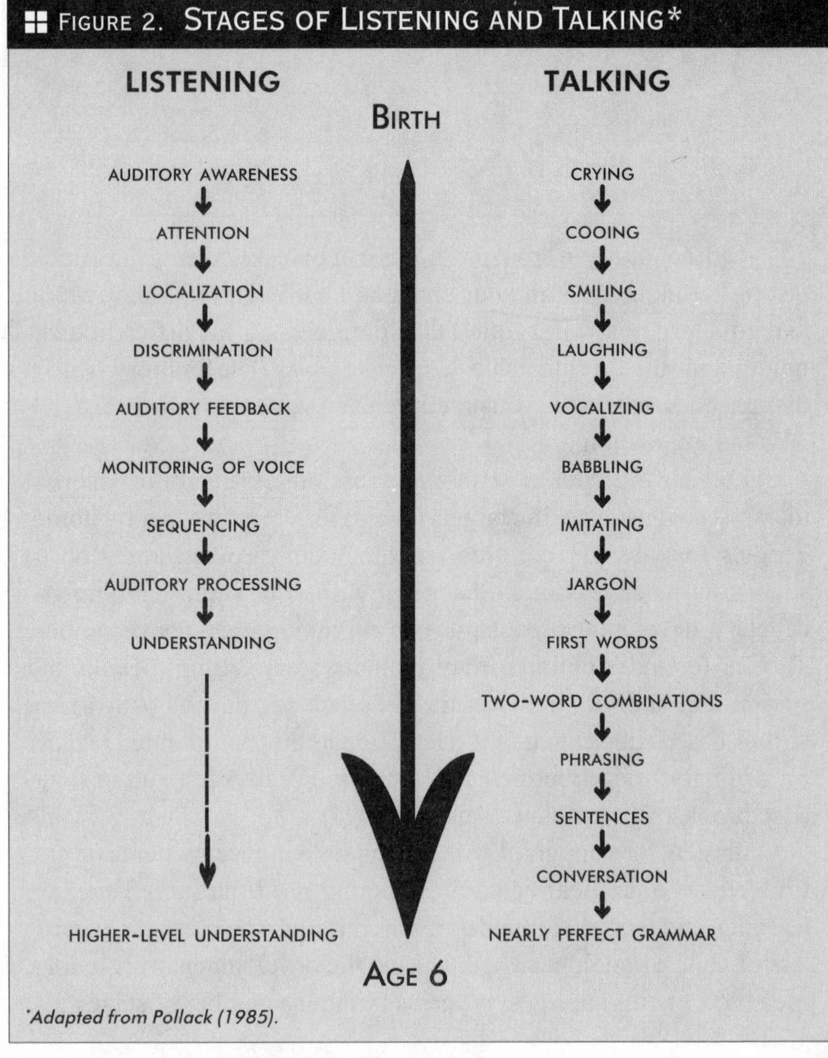

Adapted from Pollack (1985).

The Auditory–Verbal Approach embraces the view that children learn language most easily when actively engaged in relaxed, meaningful interactions with supportive parents and caregivers. (Kretschmer & Kretschmer, 1978; Ling, 1990; Ross, 1990; Estabrooks, 1994). In auditory–verbal sessions, therefore, you need to *observe, participate,* and *practice* to learn to:

- Model techniques for stimulating speech, language, and communication activities at home;
- Plan strategies to integrate listening, speech, language, and communication into daily routines and experiences;
- Communicate as partners in the therapy process;
- Inform the therapist of your child's interests and abilities;
- Interpret the meaning of your child's early communication;
- Develop appropriate behavior management techniques;
- Record and discuss progress;
- Interpret short–term and long–term goals;
- Develop confidence in parent–child interaction;
- Make informed decisions.
- Advocate on behalf of your child

(Estabrooks, 1994).

TECHNIQUES IN AUDITORY–VERBAL THERAPY

A variety of specific auditory–verbal techniques are used in each session. These might include:

- rewording what has been said;
- waiting or pausing to allow your child time to respond;
- directing your child to "listen closely";
- repeating a previous word, phrase, or statement;
- moving closer to your child;
- providing a visual clue and "putting it back into hearing";
- providing "acoustic highlighting" such as whispering, singing, or emphasizing specific elements of spoken language; and
- the often–misunderstood technique called the *hand cue.*

The hand cue is used to varying degrees in most auditory–verbal therapy programs to place emphasis on the use of listening to acquire spoken language.

The hand cue may consist of:

- The therapist, parent, or caregiver covering his or her mouth briefly, from time to time, when the child is looking directly at the adult's face. This encourages listening rather than lipreading. When the child is playfully engaged and not "looking," the hand cue is unnecessary. The adult, however, must be close to the microphone of the child's hearing aid or cochlear implant (within "earshot"), as explained in the section on "The Listening Environment," below.
- The adult moving his or her hand toward the child, in a nurturing way, as a prompt for vocal imitation or as a signal for turn–taking.
- The adult talking through a stuffed animal, a toy, a picture, or a book placed in front of his or her mouth.

The hand cue signals the child to *listen intently,* and is used as a stepping stone to assist the child to integrate all five senses. The hand cue must only be used when necessary, because its use can sometimes muffle or distort the sound arriving at the microphone. As children come to rely on hearing, the use of the hand cue is reduced (Simser, 1993; Estabrooks, 1994). Once the child has "integrated hearing into his or her personality" (Pollack 1985), the *hand cue* is rarely used.

THE LISTENING ENVIRONMENT

Since the Auditory–Verbal Approach encourages the maximum use of hearing in order to learn language and stresses *listening* rather than watching, therapy needs to be carried out in the best possible acoustic (listening) conditions. The acoustic environment is enhanced by:

- parents and/or therapists sitting beside the child, on the side of the *better* ear (within "earshot");
- speaking close to the child's hearing aids or cochlear implant microphone;
- speaking at regular volume;

- minimizing background noise;
- using speech which is repetitive and rich in melody, expression, and rhythm;
- using "acoustic highlighting" techniques to enhance the audibility of spoken language (moving from most audible to least audible).

Sessions may be held in a variety of settings, including a hospital clinic, a private practice, or a school. Although much can be learned in these settings, they are a far cry from the natural learning environment of the child. To make them more homelike, objects and toys found in the child's home may be used, as well as miniaturized versions of real objects. These toys help you in transferring activities and targets to your home (Simser, 1993). In the Auditory–Verbal Approach, attention is given to the personal interests of the family and its culture.

VARIABLES AFFECTING PROGRESS

Each family and child is unique, with a specific living and learning style (Luterman, 1991). Listening and communication development vary from child to child and from family to family. Progress, of course, is dependent upon a number of variables, such as:

- Age at diagnosis;
- Cause of hearing impairment;
- Degree of hearing impairment;
- Effectiveness of the amplification devices (hearing aids or cochlear implant);
- Effectiveness of audiological management;
- Hearing potential of the child;
- Health of the child;
- Emotional state of the family;
- Level of participation of the family;
- Skills of the therapist;
- Skills of the parents or caregiver;
- Child's learning style;
- Child's intelligence.

CONCLUSION

The important partnership in the Auditory–Verbal Approach is exemplified in the following by an unknown poet:

I DREAMED I STOOD IN A STUDIO
AND WATCHED TWO SCULPTORS THERE,
THE CLAY THEY USED WAS A YOUNG CHILD'S MIND
AND THEY FASHIONED IT WITH CARE.

ONE WAS A TEACHER: THE TOOLS HE USED
WERE BOOKS, MUSIC AND ART.
THE OTHER, A PARENT, WITH A GUIDING HAND,
AND A GENTLE LOVING HEART.

DAY AFTER DAY, THE TEACHER TOILED,
WITH A TOUCH THAT WAS DEFT AND SURE,
WHILE THE PARENT LABOURED BY HIS SIDE
AND POLISHED AND SMOOTHED IT O'ER.

AND BOTH AGREED EACH WOULD HAVE FAILED
IF THEY HAD WORKED ALONE,
FOR BEHIND THE PARENT STOOD THE SCHOOL,
AND BEHIND THE TEACHER, THE HOME.

Recent scientific advances in amplification and cochlear implant technology have provided great potential listening opportunities for children all over the world. The Auditory–Verbal Approach is a natural companion of such technology.

It is the vision of the Auditory–Verbal Approach as an "applied science with its objectively measured goals" (Ling 1994), to encourage a little hearing to go a long way.

ACKNOWLEDGEMENT

The author is grateful to Judith Simser, O. ONT., Cert. AVT, and Rhonda Schwartz, M.A., Reg. OSLA, S-LP(C) for their consultation in preparation of this chapter.

REFERENCES

Estabrooks, W. (1994) *Auditory–Verbal Therapy for Parents and Professionals.* Washington, DC: A.G. Bell.

Estabrooks, W. & Birkenshaw–Fleming L. (1994) *Hear & Listen! Talk & Sing!* Toronto: Arisa Press.

Estabrooks, W. & Samson, A. (1992) *Do You Hear That?* Washington, DC: A.G. Bell.

Flexer, C. (1994) *Facilitating Hearing and Listening In Young Children.* San Diego, CA: Singular.

Kretschmer, R.R. & Kretschmer, L. (1978) *Language Development and Intervention with the Hearing-Impaired.* Baltimore, MD: University Park Press.

Ling, A.H. (1977) *Schedules of Development in Audition, Speech, Language and Communication for Hearing–Impaired Infants and Their Parents.* Washington, DC: A.G. Bell

Ling, D. (1978) *Aural Habilitation.* Washington, DC: A.G. Bell.

Ling, D. (1990) *Foundations of Spoken Language for Hearing-Impaired Children.* Washington, DC: A.G. Bell.

Ling, D. (1994) *Introduction in Auditory–Verbal Therapy.* Estabrooks, E. (Ed.) Washington, DC: A.G. Bell.

Luterman, D. (1991) *When Your Child Is Deaf.* Timonium, MD: York Press.

Pollack, D. (1985) *Educational Audiology for the Limited Hearing Infant and Preschooler.* Springfield, IL: Charles Thomas Press.

Ross, M. (Ed.) (1990) *Hearing–Impaired Children in the Mainstream.* Timonium, MD: York Press.

Simser, J. (1993) "Auditory–Verbal Intervention: Infants and Toddlers." *The Volta Review,* Vol. 95, No. 3, Summer 1993.

Simser, J. (1993) "A Hospital Clinic Early Intervention Program." *The Volta Review,* Vol. 95, No. 5, November 1993.

SUGGESTED PROCEDURES FOR AUDIOLOGICAL AND HEARING AID EVALUATION (AVI, 1993)

The audiological test procedures indicated are recommended for use with children in order to ensure that maximal use of residual hearing can be achieved in the auditory–verbal approach. A battery of audiological tests is always suggested since no single procedure has sufficient reliability to stand alone. Optimally, every aural habilitation program should have on-site audiological services, but, regardless of setting, close cooperation between audiology and therapy service providers is essential. Parents should be present for and participate in the administration of all assessment procedures to include them in this aspect of the child's care.

AUDIOLOGICAL EVALUATIONS

PROCEDURES TO BE INCLUDED IN ALL ASSESSMENTS, REGARDLESS OF CHILD'S AGE.

- Case history/parent observation report
- Otoscopic inspection
- Acoustic immittance: tympanometry, physical volume test, and acoustic reflexes

Cautious interpretation is recommended if the child is younger than six months.

0–6 MONTHS: AUDITORY BRAINSTEM RESPONSE (ABR)

- Alternating click and tone pip response by air conduction and by bone conduction.

Caution: ABR should not stand alone for diagnostic purposes. Lack of response to ABR testing does not necessarily indicate an absence of usable hearing.

Amplification and auditory learning are recommended as the first option unless special imaging (CT scan or MRI) confirms an absence of the cochlea. Behavioral testing, amplification, and therapy are otherwise indicated before a decision of no usable hearing is made.

6 MONTHS–2 YEARS: BEHAVIORAL OBSERVATION/ VISUAL REINFORCEMENT AUDIOMETRY

- Detection/awareness of voice and warbled tones from 250–6000 Mz in the sound field and/or 250–8000 Hz under headphones.
- Startle response in sound field, under headphones, and by bone conduction.
- Evaluation of auditory skill development.

2–5 YEARS: CONDITIONED PLAY AUDIOMETRY

- Responses to pure tones from 250–12,000 Hz by air conduction and bone condition from 500–4000 Hz with masking (at 3° years+).
- Speech Awareness Threshold (Speech Recognition Threshold if Language development allows) using Ling Five Sounds, body parts, speech perception tasks, or formal tests such as the WIPI.

5 YEARS+: STANDARD AUDIOMETRY

- Air and bone condition, speech recognition and speech/word Identification.

AMPLIFICATION ASSESSMENT

ELECTRO–ACOUSTIC ANALYSIS OF HEARING AIDS

- On day of fitting.
- At 30–90 day intervals at user volume as well as full-on volume.
- Whenever a hearing aid is repaired, in addition to a close check of internal settings.
- Whenever parental listening check or behavioral observation raises concern.

SOUND FIELD AIDED RESPONSES

- Parents and therapists can prepare the child by teaching him/her to respond consistently to voice and the Ling Five Sounds.

- Aided measures should include: Speech Awareness or Recognition, Word Identification at 55 dB HL in quiet and, if possible, in noise; response to warbled pure tones from 250–6000 Hz wearing binaural hearing aids, or nonaural measures to compare responses at each ear.

Caution: It is important that the aided results be evaluated in relation to the unaided audiogram. Recommended aided results for the "left corner" audiogram with optimum amplification should be in the 35–45 dB HL (ANSI) range at 250, 500, 1000 Hz or better.

Probe Microphone (Real Ear) Measures

- Unoccluded measurement of External Ear Effect as well as full occlusion with the hearing aid OFF to measure insertion loss.
- Insertion gain measured with hearing aid at customary settings to verify appropriate gain and output levels and to compare changes in settings.

Caution: Existing amplification gain formulas may underestimate the actual gain required by children with severe to profound hearing impairment.

FM Systems

When FM systems are in use, they should be evaluated at the time of the complete audiological and hearing aid assessment using the same format described for amplification.

Frequency of Assessment (Aided and Unaided)

- Every 90 days once diagnosis is confirmed and amplification fitted, until age 3. As early as possible, but at least by age 3, a complete unaided and aided audiogram should be obtained (preferably under headphones, but at least in the sound field.) New earmolds may need to be obtained at 90 day intervals or sooner until age 3–4 in view of the typically rapid growth rate during this time.

- Assessment every 6 months from age 4–6 is appropriate if progress is satisfactory.
- Above age 6, assessment at 6–12 months from age 4–6 is appropriate if progress is satisfactory.
- Immediate evaluation should be scheduled if parents or caretakers suspect a change in hearing or hearing aid function.

Caution: Modifications of this schedule are appropriate when middle ear disease is chronic or recurrent or when additional disabilities are present.

REPORTS

Reports should be supplied promptly upon receipt of written release to parents, therapists, physicians, educators. Reports should include:

- Test procedures and reliability assessment.
- The complete audiogram with symbol key, calibration standard, and stimuli used.
- Hearing aid identification - make, model, output and tone settings, compression or special feature settings, volume settings, earmold style, and quality of fit.
- FM system identification and settings.
- Interpretive information regarding relationship of audiological findings to acoustic phonetics, especially with respect to distance hearing and message competition.
- Analysis of auditory behavior and development of the listening function.

Printed with permission from Auditory–Verbal International (AVI).

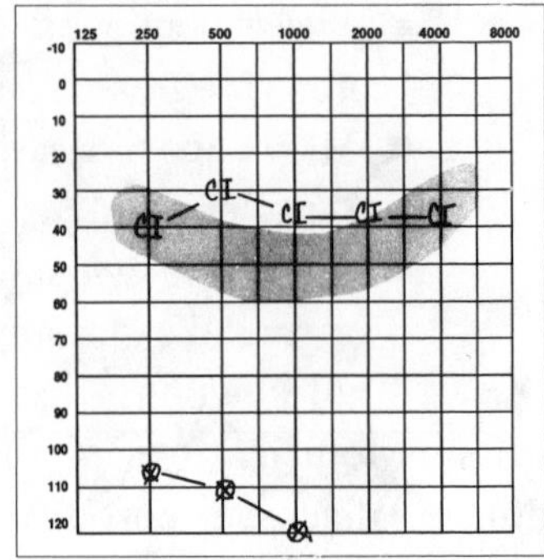

Dara's Story

Shirley Keller

On April, 24, 1986, our family was blessed with the arrival of Dara, our perfect little girl. Dara was cute, good–natured, a good sleeper, and an absolute pleasure. Along with her two older siblings, Jeremy and Josh, my husband, Julian, and I knew that she made our family complete.

For eight and a half months, life was perfect. I was blissful and nobody felt that anything could go amiss. Dara was alert, happy, and vocal, and since we did not know anybody who had a hearing loss, we never looked for *the signs!*

One day Julian wanted to take a picture of Dara and her baby cousin, Daniel. When their names were called, Daniel responded but Dara did not.

We ran the gamut of doctors, who clapped their hands or jingled keys behind Dara. One even told me to *"have a nice day"* as he left the examining room. They all acknowledged that there was a problem and that further investigation was necessary. We already knew there was a problem, but we were certain that in this age of technological wizardry it could all be fixed! We did not want our daughter to grow up in a world of silence, when we knew she could have the same opportunities as her brothers.

Eventually we learned that Dara had a profound hearing loss with hearing only in the low frequencies. There were many nights that I stayed awake wishing she had just a few more decibels of hearing. The word "profound" paralyzed me with fear and I could not help but compare Dara with all other children.

We weighed our options and chose the Auditory–Verbal Approach because we wanted her to develop the ability to communicate with anybody...neighbors, friends, family, and peers. We learned about other modes of communication, but strongly felt that the Auditory–Verbal Approach was the least restrictive for Dara and our family.

Dara received binaural hearing aids by the age of ten months and began auditory–verbal therapy one month later. Auditory–verbal therapy continued for a few years, during which time Dara developed a large language base. Her speech, however, remained very poor and the only people who understood her were our family, close friends, and her auditory–verbal therapist. At times, even *we* misunderstood her and she would throw temper tantrums out of frustration.

Even though she was an auditory child with *a listening attitude,* we could now tell that her hearing loss was so profound that her hearing aids could only do so much. After all, zero amplified is still zero and Dara fell below the speech banana in many of the higher frequencies. There were too many sounds she would never hear with hearing aids. Gradually, we began to understand the severe limitations of even the best hearing aids.

We began to seriously consider the possibility of a cochlear implant. After Dara had gone through a battery of tests, she was deemed an appropriate candidate and received her cochlear implant in New York on July 26, 1990.

The surgery was successful and Dara started along a new path of milestones, setbacks, and miracles. For several months, she exhibited very slow progress and even regressed in some areas. She had to relearn many basic language and auditory skills. She did not even recognize her name for quite awhile.

For about four years following surgery, Dara received auditory-verbal therapy in Toronto, with two programs in New York providing additional support and expertise. Everyone worked together to ensure that Dara's needs were met.

When she was about eight, a hospital in Toronto assumed responsibility for Dara's audiological needs and provided information and seminars to professionals working with children who received cochlear implants.

Today, Dara is almost nine years old and continues to be mainstreamed in our local school, where she is finishing third grade. She is at grade level or above in all subjects, loves to horseback ride, ski and swim, has many friends and even talks on the telephone. She is a happy, well-adjusted child who *still has a hearing loss*. This is a part of who she is, but her life does not revolve around it.

Since the age of three, Dara has received excellent itinerant support services which are provided by our school board. A teacher of the deaf visits the school for about six hours each week and helps her to keep up with the curriculum, which includes the study of French. The itinerant teacher helps Dara with language, speech, and auditory memory, and is a liaison between me and the classroom teacher. She also explains hearing loss to Dara's classmates by providing the children with earplugs followed by a spelling test. This simulation of mild hearing impairment helps her peers to appreciate some of the challenges of a person who has a hearing loss, especially since most of the children do very poorly on the spelling test.

A good itinerant teacher makes sure that Dara not only *gets by,* but excels whenever possible. Within the school walls, the itinerant teacher is Dara's best advocate.

Dara is truly a child of the '90s. While *she* takes many things for granted, *I* do not. I feel extremely lucky to have had the good fortune to hook up with professionals who have appreciated Dara as a child, first and foremost, and then as one who requires special services and deserves to realize her potential.

Technology is not to be feared or ignored. The cochlear implant is still in its infancy and the future will only bring good things. Auditory-verbal therapy is a logical companion of such technology. Cochlear implants will become more sophisticated and eventually more compact. Down the road, the current surgically implanted portion of the implant may become obsolete. However, Dara will have become master of her own destiny.

The cochlear implant along with auditory–verbal therapy has helped Dara to develop a natural sounding voice accompanied by spoken language which is understood by almost everybody. She has developed good interpersonal skills and is extremely self-confident. Dara has received the love and support of family, friends, and professionals.

When I hear her playing with a friend, ordering food in a restaurant, telling a joke to her brothers, arguing with her father, or talking in her sleep, I am very content that Dara has learned to use the tools necessary to live her life to the fullest.

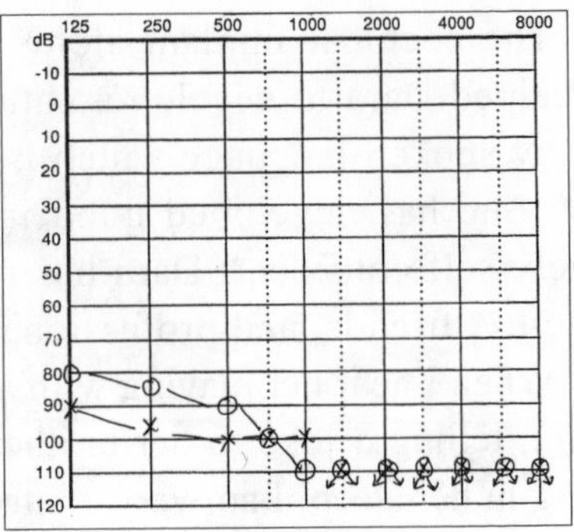

JONATHAN'S STORY

ARIELLA BLUM SAMSON

I first suspected Jonathan's deafness the day we came home from the hospital. He was five days old and our new nursery was still in transition from sewing room to baby room. As Jonathan looked peacefully about from his crib, the ironing board crashed to the floor, startling my tranquillity. Jonathan, however, smiled on, undisturbed! The first seeds of doubt were firmly planted. Still, this was our first baby and I was not yet ready for any shattered dreams. As long as I didn't talk about **it**, I could pretend **it** did not exist.

It took almost two months to muster up the courage to finally open up to my husband, who must have been doing his own dance of denial. We could no longer hide in our own protective corners. But, the pediatrician, on our next visit, convinced us that we were neurotic, over–anxious parents, expecting too much from our firstborn.

A month before his first birthday, in a crowded hospital hallway, the otolaryngologist blurted out that Jonathan was profoundly deaf. The audiologist then made earmold impressions and booked a return appointment for the hearing aid fitting. Approximately half an hour after the "official" diagnosis, we left the hospital. No further information was volunteered, no materials dispensed for study at home, and no hope extended.

Nevertheless, aside from initial numbness, our predominant feeling that day was *relief.* Relief that what we suspected was finally confirmed, relief that Jonathan was not cognitively impaired but *only* deaf, and relief that we could take some action. Yet, we knew *nothing* about deafness!

Armed only with our ignorance and the impetus to do something, we went to the library. We also visited the local school for the deaf after school hours, where the three of us were left to our own devices in the empty building. We peeked into classrooms and perused the walls that lined the hallways. This was our first confrontation with academic expectations for the deaf. We were appalled. My husband and I spent the weekend reading, talking, and crying, but we made our decision!

In the weeks that followed, Jonathan was confirmed to have a left corner audiogram (hearing only for low frequencies) with 105dB hearing loss in his better ear. Yet we still had the same child we had *before* the day of diagnosis: a bright, inquisitive little boy who did not hear the way we did, but who was still a member of our family. We decided that we were going to capitalize on the hearing that Jonathan had, and concentrate on the sounds available to him.

Our goal was single-minded: we wanted the best *for* our children, and the best *from* them. We felt the auditory-verbal approach was the best choice for Jonathan and our family. We began our odyssey with weekly auditory–verbal sessions and we worked on structured lessons daily. Most learning, however, took place during play and regular daily activities. Everything we saw, experienced, and heard was pointed out and reiterated linguistically in as many ways as possible.

I became the teacher who planned the daily lessons and developed the structured sessions, while my husband took on the supportive role of reinforcing language during playtime. More importantly, he was my support in times of stress.

At three, Jonathan began regular nursery school and at five he enrolled in our neighborhood public school. Throughout the primary grades, I was Jonathan's intermediary within the school system. I would introduce ourselves to each new teacher, give some brief background information specifically about Jonathan and generally about hearing loss, and distribute some useful handouts. I tried not to be overbearing and usually focused on our part in Jonathan's education. I also spent a lot of time volunteering in school.

From grade two onwards, our days were stretched to accommodate even more: an itinerant teacher, an F.M. system, Scouts, swimming and skating lessons, as well as the addition of a brother and sister. Jonathan also began to attend Hebrew school, which he continued for ten years. At thirteen, he confidently read his Bar Mitzvah portion in Hebrew.

When Jonathan turned seven, he began asking for piano lessons. Outwardly, we were enthusiastic and encouraging but inwardly, we again felt the initial pains of diagnosis and loss. How was I to tell my son to lower his goals and to select a more realistic and attainable interest? With great trepidation, I put his request on mental hold. Jonathan's confidence and determination, however, never lagged and we finally capitulated. He deserved the same opportunity to succeed, and more importantly, the opportunity to try and fail.

We found a music teacher willing to teach a deaf child to play the piano and to forego the theory. The rigors of daily practice and weekly lessons began. Eventually he took keyboarding as a high school credit and not only received an A, but acted as a peer tutor in that subject. I learned more from these music lessons than Jonathan did. I learned to give my son room to grow, flourish, and excel, but more importantly, to occasionally stumble.

When all the neighborhood children began to use the local public transit system on their own, Jonathan's umbilical cord was severed. On his first solo trip, he also learned to use the pay phone. Though it was a one-sided conversation, he informed us that he had arrived safely. Even though he was only ten years old, he gained immeasurable confidence and enjoyed the feeling of independence.

Through our local school board, we were given an F.M. system for use in the classroom and an itinerant teacher who provided extra tutorial work in academic areas. While working as a liaison between family and school, the itinerant would bring school staff together to acquaint them with the issues of deafness, a role previously left to the family.

Whenever there was spare time and Jonathan seemed to be on top of things, he had extra auditory games and speech. At the age of nine, we spent a great deal of time on telephone practice: learning basic skills, a stock of commonly used phrases, names of people, days of the week, and finally putting together a coded alphabet to help spell out difficult to hear words. Jonathan also learned strategies for controlling a telephone conversation, eliciting "yes" or "no" answers and repeating information he thought he heard, to confirm whether he had indeed heard accurately. These skills transferred readily to other areas. He used the auditory-verbal skills of acoustic highlighting and other adaptive strategies.

At home, Jonathan enlisted the help of all family members to help oral interpret. He would use a second telephone within visible range and while we mouthed the conversation from the other end of the line, Jonathan could use his own voice. In this way, the flavor of the conversation remained natural, didn't slow down to a TDD pace, and Jonathan could talk regularly to his hearing friends.

The summers offered a wonderful variety of experiences. In his early years, Jonathan attended local day camps, but from the age of ten he enjoyed a month away at overnight camp, where he learned to function without home support.

In junior high, the itinerant teacher's role expanded and help was extended to three hours a week. This was reduced to two hours in the first years of high school and finally to one hour in his senior year, a gentle and natural weaning process.

Junior high was Jonathan's first exposure to social isolation. He left the small neighborhood elementary school, where the children knew one another and played together in the neighborhood. He found a less homogeneous group which seemed less tolerant of anyone who was somewhat different. He had a very small group of children that he called *friends* but which we recognized as *acquaintances.* Lunch periods during the first year were most often spent in the computer room, rather than alone at the lunch table, or as a bystander on the sports field. This was a tough time.

In those early pre–pubescent years, the F.M. became a focus of rebellion. The F.M. was conveniently forgotten in the locker or left at home. The classroom teacher, parent, and itinerant teacher were all given a different story. When actually forced to wear the F.M., Jonathan regularly reported intermittent problems that could not be detected on the spot, thereby gaining two or three weeks of repair time. Jonathan concentrated all his energy on the demise of the F.M. system and eventually succeeded. By the time he began high school, we had conceded defeat.

When he reached high school age, there were two schools from which to choose. One was traditional, requiring students to study eight subjects throughout the school year, which was divided into three terms. The other ran on a semester system with four subjects each semester. In this school each subject was doubled in actual class time. Together with Jonathan, we chose the latter. The lengthier classes required longer listening and looking periods, which potentially would be more exhausting. The time allotted to master each subject was condensed into half the school year. Clearly, Jonathan would have to be on top of the work at all times. One or two sick days might equal a week of missed work. A problem not detected early might not allow us enough time to get extra help. There would also be no extra time to catch up on reading. Jonathan, nevertheless, felt this school fitted better with his personality. He always had trouble juggling too many items at the same time, so at this school he could focus all his energies on the four subjects. The decision proved to be the best choice.

High school was a total change. For the first time Jonathan took the initiative of talking to teachers before classes began, introduced himself, identified his needs, and periodically met to evaluate progress. Though at first reluctant, he experienced numerous benefits from this new obligation. His confidence grew, he felt a sense of comfort with the staff, and he learned new networking skills.

While many of his junior high peers moved on to this high school, he met them on fresher ground. A circle of new friends grew, and old friends became *real* friends. High school was a difficult adjustment, as classes rotated and there were new teachers for each subject. Each class contained a new group of students and even though he was exposed to a greater number of people, Jonathan seemed to thrive. Grades improved dramatically and he achieved the honor roll. His self–esteem flourished and there was a healthy respect between himself and his peers.

French is a compulsory subject in the Canadian school system but it was Jonathan's most hated subject. Throughout elementary school and junior high he maintained an average grade but he disliked French intensely. He discovered a loophole for special–needs students and was quick to negotiate a release from this required credit. Principal and student finally agreed to exchange French for music, to be followed by three years of Latin. To this day I don't think the principal realized the discrepancy in this unique release: that a deaf student dropped his compulsory unwanted subject on the grounds of his disability! Surprisingly, Latin proved to be a very positive choice. Since its study is predominately in written form, Jonathan was on solid ground. He achieved high grades and became a peer tutor once again.

In grade eleven, Jonathan's social life blossomed. He joined student council as treasurer and spent more time with friends and teachers, both during and after school hours.

During the summers, when he outgrew camp, Jonathan took a YMCA leadership training course. Eventually he worked as a program supervisor in a day camp, where he was required to interact with counsellors, campers, and parents. He also worked as a research assistant in a charitable organization. Here he researched and developed a proposal for the government on the victimization of the disabled and helped create a computerized filing system for the organization's reference library.

Life has a strange way of coming full circle. My mother, who has suffered from cancer for a dozen years, came to live with us a few years ago. Her condition deteriorated drastically. After her latest operation, one of her vocal cords had to be severed and she now has a tracheotomy tube. Her most difficult adjustment centered around her communication skills.

Though she was housebound for years, she still had her friends through personal visits but especially through the telephone. Presently, however, she is only able to manage a whisper, which all of us are able to hear, though sometimes with difficulty. My mother's best friend has a severe hearing loss due to old age, and the telephone once again posed a particular problem in our lives.

But we are an innovative family. Now Jonathan, with expert lip reading skills, became the oral interpreter (in reverse), voicing for his grandmother, while her friend replied at the other end. The TDD (Telecommunication Device for the Deaf) is now my mother's newest gadget: she keys to her friend and then lifts the receiver to hear her friend reply.

Our family's experience has been much enriched because of Jonathan and we have become a tightly knit unit. Our horizons have broadened and our children have learned to accept all people for who and what they truly are.

During Jonathan's high school years, the Ministry for the Disabled ran a series of commercials for public awareness. Jonathan auditioned and won the major role in one of the four commercials, which were non–scripted and used clips from the individuals' own conversations. They were a great success, airing in key time slots on national television. In his commercial, Jonathan stated that he did not often get invited to parties because friends did not think he could enjoy music and dancing. "Don't judge a person from the outside," he concluded. The commercial aired for four subsequent years and much to Jonathan's delight, his party invitations flourished.

In his senior year, Jonathan ran for student council president and won with a respectable majority. His platform was to increase school spirit and involve the student body in community projects, both with the elderly and the environment. His campaign slogan "I may be deaf but you're not blind, so when you vote keep *me* in mind" emphasized, as usual, his concept of self and healthy self-esteem.

University life reflected this growth and maturation. Because he was determined to try his own wings, and to be his own advocate, Jonathan chose an out–of–town university. Although he lived in residence for two years, he eventually moved into a house with four other students to experience "true" independence. Here he added to his high school coping strategies by hiring note takers so that he could properly concentrate on the professors' lectures. Always politically involved, he functioned as treasurer of his dormitory for one year, and as vice–president of the university student council in his senior year.

Jonathan graduated in the spring. He is now working in business before proceeding with his future plan of acquiring a Masters of Business Administration degree.

Jonathan is who he is in spite of and because of his hearing impairment. Twenty–three years ago, when we began our journey, we chose the auditory–verbal approach. We wanted to focus on Jonathan's abilities, not his disabilities, and to maximize the use of his residual hearing. Taking on an additional language, even sign language, seemed unreasonable to us because we viewed it as very segregating. In those apolitical and pre–deaf culture days, we felt confident in maintaining our own heritage, whilst nurturing our differences, yet all the while part of the greater community.

This is what we wanted for *all our children,* and our deaf child deserved no less!

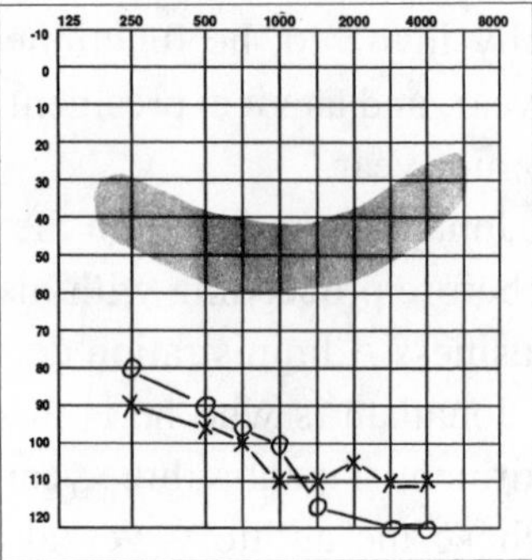

KIMBERLY'S STORY

SHERYL FORREST

Kimberly was born with a profound sensorineural hearing loss. She began wearing hearing aids at the age of 22 months and has learned to use her residual hearing to listen and to speak quite effectively. We applaud her for the determination she has shown in confronting her challenges.

Parents who have anticipated the birth of a child know the extraordinary delight associated with it. Similarly, the grief that accompanies the diagnosis of a hearing loss is familiar to every parent who has received the painful news. Delight gives way to despair, and then despair to the realization that decisions have to be made.

Deafness will not be denied, nor will it yield to a cure. Hearing cannot be restored through a technological miracle. The grief must give way to action, to an intervention which will maximize the child's abilities. Deafness did not threaten our deep love for Kimberly, nor did it alter our commitment to provide her with as many opportunities in life as we could. We found ourselves, however, confronted with choices we had never anticipated. We had no experience or knowledge with which to make a decision, but we knew we would have to make choices on her behalf. Our goal was to enable her to become independent, and to become her own advocate.

We looked at many options, many programs, many opportunities—always in the light of the end result. Decisions made on behalf of our toddler had to be made in the context of the impact they would have on her adult life. We sought out highly competent professionals who were able to translate the technical jargon into words we could understand. We observed children in various programs, using various modes of communication. We persevered until we felt knowledgeable enough to choose a communication approach and an educational setting which would give her as many advantages as possible. We talked to many professionals who looked at her audiogram and said she didn't have much hearing with which to work. Then we met an auditory-verbal therapist who believed in the power of Kimberly's aided hearing, in the potential for developing spoken language and in the possibilities for spoken communication.

We chose auditory–verbal therapy. The auditory–verbal therapist helped us to follow a program which has enabled Kimberly to listen, to learn language, and to develop intelligible speech. Between clinic visits, we implemented the program at home. Kimberly and I commuted six hours to therapy once a week for six years. After she graduated from the clinic program at the age of nine, she began working with a speech pathologist weekly and a special education teacher daily at her school. Her successes are the result of the efforts of a team of people: an audiologist who prescribed hearing aids which would provide Kimberly with access to her residual hearing, an auditory-verbal therapist who knew how to enable her to use it, and a family willing to provide a loving, nurturing environment rich in sound, spoken language, and music.

My recollection of those early years of intensive auditory-verbal therapy are quite blurry. It is difficult to remember specific events now, but I clearly recall that sometimes her lessons were fun, and sometimes *learning to listen* was just plain hard work. The first time our preschooler told the waitress that she wanted a hamburger and orange pop for supper, I was thrilled. The day she insisted on going to the office at the campground where our family was vacationing to find out what time the swimming pool opened and came back with an answer to her query, I was delighted. For a child with normal hearing, the ability to communicate this way is a simple task. But for anyone with Kimberly's degree of hearing loss, these events represent a monumental accomplishment.

If I could cure Kimberly's deafness, I would. If being the parent of a deaf child makes me *special*, I want to be *ordinary*. If I could choose, I would be the educator, not the parent. Teachers get weekends off! Yet it is nothing short of amazing to realize what she is able to do in spite of such a significant hearing loss. She is realizing the potential that all the team members hoped for. The investment we made in enabling her to learn to listen and to speak has paid great dividends. It is hard work, but it is also very rewarding.

Kimberly is now fourteen years old. She is a grade 9 student and attends classes with her hearing peers in a high school where she also has the advantage of spending one period each day with a teacher of the hearing impaired. Being deaf still presents her with many challenges, but she is better equipped to face those challenges because of the opportunity she has had to benefit from auditory–verbal therapy.

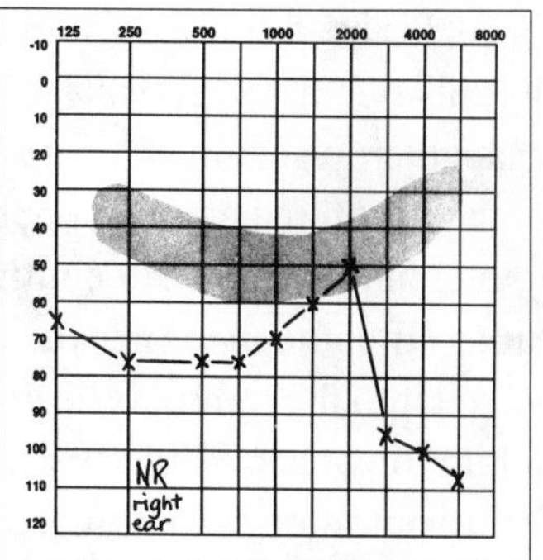

Sol's Story

Harriet Susan Fried

Sol recently celebrated his twelfth birthday, and celebrate we did!

One Sunday morning, when Sol was two years old, he awoke not quite himself. He decided to watch "Superman" instead of running around as usual. Halfway through the movie, Sol suddenly cried out "Mommy!" Then his body turned stiff, as his eyes stared off into space. Within twenty minutes we were in the Emergency Department at the local Hospital. The pediatrician on call did a spinal tap. Sol's spinal fluid was so thick, the doctors had to suction it with a syringe. Blood tests were taken and an IV was started.

Sol was admitted to the hospital and later in the day the diagnosis was confirmed that Sol had Hemophilus Influenza Type B Meningitis. For the next three weeks he was treated with massive dosages of Ampicillin, Chloramphenicol, and Hydrocortisone. Numerous tests (CAT scans, EEG, E.C.G., blood tests and spinal taps) were done. Only after ten days did Sol slowly begin to improve. We came home three weeks later.

Sol arrived home a very different child. Before his illness, he was a very active boy, and weighed thirty–five pounds; when he left the hospital, only weighing twenty pounds, he had regressed to bottle feeding and wearing diapers once again; he could not walk, sit, or even hold his head up, without support; he had very little movement on the left side and his left elbow and right knee were so swollen they could not be straightened; his head could not turn to the left. The worse part was that he had left his bubbly personality behind somewhere.... There was no smile or laughter, just pain and frustration.

For the next three months, I put Sol through exercises every hour to strengthen his muscles. He continued to drink milk from a bottle. He screamed if someone other than his three elder siblings, Dad, or Mom walked into the room. As he got stronger, we put him in a stroller and took him for walks. While strolling along, I would be talking away and pointing out interesting things, but Sol did not respond.

At the end of August, an E.N.T. specialist confirmed our fears that Sol could not hear and that he was "severely to profoundly deaf." His right ear had no response and the left ear tested at eighty decibels up to two thousand Hertz, and then dropped off. We asked the doctor, "What, if anything, can be done?" He gave us a short–term (two week) dose of cortisone to see if it would shrink swelling further in the brain. But he really thought it was irreversible nerve damage. The doctor also informed us that there were schools for deaf children and that there were special teachers for children who are deaf at the local hospital, as well as at another hospital in Toronto.

We left the local hospital and went across the street to have Sol fitted with two hearing aids . . . not an easy task. Within minutes after Sol was fitted, he pulled the hearing aids out. The miracle that my husband, Oded, and I had hoped for did not happen. We thought they would work like glasses; once on, you could see clearly. Once the hearing aids were on, however, Sol could not understand environmental sounds or words. How much there was for us to learn!

On the way home, we discussed our options, including moving to another city to be near a residential school for deaf children. That journey home seemed so long! Sol still was yelling a lot and banging his head against the nearest surface. Upon arrival, we sat down with our older children, Golda, Ari, and Shawn, and explained to them as much as we could.

Understandably, they too were quite upset, especially when told that hearing aids were not like glasses. But we all understood better some of what Sol had been going through for the preceding three months. For example, the only movie Sol wanted to watch was "Superman." He rarely spoke and when he did, his speech was so loud and slurred that we couldn't understand him, and we knew he couldn't understand us. No wonder he yelled whenever people were around! They were just faces with moving lips, similar to a TV with no sound.

That night, thanks to a concerned relative, I was put in touch with a mother of two children who had hearing loss. She talked at length about residual hearing and that excellent, high powered hearing aids could augment the environmental sounds and speech. She went on to explain all about auditory–verbal therapy, and how, hopefully, Sol could learn to listen and talk. This all sounded foreign and unbelievable. It was hard for us to comprehend the technical language, let alone the audiogram! The mother went on to say that her daughter had just graduated from high school and was spending the summer in Europe. She gave us the phone numbers of two therapists: one in Toronto and one at the local hospital in case my husband and I were interested and would like to ask them questions.

Interested! How could we not be? A chance! A hope! The dreams and hopes that emerged when Sol was born might still develop and materialize. Oded and I talked long into the night and made our decision before we actually met with the therapists. If there was a space available in either auditory–verbal therapy program, we would go. We wanted to be able to give Sol every opportunity: to be able to communicate with everyone, to hear, listen, and to speak, to be integrated in the regular school and get the same education offered to our other children. We would offer this to Sol and our family.

During the following week we used bribery to coax Sol into wearing the hearing aids and it worked, but we had to wait until after Labor Day for our appointment at the auditory–verbal programs. During that time we read everything we could get from the library about deafness. Finally we met the staff, who explained in detail the Auditory–Verbal Therapy Approach. The auditory–verbal therapist stressed that, primarily, it would be the parent who learns to help the child. There would be only one hour of therapy per week and then we would go home and work and play with Sol every day.

After another week of more tests and interviews with a psychologist, social worker, and audiologist, meetings through which Sol continued to scream, we began auditory–verbal therapy. We were thrilled! But *I* was petrified! What if I wasn't capable of doing all that was required? In the end, I just went ahead and tried my best.

Three months later, Sol began to walk again like a drunken sailor, but walk nevertheless. Do you know how exciting a child's first step is? Well the first step *the second time around* is incredible! Then, one morning eight months later, Sol awoke and smiled; a sight for sore eyes. We were all so excited. Later that day he laughed; I started to cry with joy. Sol's personality was coming back! We were all going to make it!

Still, for the next few years, Sol only slept three to four hours a night. So, there were many hours to do our "lessons." We had structured lessons, read stories, acted with puppets, and played with miniature toy animals. Sol played many games with his brothers and sister and took many trips to the park with his dad. It was about a year until Sol said "Mom," but that was music to my ears. After that, words came slowly. Those words were not always understandable, but they were always exciting! It took us eight more months to learn colors, and to answer simple questions such as "What's your name?" Everything in our house was labeled and our lives revolved around teaching Sol and caring for our other children.

Before we knew it, it was time for Sol to begin school. Our three older children went to a parochial school, but we felt that the two languages required there would be too much for Sol. So, off he went to a nice, small public school with individual classrooms, not the open school concept which was popular in our city at that time. There were only a hundred and fifty children from kindergarten to grade six with a class for each grade.

Sol is now in sixth grade at school; everyone knows Sol and Sol knows everyone. From the beginning, Sol has been fully integrated into the school. He also receives several hours of special support every week from his excellent itinerant teacher, who, fortunately, has been with him for the past six years. Sol enjoys school and does well there.

Sol also keeps very busy outside of school. He is an accomplished swimmer, has attained all the Red Cross color badges, and Royal Lifesaving 1, 2, and 3 badges, and has won two swimming trophies at the overnight camp he attends. He enjoys skiing, camping, canoeing, and fishing—last summer he caught a twelve–pound pickerel, 27 inches long. He takes piano and flute lessons, and, for the last few years, he has taken Hebrew lessons as well. His greatest love is for animals! He goes horseback riding at least once a week and competes in shows where he has won numerous ribbons. Sol's riding instructor recently wrote, "I just don't think of Sol Fried as a child who has a hearing loss and coping well; rather, I think of Sol as an extremely bright, friendly and enthusiastic child who is a pleasure to teach and with whom I am very proud to have associated." Sol is a happy and well-adjusted twelve–year–old. He has a strong desire to become a veterinarian and we hope he makes it!

Last year Sol received the Alexander Graham Bell Oral Hearing–Impaired Section Youth Achievement Award.

When we are asked if auditory–verbal therapy was worth all the hard work, the roller coaster ride of ups and downs and plateaus, and whether we would follow the auditory–verbal approach again, our answer is irrevocable. **YES!**

5

The Bilingual-Bicultural (Bi-Bi) Approach

A Professional Point of View

Laurene Gallimore, M.A., and Susan Woodruff, M.A.

The choice of an educational program for your deaf child is one of the many important decisions you will make in the coming years. Your choices will be greatly influenced by your knowledge of and your attitudes toward deafness, deaf people, and the current state of deaf education. Educating yourself fully about the different programs and their philosophies will aid you in making the best decisions possible.

What Is Bi–Bi?

Bilingual–Bicultural education is an approach to educating deaf children that incorporates the use of American Sign Language (ASL) as the primary language of instruction in the classroom. English is taught as a second language through reading and writing print (Reynolds, 1994).

In addition, the Bi–Bi approach supports instruction in deaf culture, including the history, contributions, values, and customs of the deaf community. In other words, Bi–Bi means "learning two languages and two cultures" (Reynolds, 1994). The goals of a Bi–Bi education are to help deaf children establish a strong visual first language that will give them the tools they need for thinking and learning and to develop a healthy sense of self through connections with other deaf people.

Bi–Bi advocates strong parent support through outreach programs. These programs encourage hearing parents to interact with deaf adults and other parents of deaf children and to learn American Sign Language and the culture of the Deaf.

The current enthusiasm for a bilingual-bicultural (Bi–Bi) approach to deaf education has gained momentum in recent years. The growing support for Bi–Bi has been fueled by the continued low academic achievement of the majority of deaf students and by a number of significant social, cultural, and legal changes in the lives of deaf people. Changes in the law and changes in rights have heightened society's awareness of people with disabilities in general. "An understanding of the importance of the role of American Sign Language (ASL) in the lives of many deaf persons is a component of this new awareness" (Strong, 1995).

In addition, in recent years greater numbers of deaf people have entered school administration, especially in residential schools for the deaf. As a result, there has been an increasing desire for a "more equal partnership" between deaf and hearing educators in designing and administering programs for deaf children (Reynolds, 1994). In the past, programs for the deaf were created and administered for the most part by hearing people. This chapter deals with this new perspective in the education of deaf children.

How Bi–Bi Differs from Total Communication and Cued Speech

To understand how Bi–Bi differs from other manual (signed) systems, one must first understand what ASL is and is not. ASL is not English made visible. ASL is *not English* at all. American Sign Language has been identified as a true and distinct language completely separate from English. As explained in Appendix A, it has its own grammar (the arrangement of words in sentences), syntax (the relationship among words, phrases, and clauses forming sentences), and semantics (having to do with development and changes in the meanings of words). Like other languages, ASL borrows words from languages it comes into contact with (in this case English). Like all languages, ASL grows and changes. Signs are continually added, deleted, and modified.

Cued speech (described in detail in Chapter 6) is a system of hand shapes that represent the sounds of spoken language—in this case, English. It is an aid to lipreading oral language in that it makes speechreading unambiguous. It allows for an exact visual representation of spoken English.

Total communication is a philosophy of educating deaf children by using a manual sign system simultaneously with residual hearing, speechreading, and speech. (See Chapter 8 for more information.) The manual systems used in the past with total communication have included one or more of the following invented systems: Signed English, Signing Exact English, Seeing Essential English, Linguistics of Visual English and others. These systems are known as MCE or manually coded English. They are all attempts to represent English visually with signs. While some total communication programs say they use ASL, supporters of true ASL argue that it cannot be done. ASL has different parameters than spoken language and it cannot be used simultaneously with speech. "Something happens when we try to rebuild English for the hands and eyes. Manually coded English (MCE) lines up in the air just as spoken English lines up words. To produce an idea by coding English on the hands takes twice the amount of time that it does to speak the idea" (Bellugi, Fischer, and Newkirk, 1979). "The short term memory has time limits and MCE goes beyond these time constraints. Thus the brain is not able to easily process MCE because of memory and cognitive limitations" (Goodheart and Gee, 1988).

In spite of numerous attempts in the last twenty years to make English visible using a variety of other manual approaches, the majority of deaf students are still not literate in English (Position paper, Indiana School for the Deaf). Studies have found that the average reading level of a deaf student graduating from high school is between the third and fourth grade level.

■ WHAT IDEAS SUPPORT BI–BI?

At the heart of the Bilingual–Bicultural theory for educating deaf children are a number of central, commonly held understandings and/or beliefs. Advocates believe the following statements are true:

- Vision is a deaf child's chief modality for learning language. Therefore, a deaf child needs access to a complete language that is entirely visible.
- ASL is the only *complete* language that is entirely visible.
- Visual learning of English through speech reading "depends on stimuli that are often ambiguous and sometimes invisible" (Vernon, 1994).
- Neither speech reading nor MCE systems give a deaf child access to a complete language during the critical language learning years.
- Acquiring native proficiency in a first language requires that an individual have exposure to a complete language during the critical language learning years—ages zero to five.
- Deaf children from deaf families who acquire ASL as their first language perform better socially and academically than deaf children from hearing families who did not acquire ASL as their first language.
- If a deaf child can acquire strong receptive and expressive first language skills in ASL, he can then learn English more successfully as a second language. Research on bilingualism suggests that people need to be proficient in one language before they can successfully acquire a second language (Cummings, 1979).
- Language is the chief transmitter of an individual's culture, so learning ASL is the most powerful tool in learning deaf culture.

- Interaction with deaf peers and the presence of deaf role models both in and outside the classroom are necessary for the self–esteem and emotional well-being of a deaf child.

WHAT ARE THE CHALLENGES FACING BI–BI EDUCATION?

RESEARCH AND EVALUATION ARE NECESSARY

Bilingual–Bicultural education is now in place at a growing number of sites across North America. (See the article by M. Strong in the References for an overview of nine Bi–Bi programs available). However, unlike Bi–Bi programs in Sweden and Denmark that are firmly established and showing promising results, programs in North America are in their earliest stages (Mahshie, 1995). Only a few of these programs are engaged in serious research on the effectiveness of the Bi–Bi model.

THERE ARE GAPS IN TEACHER TRAINING PROGRAMS

In spite of enthusiasm for Bi–Bi, teacher training programs have not adapted their instruction to provide adequate skills for teachers of Bi-Bi education. As a result, there is "a great barrier due to a lack of appropriate training and skills in American Sign Language" (Gallimore, 1993). Successful Bi–Bi programs require educators of the deaf to "have fluency in and understanding of American Sign Language, Deaf Culture, linguistics, human development and bilingual-bicultural education. Furthermore, they need to develop and maintain cultural sensitivity by being immersed in the Deaf community" (Gallimore, 1993).

DISAGREEMENTS ABOUT WHERE AND HOW ENGLISH WILL BE TAUGHT

There is much controversy and not much agreement on this issue among supporters of Bi–Bi. Some programs indicate they will use E.S.O.L. (English for Students of Other Languages) methods.

E.S.O.L. methods, however, often demand total immersion in English, so this would seem incompatible with a Bi–Bi program. Other programs teach English through reading and writing. Dr. Orin Cornett has suggested that the cued speech method, which he developed, would be an effective way to teach English because it is the most accurate visual representation of English on the hands. He has stated that "ASL English bilingualism is feasible if and only if both languages can be learned efficiently and successfully with a specific educational program" (Cornett, 1994).

ASL/English Bilingualism and Hearing Parents

What will the effects of Bi–Bi be on parent-child relationships? Even though extensive outreach to hearing parents is part of the Bi–Bi model, it is highly unlikely that most hearing parents of deaf children will achieve fluency in ASL. According to Shawn Mahshie, parents in Denmark and Sweden who immersed themselves in learning Danish Sign Language (Denmark's native Deaf language) were more relaxed and better able to understand their children. The emphasis on native sign as opposed to signs in the order of Danish had enabled parents to better develop their skills. They were able to have more meaningful conversations with their children and with deaf adults (Mahshie, 1995).

Curricula and Supporting Materials

Because Bi–Bi programs are so new, supporting materials and specific curricula have not yet been fully developed or tested. Teacher training programs and materials must be developed before programs can be optimally implemented (Vernon, 1994).

Summary

A growing number of residential programs for deaf children are moving toward a Bilingual–Bicultural model. The Bi–Bi approach aims to help deaf children acquire skills that will allow them to function effectively within both the deaf and hearing community. Through the use of American Sign Language in the classroom, deaf children are provided a completely visual first language for thinking and communicating while learning English as a second language. Specific education in deaf culture and interaction with deaf peers and deaf adults is critical in Bi–Bi education to foster self-esteem. The Bilingual–Bicultural perspective provides a new dimension in deaf education with the goal of achieving better outcomes for deaf children.

REFERENCES

Bellugi, U., Fischer, and Newkirk, D. (1979) "The Rate of Speaking and Signing." In E. Klemer and U. Bellugi (eds.), *The Signs of Language.* Cambridge, MA: Harvard University Press.

Bragg, B. (1994) "Culture, Language and Deafness (Collectivism and Individualism)." *Deafness, Life and Culture. A Deaf American Monograph.* Vol. 44. Silver Spring, MD: National Association for the Deaf.

Cornett, O. (1994) "Who Am I." *Deafness, Life and Culture. A Deaf American Monograph.* Vol. 44. Silver Spring, MD: National Association for the Deaf.

Cummins, J. (1979) "Linguistic Interdependence and the Educational Development of Bilingual Children." *Review of Educational Research.* Vol. 49, 222-251.

Gallimore, L. (1993) "How to Utilize American Sign Language as the Language Instruction in the Classroom." *Conference Proceedings. ASL in Schools' Continuing Education and Outreach.* Washington, DC: Gallaudet University.

Gee, J. and Goodhart, W. (1988) "ASL and the Biological Capacity for Language." In M. Strong (Ed.), *Language, Learning and Deafness.* New York: Cambridge University Press.

Indiana School for the Deaf Position Paper Committee. (1992) *Foundations for Bilingual/Bicultural Education and Implications for Educational Residential Programs.* Indianapolis: Indiana School for the Deaf.

Mahshie, S. (1995) *Educating Deaf Children Bilingually.* Washington, DC: Pre College Publications, Gallaudet University.

Reynolds, D. (1994) *Parallel Views. The Spirit of Bi–Bi: Two Languages and Two Cultures.* Washington, DC: Gallaudet University Press.

Strong, M. (1995) "Bilingual/Bicultural Programs for Deaf Children in North America." *American Annals of the Deaf.* Vol. 140, No. 2.

Vernon, M., and Daigle, B. (1994) "Bilingual and Bicultural Education." *Deafness, Life and Culture. A Deaf American Monograph.* Vol. 44. Silver Spring, MD: National Association for the Deaf.

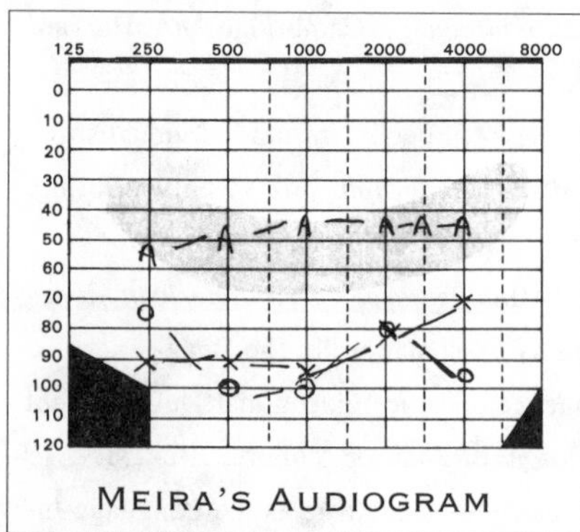

MEIRA'S AUDIOGRAM

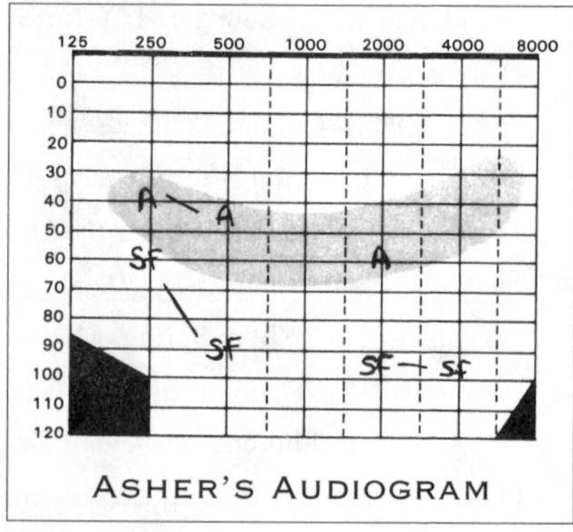

ASHER'S AUDIOGRAM

MEIRA AND ASHER'S STORY

BARBARA RAIMONDO

Meira and I are sitting in the audiology booth of a large Washington hospital. She is ten months old, with dark, sparkling eyes and curly hair. I am cranky. We got lost on the way to the hospital and then when we finally arrived, we got lost in the hospital itself. Anyway, we are wasting our time. Of course she can hear. How could she not hear? We have no deafness in our family, I had a normal pregnancy, and Meira was never sick a day in her life. The audiology booth is a tiny, soundproof room with a thick door. I feel like I am in a bank vault. No money here. The audiologist will test Meira's hearing using play audiometry. When Meira hears a sound, she is to look at a toy clown in the corner of the room. When she looks at the clown, it will light up and dance. She will be conditioned to look at the toy whenever she hears a sound.

That sounds simple enough. In a few short minutes Meira will give the expected responses, we will see that her hearing is perfectly normal, and we will chuckle, "Oh, gosh, imagine thinking she had a hearing problem! She just listens when she wants to. Good for you, Meira!" My husband, Dennis, and I will go home flooded with relief, and we will give up the pot banging.

I hold Meira on my lap during the testing. I am supposed to amuse her with a toy while the audiologist makes a sound tone with her big audiology machine. I am not supposed to respond in any way. Then Meira will look up to see where the sound is coming from. The sounds come. Meira continues playing with the toy. The sounds are louder. Meira continues playing with the toy. More, louder sounds. Meira continues playing with the toy. The audiologist starts to look frustrated, or maybe annoyed. Meira continues playing with the toy. The sounds are booming. Meira looks up.

After the test is complete, the audiologist is talking to me. I am dazed. The words "severe to profound hearing impairment" seem to drift through the air and then hang there. I say nothing. I think, "Impossible." The audiologist asks, "Is she stubborn?" "Oh, very much so," I reply. So that's it. She's just stubborn.

After more testing we could no longer deny that Meira was—although we were afraid to say the word at the time—deaf. I liked the term "hearing-impaired." It was so polite. You never had to say that your child couldn't hear. I had never met a deaf person in my life. I tried to imagine what kind of life deaf people led. Dark, lonely images filled my head along with questions that were too frightening to ponder. Can deaf people work? Can they be independent? Will Meira be a part of our family?

At home, I cried and felt sorry for Meira. I didn't know how to raise a deaf child. I felt guilty that she had the burden of deafness and that she had been born to the wrong mother. I had never felt so helpless in my life. Another frightening thought occurred to me. Time was moving on. From the time she was born we had talked to her constantly, describing the world around her, naming objects, singing songs. I realized that this had all been wasted. We had to start fresh with a new way to communicate. I had no idea how.

But I tried to be optimistic. I figured there must be things I could do with Meira. She is not the first deaf child there ever was. Other people have raised deaf children. I will find the people who have been successful at it and do what they did. Surely, there must be a national, effective way of approaching this.

I went to the library and took out their books on deafness. I consumed them. I learned a lot about controversies and philosophies but got no answers. I called the audiologist with a torrent of questions. Will she learn to talk? Where will she go to school? How will she be able to succeed in the "hearing world?" The audiologist's answers were vague. But the most important question of all: "What can I do now?" I wanted to be sure that no more time was lost. "Well," she said slowly and, I thought, rather reluctantly, "you could learn sign language."

Sign Language. Now that was an idea. But isn't she too young? No, deaf babies who are signed to from birth can understand and sign back at a very early age. How would I learn sign language anyway? It seemed so mysterious. I asked her to explain some signs. Over the phone she described how to sign "milk" and "ball." In a strange way, knowing those two signs made me feel like I had some kind of power over our situation. Meira's deafness was not just something that was happening to us. I could form a response. Now I had something to give Meira. I could sit down with her and point to a ball and sign and say "ball." Yesterday I could not do that. Today I can give her meaning.

I gathered loads of information. I contacted all the organizations that were listed in the library books. I bought sign language books. I watched videos on Deaf culture. I called teachers and parents. Dennis and I registered for a sign language class. I made an appointment with one of the top ear nose and throat specialists in the country (whose sophisticated hearing test consisted of banging two metal blocks together and whose advice went something like, "Hmm...She definitely can't hear...I'm not sure what you should do....").

But by far the most important people I talked to were parents of deaf children and deaf adults themselves. Some of the parents I talked to signed, some didn't. To me it seemed that the signers seemed more at ease with their children. They could communicate effectively with them. They could read them stories, help them with their homework, discipline them when necessary. Their lives were—well—normal. They described meeting deaf adults and learning about deaf culture as positive experiences. Talking to these parents made me feel like the sun suddenly appeared on a cloudy day. I went from being burdened with the fears, worries, and confusion of finding out my child is deaf to thinking that it was something that could be positive.

Meeting deaf adults, while scary at first, was enlightening. They were very patient with my beginner signs and my constant requests for them to repeat what they said. Over and over they told me what a wonderful thing I was doing for my daughter by learning to sign and how they wished their parents signed. Learning about their experiences was important to me. It helped inform my decisions in a way that my own experiences as a hearing person could not.

While we wanted Meira to learn to use her residual hearing and learn to speak, we knew that might take years, if it happened at all. We chose to sign and speak with her at the same time. It was a somewhat awkward process at first. Whenever we wanted to say something we would rush to the bookshelf, grab the sign language dictionary, flutter through the pages looking through the index, then searching for the page, run back to Meira, get her attention, try to remember the sign, oops, forget, gotta go back and check again, okay found it, race to Meira, try to remember the sign (successfully this time) and keep her attention, then sign it. Whew.

Despite the apparent disorganization of this method, it was surprisingly effective. Within weeks Meira was understanding our signs, and shortly after that she began singing back, in the nondistinct motions of sign babbling and baby sign, then in real signs. Although in some ways it was strange to us that these were our child's first words—we had been expecting something quite different, to say the least—it was every bit as exciting. We were communicating. As we signed more and more with Meira, as we attended sign language classes, and as we met more and more deaf adults, we consulted our dictionary less and less.

Eventually we gave up "sim-com" (simultaneous communication) and moved to a bilingual-bicultural philosophy. It was not something that happened overnight. Like any parents of deaf children, we wanted to be sure that Meira acquired fluency in English. In the beginning we felt that speaking while signing would be the best way to accomplish it. The more exposure to English, the better, right? But as the concepts we were trying to convey became more complex, using both languages at the same time caused each language to lose its integrity. The spoken English would be somewhat understandable (to a hearing person already fluent in English), but the signing simply confusing. It is difficult to try to use two languages at once. It was not fair to make Meira guess what we were trying to convey. We found that turning our voices off while signing improved clarity, so that is what we did. We continued to encourage her "reading" and attempts at writing and sending her to both private and in-school speech training. We began explaining to her (in ASL) the differences between English and ASL. In addition, we continued improving our signing skills through classes and interactions with deaf friends and acquaintances. We still do, even though we are quite competent signers.

We are committed to her developing the best English skills possible—in reading, writing, and to the extent possible, speaking. We reject the notion that because she is deaf or because she uses ASL she will not acquire age appropriate English skills.

We feel fortunate that we have the opportunity to send her to a school for deaf children, where she has free and easy communication with everyone, from the bus monitor to the teacher, from the children in her class to the principal. Natural access to communication is the norm for a hearing child, and we believe that it is in an accessible environment that a deaf child develops the knowledge and skills needed to succeed in the world at large. We are pleased that Meira's school provides a Deaf culture curriculum. We want her to learn the history of the deaf community and to know about successful Deaf adults.

At times I have met other parents of deaf children who are shocked when I tell them I want my daughter to use ASL and to be a part of the deaf community. "Aren't you afraid of losing her?" they ask. Never. If we communicate clearly, have mutual respect for each other's primary language and culture, and love each other the way parents and children normally do, we won't lose her merely because she is part of the Deaf community.

Today, at age six, her reading level is above grade level as compared to both hearing and deaf peers, her speech continues to improve, and she is fluent in ASL. Her academic knowledge and her knowledge of the world in general is on par with that of bright, hearing six–year–olds. She sends us e–mail from school, has lots of friends, goes to Brownies, creates finely detailed art work, and knows a lot about animals. She is a light in our lives.

Almost two years ago our son, Asher, was born. He's deaf too. He has been seeing signs since his first day of life. His first expressive sign, at age nine months, was "Daddy," and now he delights in watching us sign stories just before his bedtime as we sit on the sofa with his blanket and books. He is a normal twenty–two–month–old child developing a solid language base, and he is a joy to us.

Before we found out Meira was deaf we couldn't have imagined how interesting she would make our lives or how fulfilling it would be to learn a second language so that we could communicate with her, and later, Asher. As we watch Meira tell stories to Asher, as we watch his attempts to make new signs, and as we experience the thrill of either of them learning a new sign or fingerspelled word, this we know: we wouldn't have it any other way.

JACKIE'S STORY

GLENN PRANSKY AND TERRY SUDBURY

Audiogram not available.

We wanted a baby. After four years of infertility, our prayers had been answered—Terry was pregnant. The first trimester was somewhat complicated, but then things seemed to be going well. Unexpectedly, our daughter was born two months premature. She was tiny, could not yet swallow, but we were reassured that she was perfectly healthy. Our tiny gift came home with us three weeks later. We were ecstatic yet frightened: was there anything else wrong with her? Our pediatrician examined her carefully, and reassured us that, no, she was perfectly fine, and charted her slow but steady progression through developmental milestones over the following months.

We didn't suspect that she could not hear until the Fourth of July parade. Jackie was ten months old, and sat in her stroller, watching the Minutemen march by in Revolutionary War costumes. They stopped directly in front of us and fired their muskets. The other children cried; strangely, Jackie was quiet. Soon afterwards, our family day care provider mentioned that Jackie's hearing should be tested—she seemed to ignore loud noises that startled other children.

Our pediatrician assured us that Jackie's hearing was fine. He shook his keys near her ear; of course, Jackie turned her head. We wanted to believe it was nothing—yet our doubts grew. Why did she never seem to hear when we called her name or when we walked into the room? Was it her prematurity? Some mild form of auditory processing disorder? There were other times, however, when we were certain she could not have responded unless she had heard us come into a room or close a door in another part of the house. We found this somewhat reassuring. Our day care provider continued insisting on the need for better testing, and we scheduled a brain stem auditory evoked response (BAER) through our pediatrician's office. Jackie was almost a year old.

We brought her into the testing area thinking of her upcoming birthday party—all of our relatives were coming in to celebrate this miracle. Jackie had beautiful, wispy red hair, and we talked about how pretty she would look in the picture. An hour later the technicians came out with drawn faces. Jackie had very little hearing; in fact, they described her hearing as little more than the ability to detect vibration. We were grief stricken. The audiologist told us that we should immediately begin using hearing aids and fitted her with ear molds before we left, referred us to a parent–infant program that specialized in oral communication.

After a few weeks in this program, the pain of our discovery had subsided, and we began to have doubts about this approach. We began a process of collecting data, discussions, and visiting programs for Deaf education that has become a continuous process. In some ways, as a physician specializing in rehabilitation research and a biomedical engineer, the two of us were well prepared for this process. As scientists, we were used to questioning assumptions and theories, and we realize the value of objective, scientific evidence.

Initially, we discovered that there were very few studies that objectively measured outcomes in Deaf children who had been educated through an oral, total communication, or sign language–based approach. The oral approach was attractive, with the promise of better English skills and perhaps Jackie becoming like us, main–streaming into society. The data that we reviewed, however, consistently showed that 30–50 percent of profoundly Deaf children had very little success with this approach. Other studies compared results with hearing aids and cochlear implants, and we were particularly interested, as this might give Jackie some auditory function. Again, the spectrum of results was quite wide.

Soon afterwards, we began to meet Deaf adults, to help us understand who Jackie might become. They had been raised in a wide variety of settings—some in residential schools, some in mainstreamed programs, and some in oral–based programs. We began to realize that many Deaf people whose primary language was not English were productive, happy, and successful members of society. Although all who had good English skills valued them dearly, they consistently emphasized the importance of early and natural communication with our child, regardless of which path we pursued for her schooling later on. All felt very strongly that early exposure to sign language would not adversely affect Jackie's ultimate ability to acquire spoken or written English skills—and many with very successful oral skills, brought up in Deaf families, cited themselves as examples. They insisted that we visit as many different programs as possible, yet in the end, reminded us that we must feel entirely comfortable with our choice.

Jackie's frustration told us that she wanted to communicate more effectively with us. We turned to a center for Deaf Children which had a parent–infant program; they said their coordinator, who was Deaf, would come to the house and meet with us next week. We began to see this person and many other Deaf adults as role models for our daughter, and, as we saw how positive her future could be, we began to accept her more and more for who she was. Through a family Sign Language class, we picked up the rudiments of sign language, and began to communicate with Jackie at home. To our delight, she began to respond. Within two months, she used 20–30 signs regularly, could tell us about her needs, and appeared to be much happier and much more connected with us. As we met other Deaf parents with Deaf children the same age as Jackie, we began to think of her more and more as a normal child.

Our next major step happened when Jackie was a year and a half old. We invited a Deaf adult to move in with us. This accelerated our understanding of Deaf culture, our ability to converse in American Sign Language, and was especially important for Jackie's language development. Her vocabulary rapidly increased, and we began to see that she had many, many things that she wanted to tell us about. Over the next eighteen months, we lived with Deaf adults, and tried to use American Sign Language as the primary mode of communication at home. Although this was difficult at first, we found that our roommates were able to help us along.

One year later, our work took us to Sweden, which is known for its remarkable success with educating Deaf children. The Swedish system is very different from that of the United States. Sign language exposure for Deaf children is legally mandated, and Swedish Sign Language is the primary mode of instruction for all Deaf and many hard–of–hearing students. Although oral skills are valued, they are not the primary emphasis for language instruction. Parents are strongly encouraged to learn sign language and use it with their Deaf infants. The results are impressive—the range of college–entrance examination scores of Deaf high school students is actually higher than that of their hearing counterparts! We visited a parent–infant program, as well as a secondary school for children, with an opportunity to meet students and teachers. This visit confirmed what we had learned up until this point—that Deaf students could succeed academically through instruction in their native language.

Jackie has been a student at a center for Deaf children since she was 14 months old. At this school, all instruction is in American Sign Language. She has had a childhood that is as normal as any other—and has friends, likes and dislikes, dreams and fears. She is idiosyncratic, artistic, expressive, intensely inquisitive about the world around her. She wants to know more about how a small group of people that argue can close down the Federal government; who is God; and what happens after we die. Confident in her ability to communicate with hearing adults, when we go to a restaurant, she insists on ordering for herself and then asking for paper and crayons. She has mastered the use of gesture and writing simple phrases with paper and pencil to communicate effectively. Her oral skills are not very good now, although she is highly motivated to improve them, and attends speech classes regularly. Most Deaf adults who meet her are very impressed with her fluency in sign language. In fact, they often feel that her sign language skills are equivalent to those of children who have been brought up in Deaf households. She is proud of being Deaf, and has a clear sense of who she can become.

Now, Jackie is almost seven and is about to enter the first grade. For us, the latest challenge has been to evaluate the alternative approaches to teach her to read. We believe that access to written English and ability to write well (but not perfectly) will be a key factor in Jackie's future academic and employment success, and to her self–esteem. Now, Jackie reads and writes at an appropriate first-grade level. She combines words to form sentences, is aware of nouns, verbs, and adjectives, and enjoys comparing ASL to English word order. We are actively exploring all types of instructional alternatives: cued speech, some total communication, signed exact English, and ASL.

Teaching Deaf children to read is a difficult challenge, one that will require far more effort for our children than for their hearing peers. However, we feel that the published studies on children who have had early and intense, full access and exposure to language through ASL, as well as research in other situations where English is acquired as a second language, indicates that our goals are indeed achievable. Again, we are asking our Deaf friends and educators to share their success stories with us. Most importantly, we are pursuing an educational process that is occurring in a setting where Jackie knows that Deaf people can do anything that hearing people can do—except hear.

KYLE'S STORY

AUDREY BYRNE

Audiogram not available.

It was 10:25 on a Wednesday morning, just over eleven years ago, that the phone rang and I was engaged in a conversation that completely changed my life. The caller was quick and to the point. "Hello, this is the doctor. I am just calling to tell you that your son is Deaf." My two-week-old baby boy, not yet reaching 5 pounds, could not hear. I responded with "Thank you" and hung up the phone.

I was in the kitchen at the time of the call. My twin babies were in incubators in the hospital and I was home alone. The tears came slowly that day and the sobbing came many months later. Somehow I drove myself to the neonatal unit at the hospital, parked the car, rode up in the elevator, and tried to envision how I would react to my son. I clearly remember entering the nursery, and as I looked across the room at Kyle's incubator, I recall the nurses doing everything possible to avoid me. Not one nurse came up to me and no doctor was present to answer questions. It seemed it was only Kyle and me in the room. As I approached him, I tried to hold back the tears because I knew it would make the staff feel uncomfortable. I wish now that I had let it out then. I stood looking at him for a short time. Finally, one nurse approached and asked if I wanted to hold him. Thank God for that. I needed to hold onto him and to reassure him that I loved him and to get to know this tiny, new life much better.

That same afternoon, I demanded and received some time with the pediatrician who had called me. I had a lot of questions. Why was I not informed that my son was being tested? Why did they suspect that Kyle was Deaf in the first place? When were the tests done? Did it hurt? The responses were perfunctory and not much help. I was told that they suspected neurological damage because Kyle had experienced some minor seizures within the first twenty-four hours of birth and he had exhibited some eye rolling. Also, these tests were extremely expensive and unless they suspected some kind of problem, they usually did not perform them. The Doctor then added, "With Kyle we were lucky, we hit the jackpot. He is Deaf."

Hit the jackpot. Hit the jackpot. Hit the jackpot. Those words have bounced around inside my head for eleven years. They have taken on so many meanings, both negative and positive. On the positive side, I started on a journey that was life changing for me. I found strengths I did not know I had. I found talents I did not know I possessed. I found a love I did not know existed.

Kyle is not Deaf because he is a twin, nor because he was born early, nor because he was a small baby. My children were born at 34 weeks gestation. Kyle weighed 4 pounds, 15 and one-half ounces and Janelle weighed 4 pounds, one and one-half ounces. And yet Kyle's twin sister is hearing. They never tested her as extensively as they tested Kyle. They looked so different from each other that it was hard to believe they both came from me! They were my first children and although I knew having a new baby at home would be difficult, I simply expected twins to be a little bit harder. In my blissful ignorance, I survived the first year of having two babies at home. I did not have a lot of time to do much research about people who are Deaf. I just remember thinking that I would have to learn that "hand thing."

Before the twins left the hospital, I was told that they had both received the Auditory Brain Response test (ABR). Kyle was then booked for another one at three months of age. At that time, I was told by the audiologist that they would do another ABR test at six months of age, "just in case his hearing develops." Not knowing any better, I just accepted what they had to tell me. I was kept too busy keeping them fed and changed and trying to keep up with daily chores. Looking back, I felt that I lost some very precious time. Kyle could have been exposed to his natural language far earlier.

When Kyle was six months old, we went to the local Children's Hospital and he underwent his third ABR. It was confirmed. He definitely was Deaf. They showed me the results on the computer screen and I could see the huge difference. Kyle basically had a flat line and Janelle had many peaks and valleys. Of course, that just reinforced to me that I had to learn that "hand thing."

We were referred to the clinic at the hospital and the nurse clinician who spoke to me handed me three pamphlets describing programs that help families who have Deaf children. I was, by then, used to hearing the term, "hearing impaired." I did not like it then and I certainly do not like it now. I have never referred to Kyle as hearing impaired. I have always used Deaf. Of the three pamphlets given to me, only one talked about a Deaf child being a child first. The others focused on the disability.

So, six and a half months after Kyle and Janelle were born, we attended our first meeting at the Deaf Children's Society of British Columbia. Kyle met his first Deaf person. Kyle spent his time on the floor with his sister and I spend my time avoiding eye contact and pretending to be listening but tending to the children. Kyle would receive weekly home visits with a Home Training teacher and I would receive weekly visits from a Deaf adult as well as attending weekly sign communication classes. That all began in October of 1985.

By January of 1986, I was getting used to using my hands to communicate and Kyle had already started signing "light." I had discovered that I needed to be reminded to constantly repeat the signs for Kyle in the same way that I automatically spoke to my daughter. I started by attaching a small reading light to the wall next to the babies' changing table. I know I would be spending a lot of time changing diapers. Every time I changed Kyle's diaper, I would sign "light on" and turn on the light. I would then sign "light off" and then turn off the light. I did this three times every time I changed his diaper. What I did not think about and no one suggested to me was that I should have spent an equal amount of time talking to his sister. Janelle started signing one month after Kyle. Her first sign was "milk." She must have learned it through osmosis because I cannot remember teaching her. I did start voicing when I signed but quickly stopped because it seemed silly to be talking to a child who could not hear me. Kyle was, and of course still is, profoundly deaf. There were so many advantages to using that "system." When Janelle was sleeping, Kyle and I could have conversations and not disturb her. This was especially helpful at night. Vice versa, when Janelle would cry, I knew it would not disturb Kyle's sleep.

Early in January, I started attending sign classes. What an eye opener! At the third class, I finally realized that I had to actually look eye–to–eye at the person with whom I was communicating. It was like a light exploding in my brain when that all–too–obvious realization dawned on me. Wow, that was so hard to do. We are taught from a young age that it is so impolite to stare at people, and here was a culture that not only required staring but considered it rude if you did not. This coupled with the need to point at people and objects made me begin to realize that I was not just learning that "hand thing" but that I was beginning to learn about a new culture: one that included flashing lights, acceptance of differences, and the need to be more open minded, forthright, and blunt. After eleven years it still does not all come naturally, but I look at this learning as a lifelong process.

I remember noticing how Kyle's eyes were always so active and animated. He could fool me into thinking that he actually did hear me. There were occasions when I would walk into their room to check on them and Kyle's back would be to the door. Before I reached his crib, he would roll over and smile at me. It did not take me long to realize that he was responding to a shadow on the wall or the vibrations he felt through the floor. No wonder most children who are born Deaf are not diagnosed until after they are a year old! They adjust naturally to accommodate to their environment and how they interact with it.

Early in my journey, I learned that my son had different linguistic needs than his sister and the rest of the family. His language came through his eyes, not his ears. That became painfully clear to me one December night prior to his first Christmas. That was when the sobbing finally happened. I gently picked him up from his crib and we sat in the rocking chair for a long time. He never woke up. He lay so peacefully in my arms, totally oblivious to my pain. I kept thinking that Christmas is a time of tradition. In our household, as in many others, the tradition included playing Christmas music. So many songs trigger such wonderful memories of Christmases past. How was I going to make Kyle's Christmases memorable?

I returned my sleeping babe to his bed and tried to return to sleep myself. It was impossible. I kept asking myself how I would create a new tradition, one that Kyle could participate in. At dawn, the time when our best ideas hit us, I realized that I would have to make our Christmases far more visual than they have ever been. The tree received double the strings of lights we usually used. Garland was put everywhere possible. Festive door-pull covers were used; red, green, and white toilet paper replaced our usual white roll; even the kitchen cupboards were "wrapped" with ribbons and bows. That Christmas season, there often were times when I had trouble locating Kyle. I would look under the Christmas tree and he would be there on his back gazing at all the lights.

Our family held its first open house that year and invited everyone we knew and their children. By the time Kyle was three years old, he knew what was happening. It was an exciting moment on December 1st that year when I started to hang the garland in the living room. He began squealing and running around and signing, "PARTY CHRISTMAS SANTA COME." I knew I was on the right path for Kyle's sake. He had been a passive observer all of this time, but had retained far more that I gave him credit for. From that time forward his expressive language just exploded. It was very hard trying to keep ahead of him.

I attended every function I could where there was either a Deaf speaker or an interpreter. I desperately needed to be exposed to American Sign Language as much as possible. The Greater Vancouver Association of the Deaf held many socials and activities for adults and also for families. Kyle learned most of his language from these natural social gatherings. I was able to sit back and let him "learn" about being Deaf. The Deaf community was just wonderful. They were supportive and helpful. As hard as it was for me to attend a function where I could not fully communicate, I knew it was the best place for my child. I sat on the fringe and let him go. He and his sister always had such a great time. Kyle became alive and far more communicative than when we went somewhere where no one signed.

To parallel his exposure to American Sign Language, I tried as much as possible to make him aware of his print environment. When

I baked, I would show him the names of the ingredients and we would fingerspell them together. When it was bed time, I would first sign, "time for bed" and then slowly that evolved to "Time for b-e-d." Finally I would just fingerspell b-e-d and he would on rare occasions march off to bed or more likely kick up a fuss because he did not want to go to bed.

I had already figured out that Kyle's adult link to the hearing world would be through written English. I was trying to give him the foundations for understanding English. What I did not know was that he also needed more formal teaching of English because once someone is fluent in his native language (ASL for Kyle), then a second language is much easier to acquire. Unbeknownst to me, Kyle needed the bilingual–bicultural approach to learning. This is when the research began.

I started my research by having conversations with Deaf adults and attending conferences focused solely on helping families who had Deaf children. I also read articles and newsletters, watched Deaf adults socialize, and, most of all, observed how my son interacted with his peers, his teachers, his family, and people who did not know him or know anything about being Deaf. It was then that I discovered the Bi–Bi method was what we were looking for. One of the biggest reasons we decided on the Bi–Bi approach to Kyle's education was that it recognized that American Sign Language (ASL) was his native language, even though I was a bit resentful that his native language and mine were so different. By accepting that fact it became far easier to see what was so necessary for him. Another reason was that English was taught as a second language—a necessity for Kyle to properly learn about the written environment. But probably what really made it all seem right for us was the realization that in every situation where I encountered a Deaf adult—either at social occasions, conferences, educational or political meetings, or through casual encounters—they all used ASL even when using interpreters.

Now that I knew what I wanted for Kyle, it was a matter of trying to find it. The school I enrolled him in had bits and pieces of what I wanted and there really was no other choice. I knew that I could try to augment his education, but I was not a teacher.

By this time, my third child, Shannon, had been born. I informed the staff that we would not leave the hospital until her hearing was tested. I was hoping for another Deaf child so that I could continue having a Deaf adult come to my home to teach me ASL. Once Kyle turned three years of age that service was no longer available to me. The ABR, however, confirmed that Shannon was hearing.

Shannon began signing prior to age one. That is because our home was a signing environment. ASL is a language, and when it is used consistently in the environment, everyone exposed to it will pick it up. (My children have been further immersed in the signing environment because the preschool for children who are deaf has allowed all of my children to attend.)

Our family continued to be involved in as many Deaf functions as possible to give Kyle the exposure he so obviously needed. Each August, we attended the annual Deaf Community Corn Roast—an all–day gathering of hundreds of people from the Deaf and hearing communities. My proudest moment up to that time as Kyle's mom came when I witnessed a conversation between Kyle and a Deaf adult. Kyle and he were chatting about the fun everyone was having at the Corn Roast, when he asked Kyle if his parents were Deaf. He looked astonished when Kyle told him that his mother was hearing. I then approached the two of them of them and had a short conversation with this gentleman. He told me that most Deaf kids Kyle's age did not sign as naturally as Kyle signed and he had assumed that Kyle had Deaf parents and was exposed to sign from birth!

Each year after we attended the Corn Roast, Janelle would ask me how many more "sleeps" until the next one. Likewise, whenever we passed the park where it was held, Kyle would ask when we were going again. That always impressed upon me the impact that event made on our family.

The summer of 1990 was a time for great change in our family. I became a single mother. Kyle started kindergarten full time at a school for the Deaf and Janelle started kindergarten at neighborhood school. Kyle's report cards were always glowing. He was a joy to have in class, his progress was excellent, and he followed directions well. However, by the time, he reached grade two, I realized that his English skills were not progressing as well as they should. This was puzzling to me. He had been exposed to closed captions on TV since he was eleven months old. He would spend hours with maps and telephone books and seemed engrossed with the printed word. I questioned the teachers, but they did not have any answers. For me, this meant that it was time for more research, more reading, to try to find out what would help Kyle's English skills to progress.

During the summer of 1993, I married a wonderful man who took on the responsibilities of three children and has done it so well. He has formed a great bond with Kyle and with the girls as well. He also happens to be Deaf. Two weeks after the wedding our happy little group packed and moved four provinces away to our new life. Andrew, my new husband, had accepted a position as a teacher at a school for the Deaf in Milton, Ontario. Kyle was enrolled in the same school with his first Deaf teacher. This was a good year for him. He was still not on a par with his twin sister, however, even though he was now in an official Bi–Bi environment. By the end of grade four, my research and Kyle's experiences led me to realize that he needed additional time with someone who would teach him only English. He now works one–on–one with a hearing teacher who focuses only on teaching him English. Since he is well on his way to establishing his first language of ASL, we know that he will acquire English skills.

Kyle can lipread a few things but really looks to the hands for communication. He wore hearing aids for a while during preschool but when he started at the school for the Deaf, I kept the hearing aids at home. I wanted his language to be concentrated on rather than his ears. It was more important to me to look at what was between his ears instead of what went into them.

During his grade two year, Kyle asked if he could take speech. I said, "Sure!" but made sure he was aware that it was difficult and time consuming and that Deaf speech is not the same as having speech. He said that was fine and he was still interested. So we found his hearing aids and off he went. By the second month, he had lost interest in attending speech lessons, but I told him he had made the decision on his own and that he must continue for the rest of the school year. He did finish that year but never went back. My husband had also taken speech lessons for thirteen years but prefers to use the culturally appropriate way of gaining my attention by a foot stomp on the floor, a flash of a light, or a wave of his hand. When people ask me why some Deaf people speak so well and others do not, I simply say that the ability to speak for a Deaf person is the same as the ability to sing for a hearing person. I can talk but no one ever asks me to sing! Deaf people can communicate but not all can speak. I learned long ago that speech does not equal language and speech certainly does not equal intelligence.

My second son was born two years ago. During that pregnancy, I fully expected to have a Deaf child. We had found out that Kyle is Deaf due to a genetic condition and my husband was born Deaf to Deaf parents. Everything seemed to be in place for us to have a Deaf child. Before Austin was 24 hours old, however, we knew he was hearing. Now I had a real problem—what did I know about parenting a hearing son! Well, luckily for us, Austin may be hearing but his first language is ASL and his second language is English. He moves with ease from one to the other. His expressive language is impressive but his receptive language is awesome. All of my hearing friends think he is some little genius, but really he is a child born into a bilingual–bicultural environment. He lives in both worlds without doing harm to either one. This is just another confirmation that I did choose the right path for my son Kyle.

Just as my journey into the Deaf world continues, so does my son's and my husband's journey into the hearing world. It is only by working together, learning from each other, and respecting each other's knowledge of our own worlds that we will finally build that complete bridge between these two fascinating communities.

6

Cued Speech

A Professional Point of View

Barbara Williams-Scott, M.A., and Elizabeth Kipila, M.A.

If you are a parent new to the world of deafness, you are faced with a variety of crucial decisions. These decisions will have to be made either based on what professionals tell you or on reading material you have been able to find and decipher. Each professional who has had success in a particular area of education or communication will most likely advocate his or her approach strongly, yet he or she should encourage you to make your own decision.

Cued Speech is a current option for educating deaf and hard of hearing children. It is also a way for these children to communicate at school and at home. Although Cued Speech has been in existence for thirty years, not enough families and professionals know the truth about Cued Speech. As a result, many families who are new to the field of deafness may not learn about Cued Speech from people in their area. We hope that you will become curious about Cued Speech and find a school program or a family that is using it. We hope you take the time to learn about the system and consider it for your child.

■ WHAT IS CUED SPEECH?

Cued Speech is a method of using handshapes to supplement speechreading. These handshapes are *phonemically based*—that is, they are based on the sounds the letters make, not the letters themselves. Cued speech is comprised of eight handshapes that represent groups of consonant sounds, and four positions about the face to represent groups of vowel sounds. Combinations of these hand configurations and placements show the exact pronunciation of words in connected speech, by making them clearly visible and understandable to the Cued Speech recipient. Cued Speech allows your child to "see-hear" precisely every spoken syllable that a hearing person hears.

Cued Speech was developed by Dr. R. Orin Cornett in 1966 because he was concerned about the low reading level of the average college-age deaf person. In investigating the skills needed for reading comprehension, Dr. Cornett learned that comprehension is directly correlated with the development of spoken language. A child needs to *have* language first to be able to read it, and the language that the child reads is the written form of the language that is spoken.

Among hearing people, language is conveyed through speech. People who are deaf, however, cannot understand what is said solely through listening. Speechreading therefore appears to be a logical skill to develop. Dr. Cornett learned that speechreading is complicated since many English words look alike on the lips. For example, the little word "met" has at least sixty other possibilities—mitt, mutt, bet, but, bit—to name a few. When Dr. Cornett discovered the difficulty of speechreading spoken English, he decided to develop a system to alleviate the ambiguity in reading lips.

■ HOW DOES CUED SPEECH WORK?

Speech is the physical production of spoken language and is comprised of sounds called *phonemes*. The twenty-six letters in the English alphabet, singly and in combinations, produce forty-three

FIGURE 1. CONSONANT HANDSHAPES

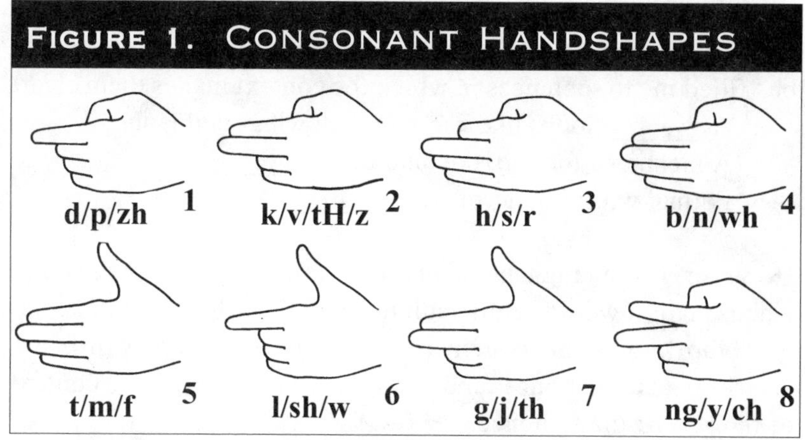

phonemes. For example, the letter "Aa" has five possible pronunciations (phonemes) in American English: /ah/ as in "father," /a/ as in "cat," /ae/ as in "may," /u/ as in "about," and /aw/ as in "tall." Sometimes phonemes involve more than one letter, such as /sh/ in the word "sheet" or /ng/ in the word "song." Spelling cannot indicate these pronunciation differences without using diacritical markings like those seen in the dictionary. Cued Speech, however, can immediately show the cue reader how something is pronounced while it is being uttered.

Dr. Cornett organized the American English phonemes into groups that always make the spoken word clear to a cue reader who is deaf. It is important to remember that Cued Speech is a hand *supplement* to speechreading. The manual cues alone are meaningless in connected speech, because they must accompany the speaker's mouth movements to be useful.

Different handshapes are used to distinguish between consonants that look alike on the mouth. For example, /m/p/b/ look the same on the mouth, so different handshapes are used. (See Figure 1.) The sound that the letter "Mm" makes is shown on the number 5 handshape; the sound that "Pp" makes is depicted by the number 1 handshape; and the sound that the letter "Bb" makes is indicated by the number 4 handshape. For example, say or mouth the words, "mat," "pat," or "bat" to yourself while watching yourself in a mirror. These three words look the same on the lips. For someone familiar with spoken English, the words could be "filled in" to sentences in which the context makes them clear:

A _______ looks like a mouse with wings and fangs.

A nickname for Patrick could be __________.

Formal wrestling occurs on a _________.

However, if the language is unknown to the listener or the child who is deaf, it would be difficult to fill in those blanks. For someone who knows the system of Cued Speech, these words are clearly readable at once, and can be learned through the context of the rest of the sentence.

Just as different consonants can look similar on the lips, so too can different vowel sounds. In Cued Speech, the vowel sounds of a word are therefore also visually represented. Figure 2 shows the vowel positions that are used to represent vowel sounds.

It is important to remember that all words are made up of consonant-vowel combinations. For instance, in the word "me," the /m/ sound is pronounced first, followed by the /ee/ sound. If that syllable is repeated, it becomes the name "Mimi"—again, the /ee/ vowel is attached to each /m/ phoneme when the name is said. Consonant–vowel combinations are done through Cued

FIGURE 2. VOWEL PLACEMENTS

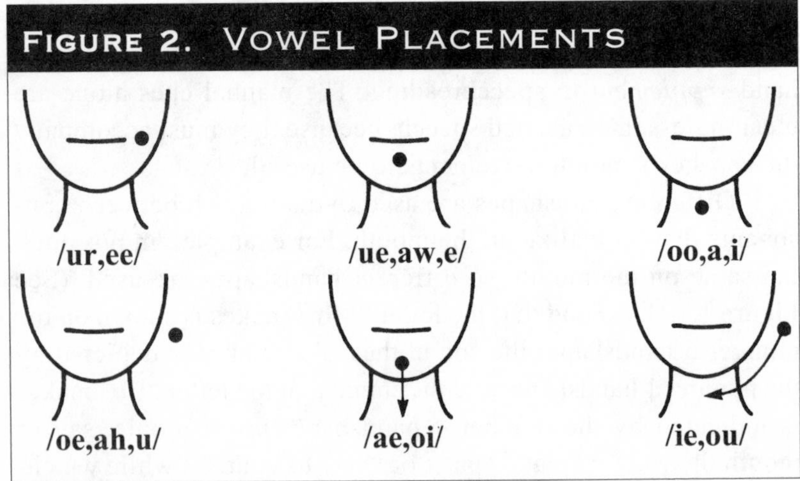

Speech by placing the appropriate consonant handshape at the proper vowel position. Thus, the word "me" is cued with the number 5 handshape at the mouth position. The name "Mimi" is cued in the same place, with two taps at the mouth to indicate the two syllables as they are uttered. Every phoneme is always cued at the same time it is said. This illustrates the most basic rule of cueing: "cue what you say, as you say it, the way you say it."

As illustrated in Figure 1, most of the handshapes are used to represent three different consonant sounds. Handshape number 5, for instance, represents the sounds /m/f/t/, which are clearly different on the lips. Likewise, most of the vowel positions are assigned three vowel sounds. For example, /ue/aw/e/ are assigned to the chin position. When uttered, the mouth is shaped differently for each sound: /ue/ is round (o); /aw/ is open (O); and /e/ is flat (-). Thus, the same principle of making look-alike sounds distinguishable on the lips is applied to the cues themselves. When the handshape or vowel position for different letters is the same, the mouth looks different.

Cueing is always used in conjunction with speaking. Cues alone do not carry meaning since they have groups of sounds associated with them. If the cuer does not talk, or at least mouth the sounds she cues, a full message is not being sent. That is why Cued Speech cannot be described as a language of its own. It is a visual representation of English.

Through the tool of Cued Speech, your child can "see–hear" the language around her. Every speech sound, and many sound effects (like crunch, rustle, bang) can be communicated without writing or spelling. A Cued Speech deaf child with hearing parents is allowed to develop in the family's native tongue, as her hearing peers and siblings do—naturally. She will find this same language written in books and will be able to read a familiar language. She will be able to learn how to read her own language as hearing children do, by sounding out new sight words that probably will have been "seen-heard" before.

■ WHAT ARE THE BENEFITS OF CUED SPEECH?

Cued Speech offers numerous benefits for individuals with varying levels of hearing loss.

1. SINCE TALKING NEEDS TO ACCOMPANY CUES, CHILDREN LEARNING CUED SPEECH DEVELOP SPEECHREADING SKILLS WITHOUT EFFORT. As spoken language becomes more familiar, speechreading alone need not be a threatening ordeal. Also, because speechreading is 50 percent of Cued Speech, it has been found that many children experienced in Cued Speech feel confident in reading speakers who do not know how to cue. The language is usually familiar enough to make accurate guesses with contextual clues.

2. CUED SPEECH HELPS THE PERSON WHO IS DEAF BE AWARE OF SPEECH SOUNDS. It shows her that letters can have different pronunciations, and that our American English spelling can be confusing. Consider these examples: "rough, bough, through" vs. "Ruff, bow, threw."

3. Cued Speech does not magically help your deaf child speak well. **CUES CAN HELP HER RECOGNIZE PRONUNCIATION BUT SHE WILL STILL NEED SPEECH LESSONS WITH A SPEECH THERAPIST.** Hopefully she will get daily reminders and drills from her teacher of the deaf. She should also practice at home with you and the rest of her family. When particular speech goals are met, i.e., spoken correctly, the cues become a tool to remind her of proper speech production. It seems that the physical motor act of cueing assists in recalling correct pronunciation. For example, the past tense of the word "pop" is pronounced /pahpt/ not /pahpid/. Remembering the final handshape number 5 and being able to mouth the proper tongue placement for the phoneme /t/, the child cuer expresses the correct tense even if she is unable to spell the word or say all the sounds involved.

4. EVEN IF YOUR CHILD IS UNABLE TO SAY CERTAIN WORDS INTELLIGIBLY, WITH CUED SPEECH SHE CAN INDICATE THAT SHE KNOWS THE CORRECT PRONUNCIATION. For example, in the word "cars," the final "s" is cued as a /z/ sound with the number 2 handshape. In the word "cats," the final "s" is cued as an /s/ sound with the number 3 handshape.

5. SHE CAN LEARN ABOUT DIALECTS AND ACCENTS: Massachusetts residents have good /ie deerz/ (ideas); South Carolinians' opposite of "no" is /yae yus/ (yes); a Spanish brother might have a /sees tur/ (sister).

6. SHE HAS THE OPPORTUNITY TO LEARN A SPOKEN FOREIGN LANGUAGE. Since Cued Speech is phonemically based, cues can be applied to fit the sounds of any spoken language. Right now, there are about forty-three languages/dialects for which Cued Speech systems have been established.

7. SHE CAN BE MADE AWARE OF HUMOR IN THE RHYTHM AND RHYME OF SPOKEN ENGLISH AND THE FUN IN TONGUE TWISTERS (FINGER TIE-ERS FOR CUERS!), RIDICULOUS WORDS, AND IDIOMATIC EXPRESSIONS.

- What's black and white and read all over?
- Horrible Hannah held Harry's hand.
- Jeepers Creepers!
- Varoooooom! Kerplunk!

8. Rather comfortably, the rules of spoken English are fully internalized by the time the average hearing child is six years old. Making the sounds of the native spoken language clearly visible to the listener who is deaf or hard of hearing, the cued message is readily accessible in real time, in the exact words and even the pronunciation of the speaker, and is left to the personal perception and interpretation of the listener alone. **YOUR CHILD IS GIVEN THE OPPORTUNITY TO DEVELOP TO HER POTENTIAL WITHOUT THE INTERFERENCE DEAFNESS NORMALLY BRINGS WITH REGARD TO SPOKEN ENGLISH LANGUAGE AND SPEECH DEVELOPMENT. SHE CAN LEARN TO THINK IN SPOKEN ENGLISH.**

9. CUED SPEECH SEEMS TO BE A LOGICAL TOOL FOR ASSISTING ANYONE WHO HAS DIFFICULTY WITH A SPOKEN LANGUAGE—foreign children for whom English is a second language, some children diagnosed as having learning difficulties when processing spoken language, and adults who have lost their hearing later in life.

10. More than 90 percent of deaf children are born into hearing families. It is the authors' preference that these children use Cued Speech both at school and at home for academic growth and for communication. **CUED SPEECH SUPPLEMENTS WHAT IS SPOKEN IN THE HOME AND SCHOOL ALREADY.** It is not like trying to learn a new language.

11. We believe that **CUED SPEECH SUPPLIES THE ELEMENTS OF SPOKEN ENGLISH THAT ARE ESSENTIAL FOR A DEAF CHILD TO EXPERIENCE SUCCESS IN A PRIMARILY HEARING SOCIETY.** Still, we see value in American Sign Language (ASL) within the deaf culture and for those who wish to be part of it in some way. We feel it is important that families and professionals realize the need to consider these children's identities as persons with hearing losses. Once English is established, ASL can be introduced as a second language. For children who are deaf who are born into deaf families where ASL is used, we have a particular interest in developing a bilingual educational curriculum in which both Cued Speech English and ASL are used. It could also benefit English oriented children of hearing parents who use Cued Speech to learn ASL as a second language.

Cued Speech is practical, accurate, and time-effective to learn and utilize. We recommend that if you are unfamiliar with Cued Speech, take the time to study it. We hope you will consider Cued Speech as a viable option in the education of your child.

Materials and information about Cued Speech are available through the Cued Speech Center in Raleigh, North Carolina at 919–828–1218. For information about the profession of Cued Speech transliteration, call the Training, Evaluation, and Certification Unit at 301–439–5766.

■ *REFERENCES*

Abraham, S. and R.G. Stoker. (1984) "An Evaluation of Methods Used to Teach Speech to the Hearing Impaired Using a Simulation Technique." *The Volta Review*. Vol. 86, No. 7 (Dec.), pp. 325-35.

Beaupre, W.J. (1984) *Gaining Cued Speech Proficiency: A Manual for Parents, Teachers, and Clinicians.* Washington, DC: Gallaudet University Press.

Beck, P.H. (1985). *Discovering Cued Speech: An Eight Hour Instructional Program and Six Hour Competency Review.* Cleveland, OH: North Coast Cued Speech Services (23070 Hermitage Rd., Cleveland, OH 44122-4008).

Cornett, R.O., and Daisey, M.E. (1992) *The Cued Speech Resource Book for Parents of Deaf Children.* Raleigh, NC: National Cued Speech Association.

Sbaiti, M.E.D. (1983). *Cued Speech Instructional Manual.* Raleigh, NC: National Cued Speech Association.

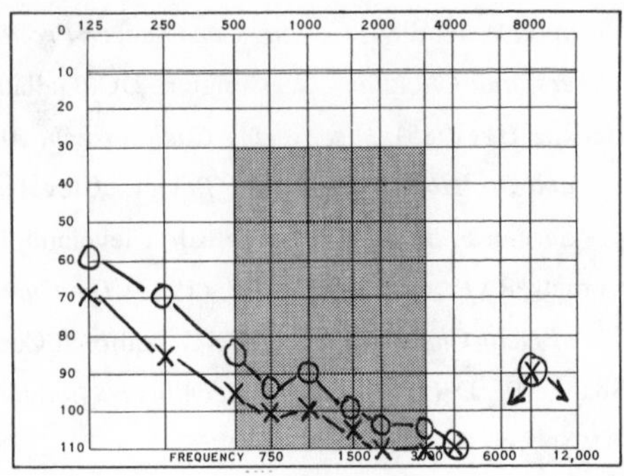

SIMON'S STORY

SARINA ROFFÉ

David and I suspected Simon was deaf long before the diagnosis. We had a door with a loud bang that never startled him. We could go behind his back and bang pots and he did not respond with even a blink. We kept asking our pediatrician to check his hearing but he kept putting us off as overprotective parents. Finally, at my husband's insistence, the pediatrician referred us to an audiology center for a hearing test when Simon was eight months old.

At the center, I was given ear defenders to protect my ears during the test. I was in the soundproof booth with Simon as the sounds got louder and louder and kept coming over and over. Simon didn't hear anything. He didn't even blink or look up. I was so traumatized that I couldn't think straight. I couldn't stay and listen to what the audiologist was saying. I had to get out of there. My husband talked for a minute or so to the audiologist, and she suggested that we come back again for more testing.

I remember being quite hysterical before I reached the car. I still don't know how I got home safely that day. All I could think of was that my baby was less than perfect. I remember being angry and asking, "Why me? Why my baby? What did I do to deserve such a fate? Why am I being punished?"

When a new baby is born, parents have hopes and dreams for that child. When we found out that Simon was deaf, we thought our dreams were shattered. Since he was our first, we had no idea about normal child development. We had no idea about the kinds of things he should be doing. We didn't understand how a hearing loss would affect his growth.

One of the worst things I had to do in my life was to tell my parents and my husband's parents that their first and only grandson was deaf. How could I tell them? What would I say? They had put so much love into him and would be so disappointed. When I finally did tell them, their reaction was to suggest seeing doctor after doctor. So we went from one to another to another. The one I remember most vividly was at a hospital in Baltimore. The audiologist sat with us for three hours explaining about hearing loss, the ear, and how it would affect Simon. She told us to go home, enroll in a local county program, and get to work. She was the first of a long line of people who told me that my work with my son would determine his success. This started many long years of guilt.

When we had first learned that our nine-month-old son was profoundly deaf, we began to learn about ways of teaching him. The ideals and goals strived for by oralists [see Chapter Seven] seemed to make the most sense to us, especially since we were hearing parents. We really believed then as we do now, that our child should learn to live in the hearing world. We expected that with time and the help of specialists in deaf education, he would be able to lipread and have understandable speech.

We were among the 92 percent of parents with a deaf child who are hearing. Consequently, we had almost no knowledge about the world of the deaf. The decisions we were attempting to make for our child were based on ideals rather than on our child's ability. We worked tirelessly toward our goals for our child for a long time. He was our only child and we had the time to give him. He was our priority because we felt that the quality time that we gave him during his language learning years would benefit his future.

We were enrolled in a parent-infant program in our county for three years. During that time, David and I learned a great deal about deafness, deaf education, deaf people, and our own feelings about our child. Simon's teacher became our lifeline, our entrance into the world of the deaf. She was our bridge into our son's life.

Simon's education became an obsession as lecture after lecture, teacher after teacher, and book after book pushed me into the role as my son's teacher. I worked with him daily on language and speechreading lessons. I remember choosing words to teach him. We would work on them for hours at a time. I had to remember to put the word I was teaching at the end of the sentence because he would be able to hear it better. We practiced auditory training in our home and in our neighborhood as he learned to use his hearing aids. We worked on lessons from a correspondence course and spent four weeks one summer at the John Tracy Clinic in California. It seemed as if time was marching on, and I could still count the words that Simon knew on my fingers. Each night I would go to bed feeling guilty that I had not done enough for my son.

By the time Simon was two years old, it was apparent that he needed a support system to help him learn language. His vocabulary was all of twenty words. Since this was our first child, we had no other child with whom to compare or gauge his progress. We did not realize that we were measuring his growth as a deaf child. Yet our goals were for him to achieve as a hearing child. On a day to day basis, we found that we expected less of him as a deaf child than we would have if he was hearing. We considered his educational growth on a daily basis instead of looking at his long-term growth. By doing this, we were closing our eyes to the time that he was losing in those crucial years.

Little by little, our lack of communication with Simon forced us to turn to Total Communication—signing and speaking simultaneously. [See Chapter Eight.] We began to use Signed English as a support system. Simon was going through stages of temper tantrums and was picking up his own form of signs through the use of gestures. He was active but we also knew that he was sharp and intelligent. His eyes took in everything around him, and he was able to use contextual clues to observe and to learn.

With Total Communication, we thought our son could continue his oral skills, yet have a support system that, we hoped, would expand his vocabulary. At the time, this approach made sense to us. Our sign skills improved and we continued with our lessons. By the time he was three and a half, his vocabulary had expanded from 20 words to 100 words. Looking back, I really had no conception of how slow his language growth was.

When Simon was two and a half, I enrolled him in a regular nursery school with hearing children. One of my objectives was to expand his social skills. His lack of language hit me one day when a little boy in the school came up to talk to me. The little boy said, "My dog pants when he is sweating." I was shocked. Simon was still learning the names of things that we were labeling in our house. This little tyke knew of abstracts such as "panting" while my son struggled with the names of things. This child spoke in sentences while my child struggled with words. This child knew colors, numbers, shapes, letters, and nursery rhymes while Simon was still learning his name. What a difference hearing makes! Meeting this child made me realize how long the road to acquiring language could be.

Gradually, we saw the limitations of Total Communication as well. Although this is one of the primary languages of the deaf, we were uncomfortable with it because we wanted Simon to live in our hearing world. We were frustrated with the number of years it would take us to learn sign language. We knew that as a deaf individual, he would eventually learn signing as a social language, but we wanted English to be his primary language. We felt that if he were able to internalize English as his natural language, it would help him with reading and writing—skills that are crucial throughout life.

I talked with mothers of older deaf children who used various communication methods. These mothers told me of the hours they devoted to helping their children with homework and re-teaching the skills learned in school. I did not like what I saw and was depressed by it. I still remember the time we learned of Simon's hearing loss until the time that we started using Cued Speech as one big emotional jumble of pain, anguish, and frustration.

We were torn between signing and oralism. We believed in the principle that the deaf child needed an early communication system and that this would foster good parent-child communication during the language learning years. We also believed that our child should use his listening skills and residual hearing and should learn to live in the hearing world. Ideally, we believed in both methods, but, in practice for us, they both failed. We were not comfortable with either system because of what we saw as the educational limitations of each. We were strong advocates of inclusion even though our son lacked the necessary skills for inclusion at this time. We were also frustrated by the silence that blocked our son's ability to achieve his potential. We knew we had an intelligent child and it bothered us that his deafness would limit him no matter how hard we worked with him.

One day, we were introduced to Cued Speech. Simon was three and a half at the time, and a new Cued Speech program would be starting in our county that September. We went with some other parents to attend a workshop. During the workshop, we learned that Cued Speech was a simple, clear, easy-to-learn method that would enhance lipreading, promote natural language, and bridge the communication gap between hearing parents and their deaf children. Another benefit from the enrichment of natural language was that this would create more success with reading. Cued Speech would provide the deaf child with a clear mental image of the English language, including its syntax, word order, idioms, and figurative language. This system has a phonetic base and can be learned in a matter of hours, although mastery takes time and practice and can only be achieved through continual use. Cued Speech seemed to combine the essence of both Total Communication and Oralism.

We met many people at the workshop who strengthened our decision to give Cued Speech a try. We felt that we had a tenuous family situation at the time, and we learned that Cued Speech had helped to ease family tensions for others. We learned that a mother could return to "mothering" and abandon "teachering." We learned that there were better family feelings between siblings and the deaf child. Perhaps most significantly, vocabulary growth was astounding. But we were skeptical. How could Cued Speech overcome all of the deficits of deafness that we had learned about so far? Nevertheless, we decided to give it our best shot.

Learning and gaining fluency in cueing was not painless. It took time and patience to gain speed. By the end of the first month, however, I was cueing all of Simon's known vocabulary as well as commonly used phrases. Little by little, I taught myself to expand the vocabulary that I was using with him. I began asking, "Do you want Rice Krispies or Corn Flakes?" instead of "Do you want cereal?" By the end of two months, I was cueing fluently and felt a new freedom with language and my child. Simon was understanding the cues and was rapidly picking up new vocabulary.

I knew that my devotion to Cued Speech and the use of it with everything that I said was to be Simon's lifeline. If I didn't say it, he wouldn't learn it. I talked and cued everything that was part of our daily routine. We took walks and talked about nature. We cooked and baked and talked all of the time. We went to the market and talked about the things on the list. We talked of animals, shapes, numbers, colors, and letters. He learned of tails that were bushy and furry, long and short, thick and thin, fat and skinny. He was a sponge as he absorbed word after word, concept after concept, and rule after rule. Frustration slowly died as he began understanding and we began communicating. Discipline improved when he understood our message.

Simon was not only learning and understanding language receptively, but his expressive language was astounding us as well. He began asking questions. He noticed the different shapes of the moon and wanted to know why it happened. He questioned everything around him. We could see the wheels turning in his mind as he absorbed new information. His curiosity opened new doors for him and the barrier of silence which previously had held him back was lifting.

When we started cueing, Simon had the receptive language of a seventeen-month-old: 100-150 words. Within the first six months of using Cued Speech, he had acquired 500 new words, as had been predicted. Within the first fifteen months, he had acquired enough language to score six months ahead of hearing children in verbal ability on tests administered at his school. By the age of five, after twenty-two months on Cued Speech, Simon had made a five-year language gain. My child was talking in sentences that had no grammatical errors. His syntax was wonderful. He had been given a clear visual image of spoken language through Cued Speech.

I felt as if I had seen a miracle happen in front of my eyes. My child was happier and had blossomed into a regular kid. Our family life returned to normal once Simon was no longer the center of our life. I was no longer feeling guilty about Simon. Now I was full of pride in his accomplishments. During those first years of using Cued Speech, his teachers worked tirelessly on language development. They were my friends and my mentors as they filled my child's needs. Together, we pulled Simon up to where he should be.

Simon needed work on his speech and he still does. Now, however, he has the language that he needs to understand how to work on his speech. Without the language base, there is no learning, no promoting of ideas, no generating of knowledge, no reading for the fun of it. I really believe this and I believe through my observations and my experiences with Simon that Cued Speech really works.

At the end of first grade, my belief in Simon's intelligence was confirmed when he was tested for the gifted and talented program in his school. He scored at the top of the entire first grade. Cued Speech made sense for Simon's visually oriented learning style.

Simon is now eleven and has excellent lipreading skills as measured on a speechreading test that has adult norms. He scored 95 percent on this test. He reads above grade level and has topped all of the language tests given to the deaf students at his school. In fifth grade, he scored in the 99th percentile on the California Achievement Test. He is an avid reader, loves to learn, and has a good attitude about school. Our son has been in a typical classroom with hearing students with the aid of a Cued Speech transliterator for five years now. He learned as hearing children do. Simon receives ongoing speech therapy to improve his speech intelligibility, continues to practice auditory skills, and sees a teacher of the deaf a few times a week to help in problem areas. He is challenged by the classes such as the Junior Great Books program that he is offered through the gifted and talented program.

Cued Speech has allowed Simon to learn a foreign language. The phonetic base of Cued Speech is compatible with learning many languages. For us, that language was Hebrew, the language of prayer for Jews. With Hebrew, Simon will be able to have a Bar Mitzvah, a rite of passage for Jewish boys, and be accepted as a man in the Jewish community.

We have provided Simon with the latest technology available for the deaf. He has a telecaptioner for the TV, and an alarm clock which flashes. We have two TTYs and a smoke alarm with a strobe. We have telephone amplifiers on all of the phones because he often uses his listening skills to talk on the phone. We are always sure that he has a pair of well-fitting earmolds and that his hearing aids are checked regularly.

Simon wants to be a lawyer as a stepping stone to Congressman or Senator and then he would like to become the first deaf president of the United States of America. We joke about whether he will be President or perhaps a Supreme Court Justice. Whatever Simon does and achieves will be because of the strong language base that Cued Speech has given him. When we first learned of Simon's hearing problem, all I kept hearing was what he couldn't do. With cueing, I know that there is really nothing that he can't do.

Simon is at an age when he is learning to understand and accept himself as a person who is deaf. We have fostered relationships between Simon and other deaf children. As much as I believe in cueing and in teaching a child the skills he needs to succeed in the hearing world, I also believe he needs to associate with other deaf children. It is possible that they are the ones that he may be most comfortable with.

We now have a four year old daughter, "Honey," who has normal hearing. We revel in her development after our years of struggle with Simon. She sings, dances, and loves to talk. Both of our children astound us at every turn. We've learned to accept them as individuals.

As a parent, I've grown in direction for both my children and myself. I've found a purpose to work for. I am a transliterator in the Cued Speech program and I enjoy working with other parents to help them learn about Cued Speech. It has worked for us and can work for other children who are deaf.

WHERE I AM TODAY

SIMON ROFFÉ

A lot has happened in my life since the first edition of *Choices In Deafness* was published. Some of it has been sad, some happy, but all of it interesting. I have gone to five different schools, made an interstate move and been accepted into a major university. I have learned to drive, having a couple of accidents along the way as well as a few parking tickets. People close to me, such as my grandmother, have died. And we had a new baby born into our family. My brother, Abraham, Abie for short, is now seven years old. He is adorable and I love babysitting for him as well as playing with him.

When *Choices* was first published, I was just entering middle school. In the two years that I was there I had a great deal of trouble socially. I felt ostracized and unaccepted. I see now that it was a growing experience and I learned about all kinds of different people. I was no longer "protected" from the real world and I learned to fine tune my antennae so that I became a better judge of character, a talent that I still have. I know by talking to a person for ten minutes if they will be a good friend, or if they are an accident waiting to happen. I also perfected a quick wit. As I got older, that talent helped me a lot with what is called "locker room talk." While at the time that I was in middle school my experiences were traumatic, in hindsight, I can see that they helped me to mature a lot. Because of these negative experiences, I decided not to stay with the deaf program's center school and instead started attending my neighborhood school.

In looking back now, I feel that switching schools was a mistake because I missed my deaf friends. I was the only deaf person in a school with hearing people. Although I no longer had to put up with the taunts of my former classmates, I wasn't fully accepted in the neighborhood school either. I was just known as "that deaf guy." However, I did learn about differences in culture. I learned about the differences between the hearing and the deaf world. While I know that to be successful, a deaf person has to be able to cope in the hearing world, I also know that to feel accepted, they have to cope in the deaf world. Now, years later, I think I have done that. I have both hearing and deaf friends and have learned how to balance both of them.

After I had spent two years at my neighborhood school, my parents decided to move back to their hometown in New York after an eighteen-year absence. My father had found a new job in New York and my mother had given up being a transliterator because of tendinitis. She returned to school to earn a BA in Journalism and began working as a reporter for several newspapers. It was a good time for us to move. We found a house in New York, sold our house in Maryland, and off we went. At the same time, I had won a scholarship to travel to Israel and although I felt guilty leaving my mother with all those boxes to unpack, I went off to discover my Jewish homeland.

On the application for the trip, they never asked if I was deaf and I never told them. I didn't have a transliterator but I had a fabulous six-week trip. I even got over feeling guilty about leaving my mom with all of the work! When I was on the flight back from Israel, I thought, "I must be the only person in New York who hasn't seen my own room!"

My junior and senior years were spent in Brooklyn, New York, at a high school that had students who were deaf as well as hearing. I felt much more accepted there than in my previous schools. One thing that was new was that I had to get a transliterator who was completely new to the field of deafness as well as Cued Speech. After a rocky beginning, my transliterator and I finally got used to each other and I began to enjoy her company. I also had a new resource teacher. She was one of the best that I ever had over the years. She knew exactly what needed to be taught and helped to keep me above water in both my science and math classes.

While I was in high school, I did several things that I am especially proud of. The first thing was joining an organization called Our Way-NCSY. It is a group for Jewish teenagers who are deaf. I held office for all four years of high school. For two years I was the secretary and was given two Executive of the Year awards along the way. When my term as secretary expired, I successfully ran for President of the organization. I held that position for another two years and was given two President's Awards for going beyond the call of duty. Only five President's Awards have been given in the last twenty years and I received two of them!

While I was in Maryland, I was a member of the Montgomery Exceptional Leaders (MEL program). This group consisted of high school students with various disabilities who would go into third and fourth grade classrooms and talk about their individual disability and how they accommodated to it. It was a spectacular success. Our goal was to make the students feel more comfortable with students with disabilities by showing them that we were, in fact, just like them. We showed them that we could do anything that we wanted to accomplish.

When I got to high school in New York, the administrator of the program I was in asked me to be the student member of the board of the New York City–wide commission on Deaf Education. That was a group of people—professionals, parents, administrators, and one student—whose goal it was to reform the deaf education system in New York City. I was chosen to be the student member of the board. As I look back, it seems surprising that I was asked to be on the board because I did not grow up in the New York system. I later realized that the reason I was chosen was because of the superior education I had received in Maryland. They wanted to put a student on the board who was well-adjusted and had grown up in deaf programs that were a part of hearing schools. When I entered the deaf program in New York, I was tested and found to have an extremely high test score. This was an indication of the superior education I had in Maryland.

During my senior year, I felt that I needed a change from the straight academic program I had been pursuing. I began an internship with a brokerage firm and worked under the guidance of a broker. I think that I learned more in the five months I spent working with him than I did in all four years of high school. I learned about how the market works and about various ways a person can invest his or her money. I learned about IRA accounts, capital gains taxes, bonds, mutual funds, and dozens of other transactions that a brokerage firm does for clients. I think this experience just whetted my appetite for a knowledge of finance.

During the summer following my high school graduation, my grandmother died. It was a shock to me although she had been sick and living on borrowed time for quite a while. She was a vital woman who was full of life and talked a lot until the last day of her life. I had grown up thinking that I was her favorite grandchild, but after she died my aunt told me a story. She said that while she was talking to an uncle of mine, they got into an argument over whom my grandmother liked more. It was then that they realized that my grandmother made everybody who talked to her feel special. She would give you her undivided attention when she was talking to you. If someone called to talk to her, and you were at her house talking to her, she would tell the person on the phone to call back because she was too busy talking to you. That was the kind of respect she gave you and that was her gift to the world.

After high school, I was ready to move onto college. Although I applied to several colleges, I knew I wanted to attend New York University. It had the second highest rating for a business program in the country. Although I almost didn't get in, I am now a sophomore at the University and commute from home every day. My plan is to major in finance and then work on Wall Street after getting my Master's in Business Administration.

After I finished high school, I had a renewed interest in Cued Speech. As I went through school, I had always referred questions about my "system" to my mother. Now, however, I was tired of knowing very little about the system that had contributed so much to my success in my trials of life. So I started asking a lot of questions of my mother and former teachers. I found that I liked talking about my system. I liked the fact that it was a success and I was a big part of it. I was one of the first children to use it. I was one of the "original" Cuekids, while now I prefer to think of myself as a CueAdult. I have been nominated for a board seat at the National Cued Speech Association. In addition, my mother and I are now forming the Cued Speech Center, which will service the New York City area. We have been actively trying to start this center because we can see a real need for it.

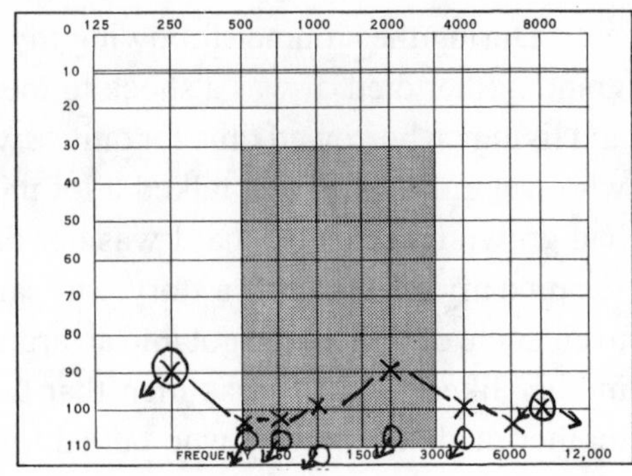

TIFFANY'S STORY

ANDY AND LINDA BALDERSON

> *I SHALL BE TELLING THIS WITH A SIGH*
> *SOMEWHERE AGES AND AGES HENCE;*
> *TWO ROADS DIVERGED IN A WOOD, AND I—*
> *I TOOK THE ONE LESS TRAVELED BY,*
> *AND THAT HAS MADE ALL THE DIFFERENCE.*
> ROBERT FROST

Although the number of roads was three, our journey to select the best mode of communication for our profoundly deaf daughter, Tiffany, parallels Frost's choice in the yellow wood. We chose to learn Cued Speech when her deafness was first diagnosed and still feel that decision was best for all of us. We would like to share that journey with you, so that you might understand how and why we made that choice.

Tiffany was born on July 12, 1973. She was our second child, full term and apparently healthy. We spent five months believing that nothing was wrong with Tiffany. Then the painful truth began to emerge. A visit to a new pediatrician on the day before Christmas in 1973 marked the beginning of our search for the answer to "What's wrong with Tiffany?" What a frustrating and frightening time this was for us. As we went from doctor to doctor and test to test, Tiffany stopped responding to everything and everyone. She would lie in her crib quietly with a blank look in her eyes. Soon it was discovered that she had a congenital heart defect that would require open heart surgery before adolescence. Medication for this condition greatly improved her activity level, but we sensed that more difficulties lay ahead. The doctors were still concerned about her overall development, and we also suspected a hearing loss. Visits to more specialists turned up additional problems, some due to developmental delays and others surgically correctable.

Tiffany had frequent ear infections throughout her first year, so her hearing loss was temporarily linked to these infections. Diagnosis of her hearing loss came after she had had tubes placed in her ears and was still unable to hear. She was eighteen months old when our suspicions of her deafness were verified.

We immediately began to search for a way to communicate with her. Her audiologist recommended that we visit all of the deaf education programs nearby. He also gave us some excellent advice. First, he recommended that we not limit our visits to only children of Tiffany's age, but also observe older deaf children in each of the programs. Second, he suggested that we observe both hearing and deaf children of the same age, whenever possible. Finally, he cautioned us to ask to see the children's audiograms and ask about the age of onset and cause of deafness of each child we observed.

We made arrangements to visit local Oral and Total Communication programs, as well as a nearby Cued Speech program. In less than a month, we had visited several programs and had made our decision—we would use Cued Speech with Tiffany. At that time, there were only four deaf children in our area using this method. Few people knew about it. We are grateful that Tiffany's audiologist was among those few! The publicly funded Cued Speech program was located in a private preschool/primary school about a forty-five minute drive from our home. Although we did not need to pay for tuition, we would be responsible for transportation to and from school. Logistically it would have been much easier to choose another program. Why did we choose Cued Speech for Tiffany?

Our visit to the Cued Speech program made a positive impact upon us. Three of the four Cued Speech children in the area were involved in this particular program. The fourth was too old to attend this school. The three deaf children we saw were ages four, five, and seven at the time. All of them had language levels at or above expected levels for hearing children their ages. The four-year-old profoundly deaf boy that we observed was working at an academic level above that of our older daughter, a bright hearing child of the same age. His speech was easily intelligible, and his personality was captivating. He was obviously doing well despite his profound hearing loss. One of these three children had unintelligible speech but his command of the English language was excellent. All three children appeared to be successful deaf students, and all had been born profoundly deaf. We were impressed! We also felt strongly that our daughter should be taught in a setting where she would have contact with hearing peers. As this school was primarily for hearing children, we felt it was ideal for Tiffany. Here she would receive individual help from a teacher of the deaf, group instruction with other deaf children, and could be integrated into a hearing class with a teacher who could cue. We felt that this educational setting was the right one for Tiffany.

In addition to the impact of our visit to the program, there were features of Cued Speech that we felt would really help our family. First, we wanted to do something concrete for our child. Learning to cue would fulfill that need. The fact that Cued Speech was easy to learn was a big bonus. We learned to cue in four evenings and have never needed to take a class since! Second, Cued Speech would allow us to say anything to Tiffany—a small sacrifice of our time for a lifetime of clear communication with our daughter. We felt that we would retain the role of parents, while making an important contribution to her learning of the English language. We would be able to communicate with her fully, an important factor in our family. We felt that Cued Speech would return a sense of normalcy to our family—a critical need for us at this very difficult time.

Educationally, Cued Speech would clarify speechreading for Tiffany, making English her natural language while simultaneously fostering her speechreading skills. The fact that the basis of Cued Speech was phonetic appealed to us because this would reinforce correct speech production. We had both worked as teachers of hearing children so we understood the importance of knowing language and phonics in learning to read. It was in this area of reading that we felt Cued Speech made its most important educational contribution. With Cued Speech, Tiffany would be able to use her understanding of the English language and her phonetic skills to become a good reader. If she was to spend her life unable to partake in activities involving hearing, we felt that it would be imperative that she be able to read easily and well. So Cued Speech made good sense to us in theory. We had seen successful deaf students using Cued Speech. Therefore, against the advice of many professionals who did not believe in the methodology, we chose to cue.

We learned to cue and began cueing everything we said to Tiffany. We were told by her audiologist that Tiffany had a profound sensorineural loss in both ears. She was fitted with hearing aids and began to respond to sounds. Her parent–infant teacher began coming to our house each week to work with Tiffany and with us. Tiffany began to try to imitate sounds. We applauded each attempt. We worked on the use of her hearing aids, listening, speech, general development, and her language. We were putting in as much language as we could. For several months Tiffany only imitated vocalizations, but less than six months after we began to cue to her, she said, "Up!" when she wanted to be picked up. This marked the beginning of her independent use of the English language. She was two years old. When she reached three, she had about a three-hundred-word speaking vocabulary and we had stopped counting the words that she understood.

Once communication was established with Tiffany, one of the strong points of Cued Speech became apparent to us. Disciplining her was no more difficult than disciplining her brother and sister. Using Cued Speech, we knew that Tiffany understood what we said to her at all times, so if she misbehaved and we had told her the consequences of her actions, we could follow through without wondering if she had misunderstood. With three young children in our house, this knowledge was indispensable.

Tiffany is now thirteen years old. We have had our ups and downs with her, but Cued Speech has been there to help us through all of our experiences. Cued Speech was there to help us explain her open heart surgery when she was six. Cued Speech was there to help her cope with the learning disabilities that we discovered when she was seven. Cued Speech was there to explain about the allergist, audiologist, cardiologist, geneticist, and urologist. Cued Speech was there when she lost most of her remaining hearing at the age of ten. She had always needed Cued Speech before and we were thankful that we had chosen a program that would meet the needs of even the deafest of children. The change in her hearing status was an unexpected blow to all of us, but Cued Speech was there, and is there to allow us to communicate with Tiffany fully every day of her life. What a difference clear communication has made.

Today, Tiffany is a student in our local public school program for students who are deaf and hard of hearing. When she was six years old, our county opened a Cued Speech program, providing the third choice for deaf children here. Because of her learning disabilities, she attends a self–contained class for youngsters who are deaf. She has had excellent teachers and has made good academic progress. She has several deaf friends and prefers their friendship to that of hearing peers. Last year, she began taking horseback riding lessons through a program for riders with disabilities and she has won several ribbons in horse shows since then. This program has helped her self-confidence and given her an athletic activity that she enjoys.

Tiffany is not an example of a deaf academic superstar but considering the additional problems she has had to cope with, we feel that she is a superstar, nonetheless. We don't know where we would have been without Cued Speech, but we know how much we have accomplished with Cued Speech. Our family, in Robert Frost's words, ". . . took the one [road] less traveled by, And that has made all the difference."

WHERE I AM TODAY

TIFFANY BALDERSON

My name is Tiffany Balderson and I am now 21 years old. The chapter in the first edition of *Choices* was written when I was in middle school and was mostly about Cued Speech. Although my parents still both cue to me at home, I started learning to sign when I made a new friend who only used sign language. I became better at signing from watching other students sign to each other in school.

Because I didn't feel that I was ready for high school, I decided to stay at middle school for an additional year. I think that was good for me, because I felt more comfortable going on to high school the next year.

When I went to high school, I enjoyed using sign language with my good friend. I used Cued Speech interpreters only for my mainstream classes, and used sign language in my classes for deaf students, because I didn't want the signers to make fun of me. Sign language students who were not my friends would tease me if I used Cued Speech. Only my good friends understood why I used Cued Speech at home and why it was good for me, but they were still happy that I could sign to them. I am glad to have some friends that know both signs and cues.

When the first *Choices* was written, I was doing horseback riding, but when I started high school I stopped riding. However, I still have the ribbons I won and the pictures of me in horseback riding shows to remember the good times I had.

During my years at High School, I took photography class for three years and enjoyed taking pictures. I stayed in eleventh grade twice, since I wasn't ready for college and I didn't want to leave home too soon. I didn't have any real jobs in high school, but I started to volunteer at cue camps. During my last year in high school I was a student aide in a preschool Cued Speech class with kids who were four and five years old. At the end of that year, I was ready to graduate, since five years in High School was enough, and I didn't want other students to wonder why I didn't graduate.

In the fall of 1994 I started going to college at Gallaudet University. I was in the Preparatory Program at the Northwest Campus, but I had a tough, terrible semester there. It started out with my roommate having her friends in the room while I was trying to sleep or do my homework. She had about five to nine friends (even boys) in the room until 2 in the morning. They all kept me awake when I needed to sleep. Also, we had fights over having the air conditioning on or off. It was a crazy month for me to deal with her friends in the room everyday! I could not get enough sleep because of the problems in the dorm, and I was very unhappy.

At the end of September, students could choose to move to new dorms. I didn't want to move out, but my roommate was trying to force me to move to another dorm. I finally agreed to move in with a student in another building. My new room was tiny, but my new roommate and I got along just fine. We became friends right away. We invited a friend of hers into the room to do homework with us, and the three of us sometimes stayed up until 1 in the morning doing homework together. I thought my year at NWC was going to be great!

Then in October my roommate had some health problems and some family problems and had to move back home. I was alone in my dorm until Christmas time, and it was too lonely. I was also having trouble in Algebra. My teacher was deaf and only used ASL, which is hard for me to understand. I had trouble for the whole semester in her class. However, I did fine in my English and P.E. classes and got good grades. Communication class was tough for me. It was mostly about Deaf Culture. The description in the catalog said that the course was supposed to teach us to respect all deaf communication. But in reality, the class only taught that we should respect ASL and nothing else. I don't think that it is a good idea, because Deaf people use different kinds of communication, like Pidgin Signed English (PSE) and Cued Speech. There were many things about the University that made me feel uncomfortable, so I moved out and came back home for the rest of the school year.

For the second semester, I started going to Montgomery College in Rockville, Maryland. So far it is just fine. I am using a taxi to take me to school and back home. At Montgomery College I can take the classes I want. I am taking Pre–Algebra class, which is helping me a bit more than at NWC. I am also taking English and reading classes. I am using a sign language interpreter in my algebra and English classes, but the interpreters use PSE and are easy for me to understand. I was able to get a Cued Speech interpreter for reading class. I enjoy being in the mainstream classes so far. I plan to continue to go to Montgomery College next year.

I have no real plans for the future, but I know that I am interested in children. I enjoyed working in the preschool class in high school and I like to work at camps in the children's classes. In the fall I plan to start taking child care classes at Montgomery College and see if I can get a child care certificate. I might like to work in a school or daycare center when I finish college. I also like to write stories. I wrote one story about a make–believe family that is 970 pages long! I also like animals, and I am teaching my dog sign language. When I move to an apartment in the future, I hope I can get a hearing dog to help me be more independent.

I am glad to know how to sign, cue, and talk. My parents still cue to me at home, but I talk to them most of the time. When I am with Deaf people who sign—well, then I sign, too. When I am with little Deaf children, I cue or sign, whichever the kid knows. I think it is important for them to know English so they can read and write well.

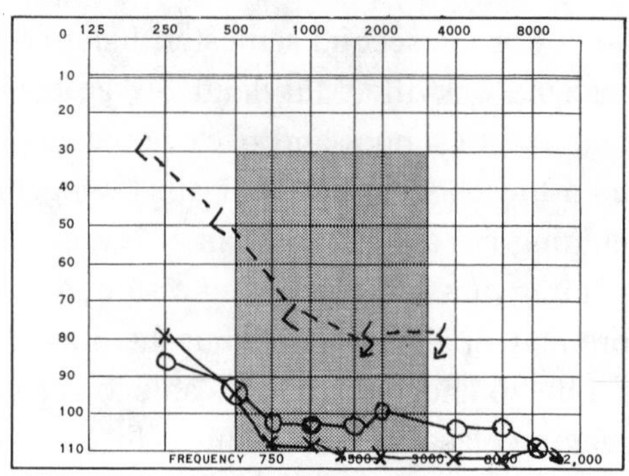

SHANE'S STORY

PAUL AND CARIN FELDMAN

After two years of fertility problems, our beautiful, healthy son, Shane, was born. He was a happy, active, alert infant, who seemed to take in visually all of his small world. Having just left a classroom where I had been teaching deaf children and children who had delayed language, I was eager to give my son the benefits of my teaching background. I often provided auditory, visual, and other sensory stimulation activities which I felt would enhance his speech and language development.

As the months passed, my husband and I noticed that Shane was not reacting to loud or disturbing noises as we thought he should. Well-meaning family and friends, however, thought that our concerns were neither well–founded nor valid.

When Shane was eight months old, we moved to Connecticut to a new home and a new job. It was at this point that we decided to investigate our suspicions of our son's possible hearing problem. Our pediatrician observed Shane in his office and felt that he was a child who had outstanding concentration skills and who was more interested in the toy that he had in his hand than in the sounds of his environment. Fortunately, he also felt that a mother is often the best judge of her child's difficulties and he suggested that we test his hearing immediately. He referred us to a group of audiologists and ear, nose, and throat specialists.

On a beautiful New England autumn morning, we started out on a half-hour trip to New Haven which ended with us in the "twilight zone." Shane's dad was seated with the audiologist on one side of a soundproof, one–way mirror and I was with Shane in the testing booth. Although we had prepared ourselves for this test by convincing ourselves that he had a middle ear infection or perhaps a minor hearing loss, we were not prepared for the scene that followed. The test sounds that were presented in the soundproof booth were loud enough to startle me and the unborn baby I was carrying. Shane did not react at all. I knew then that something was wrong. My husband, on the other side of the mirror, was unable to hear the sounds and was not yet aware of the reality we would soon face.

Our son had a major hearing loss: profound, off the chart, unable to hear a jet plane unless it was right over his head. He would not be able to hear our voices, never hear his record player, other noise-making toys, or a radio . . . DEAF! My husband remembers hearing the news and feeling as though someone had just dropped a ten–ton weight on his back. We heard little else that day even though a lot of professionals spoke to us and friends and family called us at home to check on the news. It was days before the REAL reality set in.

Once we were convinced that our son was, in fact, deaf, we began the usual process of grieving that often comes with suffering a loss of this magnitude. We felt denial, guilt, anger, depression, and finally, slowly, acceptance. Our once strong marriage suffered with our tremendous grief. Since we each went through the process of grieving at different times and in different ways, we were able to support each other's needs. With acceptance came the restoration of our marriage and our friendship.

At this time, I was six months pregnant with our second child who merrily kicked the seat belt as I traveled all over the Connecticut shoreline from New Haven to Hartford getting as much of the testing done in the shortest amount of time. This was not only to give Shane a well–fitting set of hearing aids as soon as possible but also to take care of all of the traveling before I went into labor on the highway. My daughter's arrival and Shane's introduction into the world of hearing aids and hearing were almost simultaneous.

Even with all of my knowledge and experience with deaf children and Paul's medical background, we still unrealistically felt that the hearing aid would allow him to function as a hearing child. The reality of his deafness hit us again and again. We felt sorry for him, for ourselves, and for our daughter. Yet, at the same time, we knew that we had to keep stimulating his active mind and expose him to language. It was time to decide on a means of communication and an educational program for him.

We were aware of two options: Oral–Aural or Total Communication. Cued Speech was only something that I had read and heard about in graduate school. We did not want to get involved in the hundred–year–old controversy over which was best; we only wanted what was best for Shane at that time. We wanted to promote as much receptive and expressive language as possible. Although the communication methods that we have used with Shane have changed three times over the past eight years, our commitment to using what was best for him at a given time has not changed.

Our first educational goal was to get Shane to use his hearing aids. We pointed out every sound in our environment all day long, the washing machine, the dog barking, the telephone, the jet plane, the baby crying, our voices, musical instruments, police car sirens, horns honking . . . every sound we heard was an important sound for our son to hear with his new hearing aids.

Using an oral-aural approach, Shane and his sister were given daily auditory and language lessons at the kitchen table. Soon we began to see results. Shane began identifying different sounds in his environment. His first word was "pop," which he appropriately used to request soda pop. As a side benefit to those early joint sessions, his sister began speaking at six months of age. As her speech and language skills improved, she became an additional teacher as well as his friend and favorite interpreter. Shane's expressive vocabulary increased tremendously, yet we were often frustrated because we could not understand all that he was saying. We felt that it was time to think of a new approach. Total Communication seemed to answer our needs.

Because I had seven years of experience using sign language, it was easy for me to incorporate this method into our family. My husband had to make the extra effort to learn sign language quickly and this helped to make the things Shane was saying to us much clearer. It also seemed to help him to understand us much better as well.

With this basis, we began to think about our son's education. It did not take us long to realize that there not many options in our state that suited our belief that the family should stay together. Our options were a residential placement or a three- to four-hour daily bus ride. After asking many educators about the various programs throughout the country, we decided to visit a county program in Maryland which had an excellent reputation.

This county program had educational programs available in Cued Speech, Aural–Oral, and Total Communication. We visited all three programs and spent the night in a hotel staring at each other and knowing that we would soon be making a move: one that would change our home and our jobs, and in return give us peace of mind about Shane's future education. To this day, we have never regretted that decision. In July, we moved to a new county and Shane immediately became involved in a summer program using the Total Communications approach. We were proud of his continuing success.

Shane soon began asking us for more words and vocabulary than we could produce through redundant signs, ad libbing when a dictionary was not at hand, or fingerspelling, which he was not able to grasp or reproduce. So we began to investigate the Cued Speech approach, which seemed to be the answer to a lot of our language needs. We spent three evenings learning this system and twelve months becoming proficient. At first, we used a mixture of the two systems to communicate with Shane. Amazingly, he did not seem frustrated or annoyed. Little by little, as we became more fluent in cueing, we dropped more and more of the signs. Soon we were only cueing, and Shane was ready to start his formal preschool Cued Speech program.

Shane has been in the Cued Speech program for five years now. He is currently fully mainstreamed in the second grade and aside from some mild language delays, his language development has been good. He is on or above level in all of his subjects. His speech has shown steady improvement over the years and he is understood by all of his friends and almost all of their parents. Shane's newest interest is to learn sign language to better communicate with the majority of deaf people. He and his sister spend evenings watching a sign language teaching video tape and many meals are spent using a combination of signs and cues. Having used Oral–Aural, Total Communication, and Cued Speech, we have found each method to have its value. Who knows what the future will bring? All we know is that each time we have had to make a decision for our son, it has turned out to be the right one for him and our family.

WHERE I AM TODAY

SHANE FELDMAN

Well, I have just reread the story where my parents have explained my deafness and their methods to adapt and cope. Interestingly, I was amused to realize what my parents have actually gone through. I am very fortunate to have great parents who really cared about the prosperity of their child's future. I will now tell you of what has happened in my life since childhood, where my parents left off.

I feel that the elementary school environment in my County school system was very comfortable and I am pleased to be have been a part of the program. In this program extensive and boring hours of practicing my speech paid off by enabling me to acquire hearing friends and deal with situations with few communication difficulties. I relied on my lip-reading skills to understand others. I was fluent in Cued Speech but knew a little sign language in elementary school. I had some problems adjusting to hearing people's fears or ignorance, which is probably very common among deaf people. However, I felt most accepted by the deaf crowd at our school.

Junior high school was probably the hardest part of my life. Many of my childhood hearing friends had changed, as did I. We had minimal contact during the course of four years. For a while I had few friends and mostly did things with only deaf people. Yet, even this was difficult for me as the "little kid" of the group, since the majority of the deaf kids were one grade ahead of me. Looking back now, I feel that the last year of junior high school was probably the loneliest and most depressing part of my life. But the following year was a dramatic change for the better.

At the end of junior high I was introduced to a high school on Gallaudet's campus by a good friend and my parents. I quickly generated an interest in this school after I visited it the first time. Even though all the deaf students were very new acquaintances to me, everyone there immediately accepted me as one of their own. Feeling so welcome and having so much in common, I made the decision to attend this school, despite hearing rumors that deaf schools had poor education and bad influences.

My first year was fantastic, although I would define it as a "culture shock" experience. It started off with a great football camp where I was able to learn signing before the school session started. Although there were a few people who ignored me, most of them helped me to improve my signing through the school year. I had much more confidence than ever in my life that I would turn out to be the person I wanted to be. The environment was very comfortable where everyone was very friendly with each other. I quickly made good friendships with many people and started to enjoy a great social life.

Academically I was too distracted and ignorant to do much homework or studying, which led to a low G.P.A. for my freshman year. Some of my other classmates fared a lot better than me. I also found the work easy except for mathematics, which I never enjoyed! My sophomore year was similar to my freshman year until the second semester when I started commuting home and regaining contact with friends I had cut off contact with for almost two years. In my sophomore year, I improved my grades and started dividing my social and school times wisely.

I have to admit that I got into lots of trouble my first quarter at my new school. My poor mother woke up almost every night around 11 p.m. to answer the phone and hear the school tell of my troubles. I eased up on them after the first quarter but continued enjoying myself in mischievous activities. Hey, you can't blame me!

My junior year, I transferred back to my former school, my hometown high school. Many people have asked me the same question, "Why did you switch?" I do not have the definite answer for that question and would like to know why myself. I usually answer people, "Oh, just many reasons mixed together, not just one major reason," which is true. One thing is definite, I do not regret transferring back, but, on the other hand, I think it is important for many people to also realize that I do not regret going to the high school at Gallaudet either. The experience made me a better person than the dismal boy I was at the end of junior high school with no expectations for the future.

I am now a student in honors classes at my local high school. I also think it's important to note that I am still playing football and started on the defensive line. The team quickly respected me after I knocked a few people on their fannies! They learned that I had the heart to play, and that my deafness wouldn't affect me in any way. My grades have gone up much higher even when the academic challenge is more difficult and I have been a step behind in some areas. I regained a great friendship with two seniors who I did many things with through my junior year. Regrettably they will be leaving for college soon. I have some hearing friends and hope to make more next year. I have kept in touch with my friends from the high school at Gallaudet and enjoy visiting them when I can.

I have not yet decided on a college to attend. I have some choices: R.I.T., Northeastern, University of Maryland, Baltimore Campus (UMBC), Lenior Rhyne, and some ideal colleges which have my interest. I have decided football is not a factor to which college I go to. It will be dependent on the deaf services and a deaf population because I feel a strong bond to it, since it is where I feel most comfortable. I am also looking for the best education in my field, which may be Physical Therapy for now. I also plan to make the best out of my college years socially and academically since it should be the "time" of everyone's lives. I have little idea of what I want to do after college now, but I have some goals which I hope to live up to.

I plan to stay with the same kind of communication method I have been using for two years now. That is to use the preferred communication by the person I am speaking with. I understand the conflict going on with different groups promoting their method of communication as the best. Honestly, I would have to say, since I've had a period of time to use each method during my life, that each side has a valid argument and there is probably no right answer. But it is possible to be able to use the method that works best for the individual or if possible more than one method. I think that an individual's choice of communication which he/she feels comfortable with should be respected.

I have many achievements in my life which I take pride in and many mistakes to be learned from. I do not regret many things I have done and look forward to a bright future. I am proud to be deaf and there is nothing I can do to change that. I sometimes feel that even given the opportunity to become hearing, I probably would consider refusing. I feel that deafness is a handicap which can be coped with and taken advantage of to make a great person.

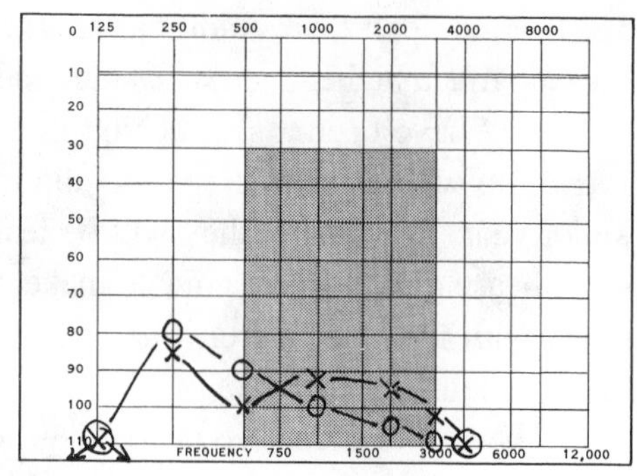

AMY'S STORY

LOIS HUROWITZ

Amy is fourteen years old and profoundly deaf. She is pretty, bright, stubborn, and outgoing with a determination and outlook which say, "Watch out, world, here I come."

Amy attends a local junior high school with the support of the Cued Speech component of the auditory program in our county. She is mainstreamed for all courses and receives the services of a Cued Speech interpreter, resource teacher, and a speech pathologist. She is on grade level and has developed independence, self-confidence, and self-motivation.

We suspected a handicap when Amy failed to develop speech at around twelve months of age. At twenty months, after a period of anxiety, frustration, false diagnoses, and numerous trips to doctors and clinics, the problem was finally diagnosed as a profound sensorineural loss with cause unknown. As painful as this discovery was, it was also a relief to finally know what was wrong with my daughter. Now, with a known cause and condition, it was time to move forward to find help and proper instruction.

At the hospital we were referred to the auditory program in our county. We enrolled in the Parent-Infant program and began the long, hard road to help Amy reach her potential. In this program I received excellent guidance, support, and instruction related to deafness and training. The program fostered a positive attitude and developed the goal that my child reach her fullest potential and compensate for her handicap as much as possible.

Another source of help during these early months was from other parents of hearing impaired children. They also provided guidance, goal setting criteria, and support. They had been there and were able to answer questions and quell my fears. One family in particular lives down the street from me. Their hearing impaired child is older than Amy and a successful role model.

After Parent-Infant, Amy entered the preschool program and her progress began to slow. Total Communication was suggested as a possible alternative for instruction. I was determined, however, that Amy would remain in the Oral program and we would just have to work harder. I wanted her to be able to function and find a place in the hearing world. I was not against sign language, but I felt that I wanted her to develop her speech and language first. I felt this could be accomplished best through the Oral approach.

I realized that no matter how good the classroom instruction was, I would need to help at home. I became fanatical in trying to find ways and methods to follow through with school work at home. I found that I had no time left for pity, hopelessness, and guilt. This was my way of coping; meeting the problem head on, and trying to beat it.

The road to success via the Oral method was not an easy one. Communication was the key issue. I developed ways to teach Amy language. Some days we would work two or three hours on formal lessons. We also talked during walks, trips to the store, on vacation, everywhere!

These were days of highs and lows, but every small achievement was a major success. I never considered the work a sacrifice and I never gave up. If one strategy didn't work, then I tried another. I was rewarded with success. By the age of four and a half, Amy was developing language both expressively and receptively and was reading on a first grade level. (The reading was a by-product of our lessons.) Because of this, Amy was able to skip kindergarten and begin in the first grade.

We were blessed with a wonderful teacher who taught both Amy and me. My daughter continued her reading progress and began to excel in other academic areas as well. I used the ideas and methods of this teacher and incorporated them in my lessons at home so that there was a link between home and school. Our intensity continued through second grade and Amy's progress was great.

Unfortunately, all of this focus on Amy took its toll on our family. Amy's older brother resented the time that was taken from him. He had had undivided attention for three and a half years and now, he not only had a new sister, but no one seemed to have time for him anymore. He felt neglected and left out. In later years I have tried to rectify the situation and have partially succeeded. By the time Amy's younger brother was born, I had learned my lesson and tried not to repeat my mistake. Now both of her brothers are proud of their sister, what she has accomplished, and how she has compensated for her hearing handicap. I believe that she is a binding and positive factor in our family life.

When Amy was in the first grade, I learned about Cued Speech. I attended workshops, talked to parents using the method, and began taking lessons. The philosophy behind Cued Speech fit my oral philosophy but would it work for us? At this point I decided that I was still content with the Oral method but continued to be intrigued by Cued Speech.

During the summer of 1977, Amy, her two brothers, and I attended a week-long Cued Speech workshop. This was the first time that we were all involved in an activity related to deafness. It was a delightful week; full of lessons, new experiences, and new friends. It was the culmination of my years of interest in Cued Speech and confirmed my decision to place Amy in the Cued Speech program when she began the third grade. Amy's brothers also enjoyed this week-long experience. They were able to see other hearing impaired students, compare their sister to them, and be proud of her accomplishments. They also felt pride in being able to help her in this way.

This decision was not an easy one but I had several reasons for doing it. I was now convinced that Cued Speech was an oral method that supplemented lipreading. Amy liked Cued Speech! She wanted to learn it, experimented with it, and was "turned on" from the start. I wanted to include her in the decision and she was able to tell and show me how much she benefited from it! An interesting phenomena occurred. As Amy learned to cue, her speech slowed down and became much more intelligible. Another major reason that we moved to Cued Speech was academics. I felt that Amy had been successful so far in her school experience, but I saw that the work ahead was becoming much more demanding. I knew that she would benefit from an aid to speechreading, and I chose to make Amy's task easier and less stressful. She had been successful and I wanted her to continue to be.

It took almost two years for Amy to fully process and benefit from Cued Speech. Through daily exposure and a minimal amount of formal teaching of the method, she was an expert cuer and receiver of cues by the sixth grade. Amy had an interpreter in her classes with her. She learned that if the teacher was difficult to speechread or turned her back, the interpreter was there. Now that she is in junior high school, where she has to speechread seven different pairs of lips, the interpreter is even more important. The interpreter has allowed Amy to receive information fully and with accuracy.

I also feel that Cued Speech has enhanced Amy's speechreading skills. Many people do not cue, but she is still able to communicate with them. By focusing on the face area, a Cued Speech reader can also become a better speechreader.

Amy's speech has improved in intelligibility over the years. Since she is able to receive unambiguous visual information about sounds, her pronunciation has improved. Vocabulary growth has improved because she has been able to see the pronunciation and eliminate the guesswork required in speechreading alone. Amy also loves to read. She is reading on grade level, is an excellent speller, and considers English her favorite subject.

The road for Amy as a deaf child is still not easy. It takes hard work at school and at home. She needs help and support from me. We work on vocabulary, language, homework, and social skills. Gaps still exist in her academic, social, and emotional development. I feel that my guidance is crucial for her. I feel that Cued Speech has helped her meet these challenges more easily, and her goals are more accessible.

Recently a professional in the field of deaf education asked me how Amy functioned in the world as a deaf child. My answer was that when Amy is with her deaf friends, she uses sign language; when she is in the classroom, she uses Cued Speech; when she goes to McDonald's to order a hamburger, she uses the Oral method. That just about sums it up. Amy lives in two worlds and in doing so is able to maximize the three methods that predominate in deaf education today.

I am very proud of her accomplishments and realize that I have been lucky. I have had plenty of help along the way. Early parental guidance is critical in helping to acquire knowledge of deafness while taking a realistic look at the future. Parental involvement is the most critical factor in helping any child, but even more so with a handicapped child.

I feel that every child, handicapped or not, has the right to achieve his full potential, and I believe this road begins at home. As I look ahead, I know that the future is still full of obstacles, but I also know that Amy has the tools and skills to overcome them.

WHERE I AM TODAY

AMY HUROWITZ

It has now been ten years since *Choices* was first published. It is a wonder so much can happen in a short period of time. The book was published back in 1986, just when I was in eighth grade and still in braces.

In the fall of 1987, I started High School not knowing what to expect....It was there that I started my journey to where I am today. I remember the days when a Cued Speech transliterator was provided to me...little did I know that I was fortunate to have the services the high school provided to me—all three tracks: Oralism, Cued Speech, and Total Communication were provided for the student's PREFERRED mode of communication.

In the winter of 1989, the Deaf Leadership Council was formed at my high school and I became the President. Little did I know that I would be faced with challenges of "not knowing" the deaf culture and the challenges of my preferred mode of communication not fitting my role as the president of the club.

During my high school years, I also became a member of the "Montgomery Exceptional Leaders" program. This consisted of many members who had a variety of unique disabilities who went around our County's elementary schools to discuss the challenges and the joys and sadness that each and every one of us went through. This turned out to be a meaningful experience for me and by the time I graduated from high school in 1990, I was ready to move on.

After considering the seven schools that I was interested in, I chose Lenoir Rhyne College in North Carolina to major in Deaf Education.

I moved to North Carolina in the fall of 1990, and during that year, I discovered my frustration beginning to show when there was not a Cued Speech interpreter available for me; and later that year, I also realized that the environment there did not meet my challenging needs. Because of this, I moved to Rochester, New York, to attend the Rochester Institute of Technology; this institute is also the home of the National Technical Institute for the Deaf, one of the largest, well-known colleges for the deaf.

It was here that I decided to major in Social Work. For the next three years, it was a whirlwind time for me as I quickly discovered my place as a Cued Speech user in the Deaf community. It was at RIT that I fought for my rights to have a Cued Speech transliterator in the classroom. It was at RIT that I discovered that no matter what mode of communication one chooses to use, there is always stigma attached. In other words, there were several "subcultures" in the deaf "culture." One culture was the "oral" culture, one was the "ASL" culture, another was the "neutral" culture, and last but not least, was the "Cued Speech" culture.

It must be kept in mind that each different communication approach strives for early development of communication and early development of personality through the use of a clear visual mode of communication.

I quickly discovered when I moved to Rochester that people would often ask me why I preferred Cued Speech transliterators when I already knew sign language. I feel that I can have access to ALL of the information that hearing students have and that's what I want! In short, the responsibility and battles for a Cued Speech student can be demanding not only in the hearing world, but, as I am very slowly discovering, in the deaf world as well.

When I started here three years ago, there were only three Cued Speech interpreters in training, and two of them are still employed by the NTID Interpreting Department. Because we have more demands for Cued Speech services, there is now training for fourteen different interpreters going on and hopefully, we will continue to provide training to the Department of Interpreting Services at NTID for quite a while.

Besides the educational aspect at NTID/RIT, the social aspects around me have changed. I often wondered to myself where I stood: in the hearing world or in the deaf world? I was fortunate to have a mother who supported me in whatever I decided to do as long as I had the English skills. I have often heard from kids who graduated from mainstream schools that they wished they had gone to a school only for the deaf, but the odd thing is that I have not heard that here at NTID, considering that Rochester has such a large deaf population.

A Cued Speech club was struggling to get started at NTID, but because there were very few support systems available, the club was put on hold. It is my hope that the club will be started in a few years as more Cued Speech users emerge into the NTID population.

Yes, I was faced with many challenges in the deaf community, once deaf people learned I was a long-time Cued Speech user, but that did not stop me. Some people here believe that I do not like the ASL language. It's not true. In fact, I think that ASL is a beautiful language and should be learned by all, but only if they want to. My philosophy has always been "Don't let others stop you from using the preferred method of communication, yet learn to respect others." I also believe that just because Cued Speech was successful and still is for me, it doesn't mean that it's successful for others. It's essential that all parents and professionals attempt to teach the deaf child the English language. Why alienate them from the hearing world? If English doesn't work for them, then let it be...at least they tried.

In May of 1994, I became an alumna of the Rochester Institute of Technology. I was handed a Bachelor's of Science in Social Work degree and decided to settle down in Rochester for a while. During the summer of 1994, I was offered a full-time job opportunity to be a program counselor for deaf, mentally ill clients at a local hospital. I accepted this job offer and have been working at the agency for some time now. I now face the challenges of working with the hearing staff and the hearing clients, but it helps me to appreciate the fact that I grew up in the hearing community. At the same time, however, I'm also glad I went to college with so many deaf peers. If it weren't for these two experiences, I wouldn't be here today.

Not only am I working full time at the hospital, I am also very involved in several activities. I am currently the Cued Speech representative for the Northeast states, working closely with the National Cued Speech Association. I have also accepted a part-time job opportunity to work with a deaf girl whose family would like her to learn Cued Speech. In addition to this, I am pursuing my Master's in Deaf Education here at RIT. I have been taking part-time Liberal Arts courses and will focus on the core courses starting in the fall of 1995. This is an exciting opportunity for me because this program is just being started at RIT, and it's really exciting to be part of this new program!

In conclusion, my years at RIT have indeed been interesting and challenging. I believe that each deaf or hard of hearing child deserves an interpreter of their choice in their mode of communication. I believe Cued Speech is an excellent tool for any deaf or hard of hearing child. I do understand that the topic of the three modes of communication, Oralism, Total Communication, and Cued Speech, is a sensitive topic for the deaf community but I also know that Cued Speech is considered to be one of the best methods of communication for deaf or hard of hearing children today. I also want to add that I really do appreciate Cued Speech now and if it was not for it, myself and many other students who have used Cued Speech would not be where we are today. I have watched myself and other Cued Speech kids grow academically and socially, and it is all because of Cued Speech.

7

The Oral Approach

A Professional Point of View

Janice Gatty, Ed.D.

What Is the Oral Approach?

Since you discovered your child's hearing impairment, you have probably been faced with many difficult decisions. Some of the decisions you have to make will have long–term implications for your child, and you will want to investigate all the facts as thoroughly as possible. One of the most important decisions will be choosing an appropriate educational program for your child. This can be a confusing, complicated, and sometimes overwhelming task. This chapter will help you understand the Oral approach to educating the deaf or hard of hearing child and give you valuable information to aid you in selecting a teaching approach for your child.

First, it is important for you to understand that there is really no single oral method of education but rather a group of methods which emphasize different aspects of the communication process. These methods, however, share one common aspect: they require children to use only spoken language for face-to-face communication. They avoid the use of a formal sign language. Some oral methods require children to wear hearing aids and use their residual hearing in combination with lipreading to understand speech. Teachers in these programs use a "multisensory" approach (hearing, vision, and in some cases, touch) to help the children learn to understand and produce speech. Other programs use the "unisensory" method. Children in these programs are asked to rely on their residual hearing without the benefit of lipreading.

The different methods of deaf education described in this book differ in the ways they provide a child with complete access to the language he does not hear. Since oral methods do not allow the use of sign, some way must be found to compensate for the fact that a deaf person may miss some speech if he is only speechreading. Speech is meant to be heard. Only about 30 percent of the speech information can be understood from lip movements. Additional information may be available, depending on the nature and degree of your child's hearing loss. If your child is in an oral program, he will have to "fill in" missing information by drawing on his knowledge of the situation, previous experience, and familiarity with the language. Your child may be able to accomplish this in daily face-to-face communication, but he may have difficulty when dealing with new material in the classroom.

Cued Speech, which is considered an oral method by some, uses hand signals to supply the missing speechreading information. (For more detailed information, see Chapter 6). The printed word, a re-encoding of spoken language, is also used by oral educators to make the spoken language patterns completely available to hearing impaired children. Although the information can be more accurately received through these two methods, neither approach would help your child directly to produce speech. The most important aspects of speech, such as the tone and rhythm of speech, are transmitted most effectively through the sense of hearing.

■ Role of Residual Hearing

The amount and quality of hearing that your child has left (*residual hearing*) is the single most influential factor affecting his ability to understand and produce spoken language. If your child has a hearing loss, he has two serious problems in hearing sounds:

1. HE IS NOT SENSITIVE TO QUIET SOUNDS.

2. EVEN WHEN SOUNDS ARE LOUD ENOUGH TO HEAR, HE DOES NOT HEAR THEM CLEARLY.

A hearing aid will increase his sensitivity to sounds by making them louder, but it cannot make these sounds clearer. In general, there is a relationship between loss of sensitivity and loss of clarity. That is, if your child has a profound hearing loss, he will have more difficulty discriminating among sound patterns than if he had a moderate loss, even when appropriate hearing aids are worn. The consequences of deafness, and the outcome of training for your child, are therefore directly related to his degree of hearing loss.

Most, though not all, deaf children can be trained to perceive some aspects of speech through the sense of hearing when using hearing aids. The process which accomplishes this is called auditory training. The amount and quality of hearing that your child may have left and the effectiveness of the auditory training contribute to his auditory performance. In general, with appropriate hearing aids and good training, you can expect children with various degrees of hearing loss to benefit from hearing in the following ways:

MILD TO MODERATE HEARING LOSS (LESS THAN 60dB). If your child has this degree of loss, he probably will develop auditory skills and acquire language spontaneously through his sense of hearing aided by hearing aids. He does not belong in special schools or classes for the deaf.

SEVERE HEARING LOSS (60–90dB). If your child has this degree of hearing loss and has good auditory management with hearing aids and auditory training, he probably will understand speech by hearing alone. (He should be able to speak on the telephone.) His speech should have good rhythm and tone and correct articulation. He should be able to be mainstreamed in schools with hearing children where there are auditory, speech, and language support services available.

PROFOUND HEARING LOSS (90–120dB). Auditory potential and performance varies the most in this category. If your child has this degree of hearing loss, even as great as 105dB, he may be able to function like those children with severe losses. He may be able to hear the rhythm and tone of speech through his aided hearing. He may learn to recognize vowels and be able to tell the difference in some consonants. He will probably, however, need to have some or all of his instruction in special schools or classes for deaf and hard of hearing children.

TOTAL HEARING LOSS (NO MEASURABLE HEARING). Only 10 percent of the population of deaf children are unable to benefit from a hearing aid. If your child has this degree of hearing loss, he should be able to understand some speech information through his sense of touch. He can "feel" the rhythm of speech, which will help him with speechreading. He can also learn to recognize some sounds around him such as the telephone, traffic sounds, and footsteps by the rhythm of these sounds. He may be able to use a vibrotactile aid which transmits sound by vibration to the inside of his wrist or he may be a candidate for a cochlear implant. Both of these devices give a totally deaf child more access to sound. You should be cautioned, however, that unreasonable expectations from these devices could lead to disappointment and feelings of inadequacy in your child. Remember, these are only tools and cannot completely make up for a complete loss of hearing.

If you would like to read more about these descriptions of hearing levels, a good description can be found in Arthur Boothroyd's book, *Hearing Impairments in Young Children,* which is listed at the end of this chapter. More information is also available in Chapter 2 of this book.

■ UNISENSORY METHODS

As I mentioned in the beginning of this chapter, advocates of unisensory methods believe that visual cues, such as lip movements, detract from the child's ability to learn to use his hearing. They believe that children should be taught to rely on hearing as much as possible and usually cover their mouth while speaking to a deaf or hard of hearing child to discourage speechreading. You may read or hear about these methods referred to as the *acoupedic, unisensory,* or *auditory verbal methods*. Most practitioners of these methods believe that the majority of deaf children can acquire sufficient auditory skills by school age so that they can be educated with hearing children. In fact, the methods may be beneficial for many deaf children, but if your child is profoundly deaf, his residual sense of hearing is probably too limited to use this approach exclusively.

Daniel Ling points out, "The crucial thing is not how much information can be presented to the child, but how much of it can be perceived and in what way the child can learn to process it" (1984). It will be up to you and your professional team to determine exactly how much hearing your child has and whether unisensory methods are options you should explore.

AUDIOLOGICAL MANAGEMENT

If your child is in a program that relies on the use of residual hearing, you should make sure that there is a strong system for checking hearing aids and auditory training units so that your child is getting the best possible acoustic signal all the time. There must be routine and frequent examination of the acoustic characteristics of the hearing aids and auditory training equipment. There should be temporary replacement aids for your child to use when his aid is not working properly. There should be routine and frequent examination of his ear canals and middle ear functions to insure the wax buildup does not affect his hearing. At least once each day, the classroom teachers should make minor repairs when necessary (Calvert, 1976).

New computer technology called Real Ear Measurement can tell the audiologist how loud the sound coming out of the hearing aid is when the sound reaches the eardrum. Real Ear Measurement does not, however, give the audiologist any information about the clarity of the sound or what is reaching the auditory center in the brain. There are also computers that can do an electroacoustic analysis of your child's hearing aid to determine how well it is working. You should check with the audiologist in your school system to see if these routine checks are being done for your child.

Clinical audiologists involved in your child's program must be trained and experienced in testing and working with young deaf or hard of hearing children. They should also be skilled in sharing this information with you, as parents, since you will be a partner in maintaining working hearing aids and in developing listening skills in your child.

An Educational Audiologist should be on staff in your child's program for several reasons:

1. To check frequently to see that your child's ears are healthy.

2. To check hearing aids and auditory training units frequently to see that they are working properly.

3. To teach the teachers how to check the aids daily.

4. To work with you to help you understand how to maintain the aids at home and how to make the most use of your child's hearing.

WHY USE AN ORAL APPROACH?

Spoken English is the natural language of our culture, and, more specifically, of the parents of most deaf or hard of hearing children. Most deaf or hard of hearing children (about 90 percent) have hearing parents. It is probably easier for you to imagine interacting richly and intimately with your child using a language that is familiar to you. If you use an oral approach, you will need to change the way that you interact with your child but you will not need to learn a new language or a new system of communication.

A second reason that you might consider for choosing an oral approach is that if your child can use spoken language competently, confidently, and effectively, he is more likely to be able to participate in classes with hearing children. It is possible that more social, educational, and work opportunities will be available to him. Ultimately, these options may lead to a more fulfilling and independent adult lifestyle.

Some Prerequisites for Using an Oral Approach

The oral approach requires children to "fill in" missing acoustic and language information by drawing on their knowledge of the situation, previous experience, or familiarity with the language. Success requires a central nervous system that is intact, good thinking abilities, and perhaps even a special listening ability. To date there are no effective ways of testing for these skills. If your child has some weaknesses in any of these areas, there is danger in expecting more of him than he may be able to reasonably deliver. Discuss his strengths and weaknesses with each other and with his professional team. Chart your expectations for him based on realistic assessments arrived at by all of you working together.

A successful oral program requires skilled and knowledgeable teachers who recognize the needs and abilities of individual children and can adapt their teaching strategies to meet these needs. Adequate numbers of teachers must be available for individual instruction and diagnostic teaching. Teachers must have training in a number of areas such as audiology, child development, teaching and learning theory, linguistics, speech, and parent counseling. The need for trained teachers is especially great for children whose residual hearing is limited or nonexistent. Make sure the program available to your child has such trained teachers on staff.

Results of an Oral Approach

Results of using an oral approach vary widely. There are successful students who have been able to complete secondary and higher education programs in the mainstream with hearing students. There are students who have been unable to continue with a strictly oral program throughout their school careers and have switched to another method of communication. Sometimes when the program is switched and more visual systems are made available, the student can be more successful. You as the parent will need to work very closely with your child's teachers to make sure that he is as successful as he can be in all aspects of his education.

In addition to focusing on spoken and written language skills, most oral programs have strong academic curricula. They report that their graduates have high achievement levels in schools. Their success reflects not only the methodology but the curricula and the high expectations for achievement held by parents and teachers. When orally trained deaf adults were surveyed, most indicated that they were glad that they had been educated orally and felt that they were able to interact with hearing people in a confident manner. It is interesting to note that most oral graduates ultimately learn sign language in young adulthood to communicate with other deaf friends.

Some Advice to Parents

If you choose to use an oral approach with your child, you should realize that observable results may not be immediate. A normally hearing baby does not usually utter his first word until one year of age. A deaf or hard of hearing child cannot begin to associate sound with the movements of the speech mechanism until the hearing aid has been worn and consistent auditory training received for a similar period of time.

An oral approach will require you to work closely with your team of professionals to find the best way to make the spoken message available to your child. Your relationship with the professionals should be a trusting and reciprocal one in which the professionals assess the individual needs of your child and then work together with you to meet those needs. Professionals should teach you the basic information about speech and hearing science so you can best help your child. You will also need emotional support and encouragement from professionals until you can see your child's progress yourself. Don't be afraid to express your feelings and ask for reassurance. You will probably hear much the same thing I have said. "It takes time." This is true, but it always helps to understand the reasons why.

When choosing an educational program, remember that programs vary widely and in practice may not reflect what theory or label they may wear. The best way to choose a program for your child is to observe the program in progress, interview the staff, students, and parents, and then carefully monitor your child's progress along the way.

REFERENCES

Bender, R. (1970) *The Conquest of Deafness.* Cleveland, OH: The Press of Case Western Reserve.

Benderley, B. (1980) *Dancing without Music: Deafness in America.* Garden City, NY: Anchor Press/Doubleday.

Boothroyd, A. (1982) *Hearing Impairments in Young Children.* Englewood Cliffs, NJ: Prentice Hall, Inc.

Calvert, D. (1976) "Communication Practices: Aural/Oral and Visual/Oral" in *A Bicentennial Monograph on Hearing Impairment: Trends in the USA. The Volta Review.* Vol. 78, No. 4.

Hubbard, G. (1908) *The Story of the Rise of the Oral Method in America.* Washington, DC: Press of W.F. Roberts.

Ling, D. (1984) *Early Intervention for Hearing Impaired Children: Oral Options.* San Diego: College Hill Press.

Ogden, P. (1979) *Experiences and Attitudes of Oral Deaf Adults Regarding Oralism.* Unpublished Dissertation. University of Illinois at Urbana-Champaign.

Vaughn, P. (Ed.) (1981). *Learning to Listen: A Book by Mothers for Mothers of Hearing Impaired Children.* Toronto: Beaufort Books.

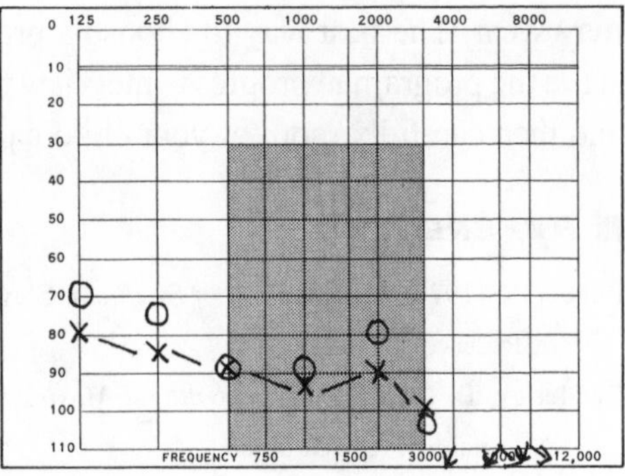

CURT'S STORY

SALLIE AND JOHN PRIDE

Curtis John Pride, our second child and only son, arrived in this world on December 17, 1968 weighing in at seven pounds, twelve ounces.

In all respects he appeared to be a normal, healthy, bouncing baby. In addition to having a wonderful disposition, he was also precocious—rolling over at several weeks of age, sitting alone at five months, walking alone at nine months, and able to climb out of his crib by a year. Because of his advanced physical development, we became increasingly concerned about his lack of normal speech development. The fact that he had not begun to babble, coupled with his unresponsiveness to household noises and our voices, caused us to seek professional advice.

His pediatrician referred us to a speech and hearing center in our area and our suspicions were confirmed. Curt was diagnosed by the center as having a moderate sensorineural hearing loss. He was nine months old. Subsequent hearing tests revealed an increased degree of hearing loss. Because of my exposure during the first trimester to the Rubella virus, a gradual loss of this type is not uncommon. However, no one could tell us whether this difference in tested hearing levels was truly due to a gradual loss of hearing or to the fact that the later tests were more reliable.

Because of our prior unsophisticated home testing, we had been fairly certain that Curt had some degree of hearing loss and were able to readily accept the initial professional diagnosis. The center recommended that we save our money and our time by not investigating cures but rather concentrating our energies on his language development.

Even though we had suspected Curt's hearing loss, it wasn't until it was finally confirmed that we both began to verbalize our concerns and raise questions about his future. We had very supportive families and friends and we tried to keep the words "feel sorry" out of everybody's vocabulary. We had a positive attitude and we wanted everybody else who came in contact with Curt to have that same attitude. We do think that having and sharing this attitude helped to educate our family and friends so that they also became significantly involved in his overall development.

At this point in our lives, we knew that we had a lot to learn and a lot to do if we were going to be able to meet the challenge of educating our hearing impaired baby. A number of decisions had to be made.

The first decision which we were comfortable in making was that I would cut short my nursing career. Curt's deafness was definitely a good reason to put my career on hold so that I could devote my full time and attention to my family. Giving up my career was not a stressful decision. On the contrary, the feedback that I got from my involvement with Curt at this time more than adequately compensated for what I may have been missing at the work place. I became involved in fun as well as meaningful activities: the PTA, the parent association for the hearing impaired, a family–oriented social organization, a bridge group, bowling league, exercise classes, and a variety of craft classes. Even while setting aside time for myself, I volunteered in the auditory and regular classes, which gave me the opportunity to talk with professionals as well as to observe classes on various levels. I found all of these activities stimulating and rewarding.

Another major decision that we had to make at this time was whether to have more children. We had always wanted to have three, but decided to wait because of the amount of time that we felt we needed to spend with Curt. Consequently, our third child, Christine, was born when Curt was eight years old. By this time Curt's education was progressing well and Christy was a welcome addition to our family.

Having decided that I should stay home and to postpone our third child, we began to face the challenge of raising our deaf son. We sought out all of the information we could relating to deafness. We knew that our baby was already lagging behind his peers in language, even though he was only nine months old. Curt's sister, Jackie, two and a half years older, had been and still is a benchmark for measuring his language development.

Upon completion of the tests by the ENT doctor and the audiology center, it was recommended that we enroll him in an Oral preschool class. Even before we enrolled him, we were told to always talk to him at eye level. It was also suggested that we use a large mirror so that he could see both us and himself verbalizing. It was further suggested that we enroll in the correspondence course that was available from the John Tracy Clinic in California. We followed through on all of these suggestions.

The preschool where we enrolled Curt met once a week. I would arrive at the center every Tuesday with Curt, Pampers, pen, and a notebook. I took notes on everything that was done with him. I was always given guidance for home instruction and I reported his progress to the center the following week. Curt's eagerness to learn and our motivation to teach complemented each other.

We knew that there were two choices of programs for teaching hearing impaired children. The Total Communication program had a larger enrollment but we decided to follow the audiology center's advice and placed him in the Oral program.

We do not want to give the impression that the entire process was easy. There were many frustrations for both Curt and the family. Both the structured and everyday normal contact with him ran the gamut from frustration to reward. During those early years it was more frustrating for us because we wanted and expected to receive immediate vocabulary feedback and were often disappointed at his seemingly slow progress. We learned very early that Curt reacted negatively to signs of our frustration because he was and still is very quick to pick up body language. To help ease the tension, we constantly inserted humor in dealing with his speech and language development. The educational process in these years involved a long series of trial and error in an environment of mutual trust and love. Our primary frustration at this time was his very slow language and speech development. We talked to professionals whenever we had the opportunity, attended as many meetings as we could find, visited other programs, and periodically had him tested. These contacts inspired us to keep on with what we were doing and provided the support we needed.

When Curt was three, he was placed in the County Auditory program and we joined the Parent Association for Hearing Impaired Children. We gained support from this group and knowledge from the books in their library and the meetings they sponsored. We met extremely successful oral teenagers and young adults. Our motivation to continue with the Oral method came from the parents of these children who constantly reinforced the fact that Curt was either right on or ahead of schedule in language development compared with their children at the same age. This was a major motivating force for us and to this day we are grateful for the support of this group. In addition to the parents' organization, I attended the formal parent meetings at the school level, along with Curt's father when his schedule permitted. The county auditory staff offered a lot of support and guidance in developing Curt's academic and social skills. Because of our continued involvement, they became more than just teachers. They became friends.

While we recognized the importance of education for our son, our primary focus was on raising him to be as normal as possible. We did not accept deafness as an excuse for poor or inappropriate behavior. We have always remembered what a psychologist told us at one of our parent meetings. He said that we should be consistent in our expectations of his behavior. Curt's behavior was not significantly different from that of our other two children at these ages. He was, perhaps, more active than our daughters. But he learned at a very early age that inappropriate behavior would result in consistent and firm punishment. We always tried when punishing him to do it in a manner which expressed our concern and caring.

Curt's education continued in the Oral program. His language and speech developed to the point where he was mainstreamed by the third grade with the aid of a resource teacher at the elementary school that housed the auditory students who were also mainstreamed. When Curt was ready for the seventh grade and junior high school, he desperately wanted to go to the neighborhood school. We sat down and talked at length with him and were finally convinced that it was important for him to attend school with his sister and meet more neighborhood children. Curt's determination and motivation carried him through this transition period. He had an oral interpreter for classes where he found the teacher difficult to lipread and auditory support several times a week. His grades were excellent and he was on his way. He continued from the seventh through twelfth grade fully mainstreamed for all his classes. When he graduated in 1986, he had a 3.47 grade point average.

During the early years, we recognized that Curt needed a physical outlet for his incredible energy level. Curt's father encouraged him to become involved in sports as a constructive way of utilizing his excess energy. To make sure that Curt could play on teams where he would understand the rules and have the opportunity to participate without his deafness being a handicap to him, Curt's dad coached five of the teams that Curt played on during these early years. When Curt participated on other teams, his father attended his practice sessions at every opportunity. When there was a conflict with his work, I was the observer. In fact, a lot of our time was spent with extracurricular activities with all three of our children because we recognize their value in the development of well–rounded individuals.

At the age of six, Curt began playing soccer and T-ball and later basketball with a boys' club. Many evenings and weekends Curt and his dad would work out in the park to improve the skills needed in these sports. Curt enjoyed playing sports and his proficiency helped him gain acceptance by his peers as well as increasing his self-confidence and self–esteem. He was involved in sports every season. In the fall and winter he played soccer and basketball and in the spring and summer, he played soccer and baseball. He averaged twenty points a game in basketball during his senior year, hit .509 with five home runs in baseball, and was the leading county scorer in soccer with sixty goals in forty career games. During the summer of 1985, Curt was chosen as one of eighteen soccer players to represent the United States in China in an international soccer tournament. He went alone with no interpreter and no other deaf individuals. He made international headlines when he scored two of the goals scored by the United States and assisted on the third. In addition to playing various sports, he coached a youth soccer and basketball team. He was also a baseball umpire and a time keeper for basketball games.

At the awards assembly at his high school, Curt was presented with the first Brady Straub Memorial Award. Straub, a football coach, had stressed to his players that they be "gentlemen, scholars, and athletes." Curt was chosen as exemplifying all three of these characteristics.

Curt's academic and sports success prompted over 200 colleges to actively recruit him. He will attend William and Mary College on a full basketball scholarship. He has been promised all of the support services that he may need in terms of an interpreter, note-taker, and tutor. We have stressed to him how important it will be for him to finish college as well as play basketball.

During the summer of 1986, Curt was drafted by the New York Mets baseball team and played with their rookie league team in Kingsport, Tennessee. Through an unprecedented arrangement, Curt will be attending college full time on a basketball scholarship and playing professional baseball during the summer. As we sent him off to Kingsport, we did so with confidence that we had done all we could as parents in dealing with Curt as a whole person. We were more certain than ever that he will continue to be a happy, confident, productive citizen. We feel that the quality of his life as an adult will not be negatively affected to any significant degree because of his deafness.

As parents of a very successful deaf young man educated in an oral environment, we hope that the sharing of our experiences will be helpful to parents of young deaf children. Because we derived so many benefits from our involvement with our local parents' organization, we strongly encourage other parents to join a parent group if it is available and to attend parent meetings at the school level. The experience will be invaluable.

WHERE I AM TODAY

CURTIS PRIDE

Photo Credit: Kathy Davison

It is the summer of 1995 and I am now a member of the Montreal Expos major league baseball team. When I made my first major league appearance in Busch Stadium in St. Louis, Missouri, September 14, 1994, I became the first deaf individual to play in the major leagues in over fifty years.

A lot has transpired since I graduated in 1986 from high school. After returning from my first summer of minor league baseball in Kingsport, Tennessee, I entered the College of William and Mary on a full basketball scholarship.

My college experience, from my point of view, was positive for the most part. I had the same apprehensions and anxieties in anticipation of college that my older sister did. Much of my anxiety was over making new friends and dealing with the higher level of academics.

As the Department of Special Needs and Minority affairs had promised, prior to my enrollment the necessary supports were there. I had the option of a note–taker or a tape recorder to record lectures. When I used the tape recorder, a transcript was available by late afternoon. In addition, I had access to tutors as needed. Gradually, the academic, social, and basketball challenges didn't seem to be so overwhelming. I credit my success to the fact that I spent a lot of time reading the text and not getting behind. Other strategies that I used were to attend study sessions, even though lip–reading was sometimes very difficult, to meet with individual professors, to review notes and old tests, and to find one person to take with me to an evening class. My parents stressed to me the importance of staying ahead in my reading so I would already be familiar with the subject matter.

The more my apprehensions decreased, the wider the scope of my interactions with other students became. Though participating in the basketball program was very demanding, both physically and in terms of time spent, there were some fringe benefits. The most significant was that because of the proximity of the college to the Washington area, there were frequent family reunions at basketball games. I still savor that I had the opportunity to have played against Dave Robinson and Blue Edwards, current NBA stars.

All in all, I feel that I had a very positive college experience, and graduated in 1990 with a degree in Business Administration. During the past five years, I have deferred the use of my college education while I climbed the minor league ladder in baseball.

The life of a minor league baseball player is not a very glamorous life. I was drafted in 1986 along with forty–eight others by the New York Mets organization. Today, there are only two players still playing baseball from that draft.

The time between 1986 when I entered the New York Mets organization (the team that originally drafted me) and my eventual rise to the major league included low wages, long bus rides, fast food, hundreds of "groupies," and numerous stops in nondescript, small towns.

Now that I have arrived in the major league, I hope that I will be able to further defer the use of my college degree for many years and to continue playing professional baseball.

As this book went to press, Curtis Pride was playing in left field for the Detroit Tigers.

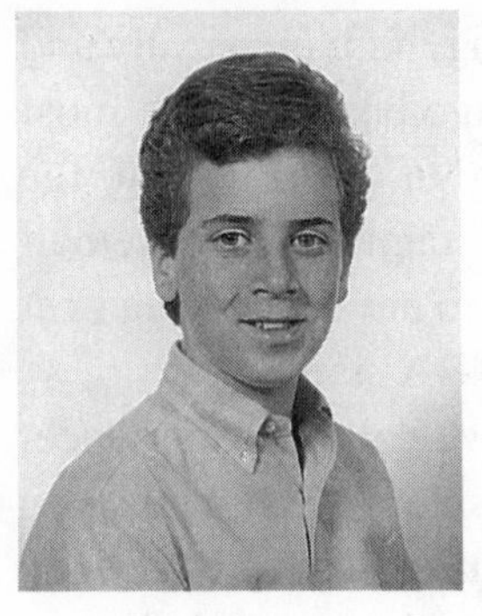

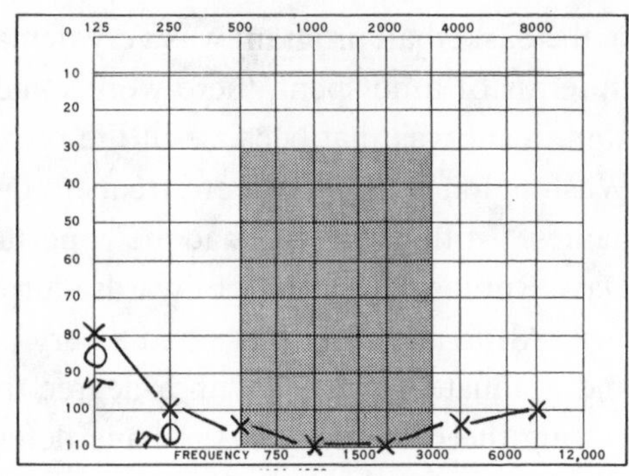

DAVID'S STORY

DEBBIE AND BUZZY COHN

It all started in June 1974. We were your typical suburban family with two young children, ages sixteen months and three years. One summer evening, David, our sixteen–month–old, started running a fever. Due to his history of repeated strep throat and bronchitis, I wasn't overly concerned. I gave him Tylenol and planned a visit to the pediatrician the next morning. By then David was seriously ill. What I had thought was a simple infection turned out to be spinal meningitis. We spent the next three and a half weeks in the hospital.

As David slowly began to improve, I noticed something was different about him. I couldn't put my finger on it, but I was pretty sure that he couldn't hear. The doctors all assured me that I was just imagining things. After all, David had been so ill that he was probably just too weak to respond. At my insistence, we called an ENT doctor in for a consultation. He performed some very informal testing on David and confirmed our worst fears. David could not hear. We later learned that hearing loss is a common side effect of H. Flu meningitis.

Life was very hectic after David returned home. We immediately took him to a hearing and speech clinic. It was explained to us that David's first test might not be 100 percent accurate due to his age. We were encouraged to go into the testing room with him to help in the testing procedure. My husband and I sat in the small soundproof room with David, listening to sounds that could wake the dead. We fought back tears when we saw that our son never even flinched at these sounds. David was then tested and fitted with the best hearing aids that were available for his particular loss. We felt sick and scared when we saw that he was fitted with two body aids that were on his chest in a harness. These were the kinds of aids that deaf people wear. Our son was DEAF! The realization slowly overwhelmed us.

The audiologist spent a lot of time with us that day explaining David's audiogram to us and the type of hearing loss he had. We learned that he had no measurable hearing at all in his right ear, and a severe-profound loss in his left ear. She tried to help us understand what David could and could not hear. She also told us that children who lose their hearing due to meningitis could lose even more hearing over the years. She talked about Total Communication, Oral Communication, special schools, you name it! Our heads were spinning with new terms, new information, ear molds, hearing aids, hearing tests, special teachers....It was too much to digest. One thing, however, was perfectly clear to us—nothing would ever be the same again.

You know, it was funny but with all of the fears and uncertainties of that day, one thought tore at me more than anything else. How could our son learn Hebrew, the language of our religion, and be able to have a Bar Mitzvah, the culmination of childhood in our faith? This became one of our goals for David.

Shortly after this audiological appointment, I was contacted by the audiologist in the county school system. Through their outreach program, they had been made aware of David and wanted to inform me about the county program for the hearing impaired. During this time, I had been doing a lot of reading and asking a lot of questions about the different programs that were available.

We scheduled an appointment and met with the staff of the Parent-Infant program. We were advised to start David in the Aural-Oral program. In this program, the children learn to make use of every bit of residual hearing they may have, through very special training. We enrolled David and he was taught to listen very hard and to respond to every sound, no matter how slight it may have been to him. He learned what different sounds mean. He learned how to speechread, even though so many sounds looked alike that it was very difficult for him to distinguish between the words.

We taught him as well. We learned that everything that you do in your everyday life can be turned into a language lesson. It took a huge amount of time and patience. We made language books about making sandwiches, taking a bus ride, nursery rhymes, and just about anything else you could think of. We felt that we wanted David to learn to speak and to be able to communicate with people the way that hearing people communicate: by listening and speaking. We felt that the Oral program offered him a more normal way of life and that eventually he would be more easily accepted by his peers. Fortunately, David did very well using this method.

I remember working hard on the words "I love you" for a long time. One Sunday night, as I held his hearing aids in my hand and spoke over and over again into the microphone those words, "I love You, I—LOVE—YOU," David looked right at me and said, "I love you" for the very first time. Even though it was late in the evening, I rushed to the phone to call his teacher and we cried together!

Our days were filled with trips to the Parent-Infant Program, follow-up language lessons at home and in the car, and daily trips to physical therapy. David had also lost muscle tone and his sense of balance as a result of the meningitis. We continued in physical therapy for the next three years. In addition to these activities, we also enrolled David in a regular preschool program. We wanted him to interact with hearing children and function at their language level. We continued these combined programs until David entered the first grade, when he was fully mainstreamed into our home school with an intense support service provided by the auditory program.

Those early years were very hard on the whole family. I had to be mother, teacher, chauffeur, educator (of family, friends, and anyone else who is involved with the hearing impaired child), all the while trying not to neglect my other children and my husband. We never dreamed how many hours of talking, repeating, and explaining would be involved with helping a hearing impaired child to learn and succeed. In our case, we involved our older daughter, Julie, in all areas that concerned David. She accompanied us on all of our doctor appointments, school, and physical therapy sessions. She learned at a young age how to talk to David and how to interpret television shows for him. She became his ears in many situations.

There were times when David and I did not get along well at all. The early years were so taken up with teaching, schools, doctors, language, that I was forgetting how to be simply "Mommy." Dave and I went to a psychologist for a short time and then worked through our problems. I had to cut back on some of the constant teaching and start being "Mom" again. After I slowed down a little, our relationship improved. During those early years my husband was completely engrossed in starting our business and he wasn't able to devote much time to our family. After a couple of meetings with the psychologist, and realizing how much his son needed his daddy, he started spending more time with his children. What a difference that has made in our lives.

We were always very strict with David and did not allow him to use his hearing loss as a reason to misbehave or to get out of doing things that were hard for him. He was expected to do everything that other children did, and he knew that we expected him to do everything that other children did, and he knew that we expected him to do it well. We felt that he must be treated as a normal child and couldn't get away with things simply because he couldn't hear.

During the years that David attended our home school, he flourished and grew. He had many friends and a wonderful sense of self-confidence. It was during this time that he was able to change from body aids to ear level aids. Even though David was doing well in school, he still had many hard times. He would miss a joke or want to know the words to songs. Many times Julie would write out the words for him so that he could be a part of the group.

When David was in the fourth grade, we realized that he didn't know all that we thought he should know. He was getting good grades but his math was only fair, and his English and grammar were not up to par. He didn't know how to sit and work independently or how to write a composition. Maybe that is typical of fourth grade boys, but we were afraid to let it continue. His classes were large and in spite of his teacher's best efforts, Dave was getting lost. Our big decision then was whether or not to put him in a private school. Our biggest concern was losing the support of the auditory program which can only serve children in the public school system. We finally made the plunge and we have been very pleased with the decision. David has been averaging As and Bs and has learned wonderful study habits. He has stayed close to his best friends from the neighborhood school and has made many new friends at his private school.

So far, anything David has been involved in, he has been the only hearing-impaired child. These activities include soccer, football, and camp. We have found that we must continue to be involved to educate the instructors about David's needs. So far he manages extremely well.

In the beginning of our experience with deafness, we learned that a little bit of hearing can be taught to go a long way. This was an important lesson to learn. We need that philosophy now more than ever. During the fall of this past year, we had some devastating news. David has what the doctors refer to as "sudden hearing loss." From out of nowhere David has lost almost all of his residual hearing. Considering that there was not that much to start with, this has left him totally without hearing. When this catastrophic loss occurred, we spent four days in the hospital with an intravenous medicine that we hoped would reverse this loss. He has regained some of the lost hearing, but now fluctuates between 95 and 110dB in his better ear.

David returned to school after missing several weeks and began to make the necessary adjustments to his new degree of loss. This was also the year of the fulfillment of the dream we had so long ago. David would have his Bar Mitzvah in February. This is a stressful time for most thirteen-year-old-boys. How much more so for David! He worked with a tutor and prepared a Torah portion and a Haftorah portion and conducted many parts of the service. Many people who had helped and supported David along this road were in the congregation that day. He made all of us proud as he stood so tall that day.

When David was six years old, we had another child. Our daughter, Suzanne, was born with a devastating handicap of severe mental retardation and blindness. We have watched with moist eyes as David handles her with a special love and never–ending patience.

He said at his Bar Mitzvah that his handicap was a mere inconvenience compared to what his little sister must overcome.

This school year has ended with his accomplishments continuing to grow. He has been the recipient of the Alexander Graham Bell Association for the Deaf's financial award for the third time in three years. He has made the Honor Roll and High Honors every year at his private school.

We know that with David's new degree of hearing loss, things will be a little more difficult for him, but we also know that he will rise to meet the challenge. Certainly we did not choose to have a child who could not hear. Certainly we would give anything if things could have been different. Being deaf in a hearing world is extremely difficult, but we know that David can deal with it successfully.

WHERE I AM TODAY

DAVID COHN

From the stoop of my apartment building, I watch the sun setting in Philadelphia: people are hurrying home from work, the ever-present mobile food trucks are closing for the evening, and I reflect upon my past as dusk settles in.

I compare myself to the towering skyscraper I see in the distance, sturdy and tall and reaching for the sky. Like the skyscraper, I am constructed by the fervent efforts of others and must compete with my seemingly flawless surroundings.

In retrospect, there is one obstacle I face daily and is far harder to contain than the various physical barriers I have confronted since I lost my hearing at sixteen months as the result of H. Flu Spinal Meningitis. This obstacle is understanding the daily conversations and classroom lectures which have been the mainstay of my life so far. When I was in high school, I used no support services at all. I had no oral interpreters, no note–takers, and managed with a great deal of struggle to be successful in my course work. In fact, in high school, I received several awards, as well as being elected Student Council President. I was twice honored with the Citizenship Award for excellence in leadership and was selected as the regional representative to the Hugh O'Brien Youth Conference.

While I cherish these accomplishments, I am most proud of being an eight-year recipient of the Alexander Graham Bell Association for the Deaf Scholarship. The annual process of applying, which required obtaining educators' professional assessments, writing an essay, and submitting current grades, undoubtedly contributed to my character. It provided me with the knowledge and insight that would later assist me in preparing my college applications.

Upon entering the University of Pennsylvania in the Fall of 1991, I began to take advantage of the resources of the

University's Office of Affirmative Actions. The oral interpreters that they provided were not ideal. As I had never before used interpreters, I did not realize that the students who had signed up for the job were far inferior to the professionals that I needed. Through my sophomore year, I used these ineffective, albeit well–meaning, students as interpreters and paid their wages when I was unable to attend class. The plight to overcome my stubborn need to be wholly self–sufficient and succumb to the very real fact that I needed assistance, escalated as my grades continued to suffer. I have since been provided with professional interpreters and have enhanced my communicative skills along with the political ones needed to deal with University Administration. Surmounting tangible barriers is time consuming and stressful but nowhere near as difficult as conquering frustration.

As I am repeatedly assured that I am not the first deaf student to enter Penn, however, I am confident that the tumultuous past four years have been an integration process, and any deaf student to follow will have it easier that I did—even if only a bit—due to my pioneering efforts. I have shown many doubters that my abilities are real, and I have learned by experience that one must lead and not follow.

Today my concern is my speech. When I was younger, people were amazed to find that I could not hear. Some did not even believe it. That still happens today, but fewer people need convincing. Although I cannot hear my own voice, it has become painfully obvious that my speech has deteriorated over the years. People suggest that I do something about my terrible cold, when I have no cold at all. Or someone may inquire as to where I am from when I stand in my own hometown. These infrequent, yet gradually increasing incidents are always a prelude to my explaining that I am deaf, and then their skepticism gives way to admiration. Still, it was much more fun when they never even knew.

Since I lipread and speak, I do not know sign language. Many are left dumbstruck when they learn of this. I do not know any other deaf people, as I have always attended hearing institutions and participated in the norms of hearing individuals. Everyone that I know, from the local dry cleaner to my very best friend, is hearing. I am not confused about my identity. I realize that I am deaf, yet I simply inhabit a hearing world with all of its opportunities. I encourage people to ask me questions about my deafness because I appreciate the inquiring mind and I wish to foster the same knowledge and understanding that I have been so lucky to seize.

Yes, my life so far is like that towering skyscraper. I reach for the sky. My opportunities are limitless. I have overcome, I have achieved. I can stand tall and sturdy amid my seemingly flawless companions.

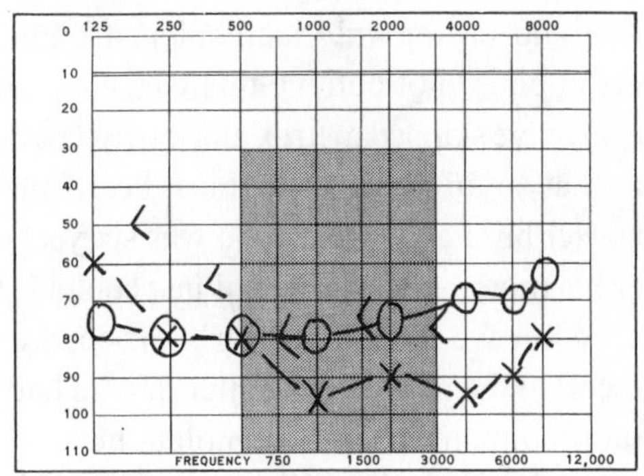

KELLYE'S STORY

LULA AND ADRIAN NELSON

We first learned of Kellye's hearing loss when she was two and half years old and attending nursery school. Her instructor at that time knew about hearing loss because her husband worked with hearing aids. She told us that when Kellye was painting at the easel with her back to the teacher, she did not respond when her name was called. At other times in the classroom when she was facing the teacher or another child, there was no problem at all.

I began to think back to when Kellye was just a few weeks old and my mother was staying with us. She had had seven children herself and she told me she didn't think Kellye was listening the way she should. I asked the doctor at our first checkup, and he said that she was too young to test, so I just put it out of my mind.

Now when the nursery teacher told me something might be wrong, I didn't want to believe it, either, but I thought I would tell the doctor again. This time the doctor made some whistling noises in Kellye's ear, to which she responded, and he said that he didn't think she had a hearing loss, but I could go to a specialist to check. We took Kellye to an ear, nose, and throat doctor just to make sure. The specialist used a tuning fork, which he put up to Kellye's ear. He said she did have a hearing loss but he could not tell us how much. He said that he thought she could lead a "normal" life with proper education and amplification. I remember walking out of that office and crying frantically. I just could not believe what I had heard. I could not believe this was happening to us.

Kellye skipped merrily along between her father and me, not knowing what awful news we had just heard and not noticing how upset I was. Her brother, Adrian, who was six years old then, wanted to know why his mommy was crying. I just couldn't find the words to tell him.

After we left the doctor's office, we went home immediately and called the audiology center that he had recommended and made an appointment to get a complete hearing test. Three days later as we sat in the soundproof booth and watched our daughter being tested, we knew the truth. Kellye had a severe hearing loss. The audiologist explained the loss to us and suggested that we get in touch with the County program for children with hearing problems. Before we left the center that day, we had made an appointment with the supervisor of the Auditory Program.

Within a week, we had our appointment and we were enrolled in the Parent Infant Program. Kellye was fitted with two hearing aids and our work had begun. I remember the day that we went to the center to pick up hearing aids for Kellye. The audiologist put them on, did some testing, and showed us how to take care of the aids. As soon as those aids went on, Kellye's eyes lit up so wide and bright. I could see what a difference those aids were going to make. When we went outside, Kellye stopped suddenly, looked all around her, and said, "Momma, waz dat?" I told her it was dirt and once again I just couldn't believe the things that she didn't know the names of.

When I look back, I can see that Kellye had us fooled a lot. She was such a good lipreader that she never seemed to miss what we said. She was talking and even though it was not clear, we could understand her and thought it was just baby talk. After Kellye got her hearing aids, a friend of mine said, "You know, I always wondered why Kellye would look at me so intently. She is more relaxed now in the way she looks at me."

When Kellye was in the Parent-Infant program, she and I went to school two or three times a week to work with a special teacher. I was in the room with her so that I could see what things she was learning and then I could work on them at home with Kellye. Sometimes I would show the teacher some of the games that Kellye and I played at home and how we worked on language. During this time, the teacher also showed me how to help Kellye use her hearing. We played games where we would only listen and not lipread. Then we would listen to sounds in the house like the vacuum cleaner, dishwasher, and blender. Kellye had to learn what all of those sounds were. Kellye enjoyed coming to classes and I enjoyed being with her and learning all that I could about hearing loss. Sometimes the teacher would let Kellye play and just talk to me about how I felt about Kellye's loss and about deafness. This helped me to understand what Kellye's life would be like.

Kellye was in the Parent-Infant program until it was time for her to enter kindergarten. Then she went with the hearing children to the regular class in the morning and with the hearing impaired children in the afternoon. In the afternoon, she got the extra help in language development that she needed.

When Kellye was ready for first grade, it so happened that the resource room for hearing impaired children was in our neighborhood school. I was so thrilled that Kellye would be able to walk to school with her neighborhood friends and still get the special help that she needed. She was mainstreamed with the hearing kids and received daily resource help from an auditory teacher. Kellye was having no problems at all in school.

When Kellye was ready for fourth grade, we had moved to another neighborhood. Our elementary school did not have a resource room for hearing impaired children and we felt that she still needed help on a regular basis. So she went to the school where the resource program was. She was still mainstreamed with regular classes and received the help she needed every day.

We were very lucky that when Kellye was ready for junior high school, the auditory program had moved to our neighborhood school. Now she had many more hearing impaired friends: some who were using sign language, Cued Speech, and Oral. Her circle of friends broadened and she still was able to have auditory help when she needed it. Kellye had never really been involved with sign language or Cued Speech before this time. Her program had always been Oral and that was the way she was learning best. Now she had the opportunity to learn other methods as well.

Kellye has never taken a class to learn sign language but she is picking it up from her friends. She and I are planning to take a class together so that I can talk to some of her new friends also. She moves easily between her hearing and her hearing impaired friends now that she can communicate with all of them.

The high school that Kellye is now attending is also our neighborhood school, so her friendships have continued. She is still mainstreamed for all of her classes but has the auditory support available when she needs it. Kellye has been active on the varsity field hockey team and has been an SGA delegate while maintaining A/B grades in her mainstreamed classes.

Kellye has also been active in her church and community. She has been a member of the youth usher board, an aide in the Sunday School. In the community, she has been a member of the NAACP youth group and the secretary for the teen group of the Suburban Maryland Tots and Teens, which is a black family organization.

I don't think that we ever really consciously chose Oral communication over other methods. We began in an Oral program and she did very well and we saw no reason to change. If, however, we or the teachers had felt she needed to switch to any other method, we would have done whatever was best for her.

Kellye has a good relationship with the hearing and hearing impaired students. We feel that because she has been able to be in the mainstream classes, and is a good student and a nice young lady, she has been included in many of the social activities which the hearing students have. She also socializes with the hearing impaired students and has enjoyed broadening her circle of friends this way. We know that she will need this ability to communicate with hearing impaired individuals throughout her life.

When we look back, we realize now that there were many things that we worried about that just have not happened. She has grown into a fulfilled teenager who enjoys school, church, sports, community activities, volunteer work, family, and friends. We are very proud of the person she has become.

WHERE I AM TODAY

KELLYE MARIE NELSON

A lot of things have changed during the years since my story was first told in 1987. When that story was written, my mother wrote it. But now it is me that is writing the story. My mother died in 1988 after a lengthy battle with cancer. I would like to dedicate this story to her.

During my senior year in high school, my mother was diagnosed with cancer. Even though my mother was sick most of my senior year, she always found the time for me. She always was at my school making sure that the teachers knew that I was hearing impaired. She always made sure that I had a note–taker for my classes or got help for my most difficult classes. Also, she always tried to come to most of my extra–curricular activities. My parents also insisted that I was going to college and *away* from home. My parents, especially my mother, felt that I had led a sheltered life due to my hearing impairment, being a female, and the baby of my family. My parents always wanted my brother and me to go to an historically black college. With that in mind, I thought about Howard University in DC; however, my mother was *not* having that!! She told me that I had to leave the state of Maryland. So I applied to Hampton University (my father's and brother's alma mater) in Hampton, Virginia, and Spelman College in Atlanta, Georgia.

In August, my father and I loaded up the car and hit Interstate 95 for Atlanta. This was both an exciting time as well as a tense time for me. Here is a funny thing that happened during that time. The day before I left for Spelman, my mother realized that she wouldn't be there to wake me up for classes. My mother had always been my alarm clock and so that day we were running around trying to find a vibrating alarm clock for me. My house was never equipped with any devices like flashing lights for the doorbell and telephone or a closed–caption decoder for the TV. My parents and I always felt that I was functioning well without these devices.

With my new alarm clock in tow, I thought I was ready for college life. However, that was not the case. For one thing, my mother died a day after I moved into my dormitory. I will always be thankful that my mother did get to see me graduate from high school, win numerous scholarships and awards and, at least, see me off to college. One of the awards that I received was "Senior of the Year" from the Montgomery County Public Schools Auditory Program. I am thankful that my mother lived long enough to know that Oral communication was the right choice for me.

On top of coping with my mother's untimely death, I found that college was a culture shock and a learning experience for me. Spelman College was a black women's college and I was one of two hearing impaired students out of 1700 women. I also had to deal with the normal anxieties freshmen go through. Dealing with my mother's death and my hearing impairment were probably the two hardest things in my life.

For the first time in my eighteen years of living, I felt very self–conscious about my hearing impairment, and not having my mother around compounded things. While growing up, my mother never let me dwell on my hearing loss and always said that it was a part of me like a nose or ears are attached to me. At first, I had a hard time making friends and I had a teacher who was not supportive of my needs. Like I did in high school, I explained to my teacher that I had a hearing loss and that I needed to sit in the front and that I speechread. I also asked if I could let the class know about my hearing loss and the teacher's reaction was, "So what, why are you telling me this?" I felt so humiliated that I didn't know what to do. I didn't have any friends that I could open up to. I didn't tell my father until much later into the semester and he then called my advisor and the dean of student affairs. They offered to give me whatever services I needed, but I declined. At that time, I felt like a burden and I wanted to show them that I was not some helpless child. By that time, I had already come up with my own system. I took my own notes, sat next to someone who wrote big, borrowed someone's notes, or just asked the teacher to go over my notes.

I should add that the majority of my professors were understanding, but I believe the students understood my needs better. They always made sure that I knew what was going on. Declining professional help was probably one of the biggest mistakes that I ever made. Undergraduate work was a challenging but a rewarding experience. However, if I could have I would have handled things differently and accepted the professional help that was offered. I realize now that there is no shame in asking for help and if most people could, they would like to have the additional help. College was hard and was very much different from high school.

I am happy to say that during my junior year, a profoundly deaf woman came to Spelman and did extremely well. The college paid for her interpreter, as well as made sure that she had notes. Sometimes, I believe that the school was not ready for a hearing impaired person when I came, but somebody had to break the ice. The school has several students with disabilities now and is more adept in handling the situation.

I graduated from Spelman College in May, 1992, with a Bachelor of Science in biology and the intention of going to medical school. However, it had been an extremely hard four years academically, and I needed a break from school. I had been going to school since I was two years old and was always in some academic program in the summers. I originally planned to take only a year off and then apply to medical school, but stayed out two years. I stayed in Atlanta and worked in a daycare center and on a research project at Emory University. I also took some courses at Emory University. Instead of going into medicine, I found my niche: public health.

Presently, I am at the University of Michigan School of Public Health working on my Master's Degree in Public Health with an emphasis on health behavior and health education. Because of my previous experience as an undergrad, I took advantage of the services offered by the service for students with disabilities office (SSD). SSD provided me with a professional note-taker and sent letters to all of my professors explaining the accommodations that I would need. Consequently, I am doing extremely well in my classes. I expect to get my degree in May 1996. I would like to work for a year with the hearing impaired community and then go for my doctorate.

I would like to say that many people think that being an Oral student has its advantages, but it can be misleading, as well. Hearing impairment has been called the "hidden disability." People have a tendency to think that if you speak well and don't use sign language, then you can hear well and that you only have a slight hearing loss. While in undergrad or graduate school, I have been in many situations where people forgot or have been uncomfortable. For example, in the classrooms, there are discussions and participation points that count towards your grade. Sometimes, I would not be able to hear everybody or people would be talking too fast. By the time I realized what they were saying, they would be talking about something different. It would be hard for me and usually I would remind them to speak one at a time and slowly or ask the professors to take my hearing impairment into consideration. Also, I would have to do presentations in the classroom. That can be very scary! Whenever I get nervous, I talk really fast and jumble over my words. Even though I have a severe bilateral loss, my speech is excellent. It is funny that a lot of people ask where I am from because they think I have an accent or that I am from New York. Most of the time, I just let people think I have an accent and don't tell them I am hearing impaired.

In another situation, the telephone can be a burden and I am not a big fan of the phone. Even though I can hear on the phone, it can be a nuisance for both parties. I always have to cut off the TV or radio and close my door to make sure there is complete silence. Then my friends have to make sure that they speak clearly, slowly, and loudly (not scream) to me. Guys are the worst! I have a hard time hearing deep voices. But most of the time, my friends know to make the conversation quick and to the point. However, throughout my internship this past summer, I have increased my confidence level using the phone. My internship required that I be on the phone 60 percent of the time. My supervisor was very accommodating; she put my office in the quietest area of the office. I don't mind using the telephone, but if I had a choice I would rather not!

Driving can be hard, too. Most people try not to talk to me while I am driving, but it can be hard to sit in complete silence. When I first got my driver's license, my mother did not allow me to drive with the radio on for fear that I might get run over by an ambulance, fire truck, or police car. However, that has never happened. I drive with the radio on now, but I have learned to check my mirrors frequently.

Finally, on the social scene, being hearing impaired can be hard. Whenever I go to parties, it can be hard trying to carry on a conversation when the music is deafening and the room is dim. Even if I tell a guy about my situation, he may not be understanding and walk away. If I go to the movies, I make sure that I am sitting right underneath the speakers. I know the movie theaters have audio loops, but those things are huge and ugly!

For the most part, I have adjusted well and the key is in educating people about my impairment. I am extremely happy with being an oral student and have done well as one. I honestly believe that if my parents felt this was not going to work, then they would have done what was best for me. Being an oral student is not for everybody: it takes a lot of work. All of those years of auditory training, speechreading, and speech lessons have paid off, but at times, I thought it was grueling. And if I had to do it all over again, I would. Times have changed, and as we move into the twenty-first century, people are becoming more aware of the needs of hearing impaired people. ADA laws have had an impact and technology is more advanced. But the most important element a hearing impaired child needs is family support. It starts in the home. I received love and support from my mom, dad, and big brother. They always made sure that I had the best and instilled self-esteem and confidence in me. And because of them, I have and will continue to succeed.

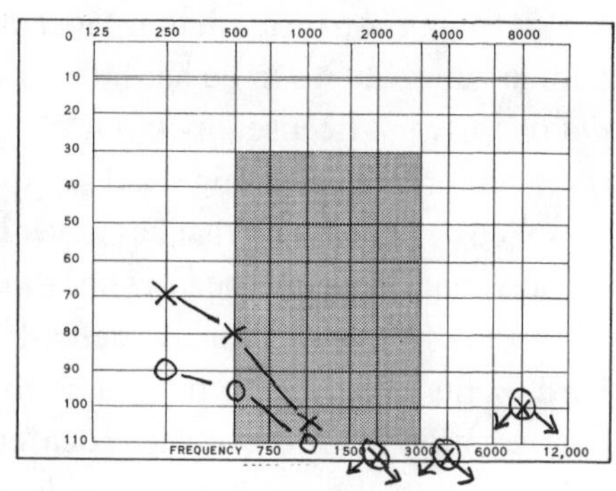

STEVEN'S STORY

LUCILLE AND SYDNEY RATTNER

"Stevie, Mommy's home! Steven, Mommy's home!" I called out in a singsong manner. "Steve?" Say, this is unusual, I thought. I stopped suddenly....I put down my bundles...stood for a minute or two and observed my twelve–month–old son sitting with his back to me, busily engrossed in putting together a play school toy. Oh, that's the reason ...he is so involved in his project that he didn't respond. I stood there still wearing my coat and feeling a little let down. Was he teasing me? I walked around the playpen and was immediately met with squeals of laughter and joy; he was so happy to see me. I picked him up, danced around the room with him, took off my coat, and proceeded to show him my purchases, putting my concerns aside. Soon his brother returned from school, and the two played together as I prepared dinner.

I had almost put the experience out of my head when I began noticing other similar things. If I walked into his bedroom, he didn't hear me. If I clapped my hands behind my back, there was no response. At first, I didn't tell my husband, Syd, about these incidents. Then one day, Syd and I were both there when Steven didn't respond. We looked at each other despondently and acknowledged that there had been frequent occasions when Steven had not responded. But we still weren't sure there was a problem. Then, during a visit to my family's home, my brother confided to us that he had noticed a lack of reaction from Steven but that he hadn't wanted to alarm us. He suggested that we make an appointment at a nationally known local hospital for an evaluation.

A team of doctors examined Steven. We will never forget their gentleness and expertise. They tested him auditorially and psychologically as well as with a galvanic skin test. They told us that Steven had a sensorineural hearing loss along with a language problem. Our fears were confirmed, yet it was still a shock for us. The doctors spoke with us for quite some time and explained how hearing and the processing of language works. They told us to place his name on the waiting list in the County Public School's Auditory Program so that when he was five or six there would be a place for him. In those days, there was little going on in the education of the very young hearing impaired or language handicapped children.

The doctors also suggested that we send for a well-known correspondence course for parents that included activities for working with young hearing impaired children. They told us to become affiliated with the national organizations serving the deaf and most of all, they said over and over, to "talk, talk, talk to your child." They said to "treat him as a normal child who happens to have a problem." They told us about a private preschool program for children like Steven, and we made plans to join the class in the fall. We ended our appointment with mixed feelings of sadness and hope.

My husband and I decided then that we would do everything possible to help Steven, and we set out to follow the instructions we had been given. We also began reading about deafness, visiting other parents with similar problems, and learning about residential and day programs for the deaf. We participated in the correspondence course, joined associations, and visited other programs in the area. Although this was a difficult and emotional period for us, we never lost sight of the need to do everything possible for Steven.

One of the first things that we needed to do was to get Steven fitted for a hearing aid. Although it took time for him to get used to wearing it, he soon realized that it was helping him. From then on he put it on with his clothes and it became a part of his routine.

Steven was a happy child, dexterous, with a keen sense of humor. He also could be very stubborn. He seemed to know exactly what he wanted. He was intrigued with the way things worked. He was always busy and always thinking. At this time, spoken language had little meaning for him and he had to be taught every word. Therefore, each word was precious to us. There were also the upsetting moments. I recall one day finding Steven's ear "glued" to the stereo, listening to a record that had stopped playing and unaware of the screeching sounds that continued. Since he didn't have the vocabulary to tell us when something hurt him, he would put bandaids over the spots that hurt and come to show us. His speech was "scribble speech" that showed us he had thoughts but not vocabulary. We had a lot of work to do!

Steven attended the private group session three times a week from age two and a half to four. The program used the Oral method. He attended sessions eagerly, but his attention span was short and progress was slow. The teacher and the aide in the classroom encouraged us with what we were doing. Each day was a special activity for us to teach language. We went to the library, the zoo, and the post office. When the post office was empty, I would have Steven hand the money to the postal clerk and "ask" for the stamps. I would stand behind him and tell the clerk what he wanted, but he felt the success of his purchase.

Steven's older brother, Barnett, would also talk with him and play with him. He thought that Steven was the smartest brother a person could have. This was because Steven was very adept at putting things together, fixing things, building, and figuring out puzzles. A large circle of family, friends, and teaching staff were interested in Steven. He felt loved by everyone and was encouraged to be included in everything.

One day when Steven was nearing four years of age, we received a letter from the school system telling us that they were starting a class for four–year–olds. We were thrilled because we had not expected them to have a program until he was five. We realize how lucky parents and children are today who can begin as infants and not lose those precious early years.

The early days of this new class were experimental. The teacher had her hands full with many children, all of whom had different problems. Some of the teachers were trained teachers of the deaf and others were not, but all were very dedicated. The method was Oral. Language was taught by lipreading, auditory training, the kinesthetic method of drawing words on his back, tracing words, speech, and reading. Steven's teacher, who had just graduated from college, was dedicated and loving. She spent extra time counseling the parents on how to work with the children at home. By mid–year, the classes were divided by special needs.

In this same year, another parent and I started an organization for parents, teachers, support staff, and friends of children with hearing and language handicaps. We felt a need for a network of people with common goals. We wanted the best education and care for our children. We wanted to educate ourselves to the needs of the children. As a group, we visited many auditory programs both in and out of state to gain insight into what other programs were doing. Whenever we became aware that prominent educators were visiting our area, we asked them to speak. In addition, the auditory and special education staff held workshops and special programs for us. Our organization is now twenty-seven years old, has grown in stature, has excellent rapport with the school system today, and continues to offer support to staff, family, and friends. The national organization for the deaf is also a continuous source of information for us.

When Steven moved on to first grade, we were told by all who worked with him that he was lovable but stubborn. The advice we got was to not let Steven run us but for us to run him! When we started doing this Steven suddenly seemed ready to work. To encourage his use of speech, we made flash cards with words and numbers, posted the famous list of fifty nouns, and hung attractive Saturday Evening Post covers next to his bed. We played word games and spoke to him in simple sentences. I did not constantly correct his pronunciation since I was afraid that he would get discouraged and not want to speak at all. I always modelled correct language for him. Although his language was minimal, he found school challenging and was beginning to learn. There were some plateaus where no progress was made, but suddenly he would soar ahead two steps.

In those early years of school, it was nothing for us to wait 35–45 minutes for the school bus to arrive. We were so happy that transportation was provided that we never thought to complain. The times spent waiting for the bus "out in the cold" were probably the most constructive language, speech, auditory, and lipreading sessions that we spent together. We counted the cars flying by, the colors, number of people in the cars, imitated animal sounds, and sang songs with varying pitches and intensity. We had a great time and I'm sure that many a car filled with people wondered what we were doing.

Steven's early years were spent in self–contained Oral classes. It was never suggested that we switch methods even when speech was very slow in coming. The program in the county was Oral, and children who were going to be educated in the manual method went to other schools in the area. In elementary school, Steven was encouraged to participate in the music program. He learned to play the clarinet and played in the school orchestra. The teachers in the school made a conscious effort to face Steven when giving instructions and to make sure that he was included in all of the activities. Toward the end of elementary school, he was mainstreamed in social science and math. On the last day of class, Steven stood up in his social science class and said, "Thanks for having me." A boy in his class immediately responded with, "We loved having you."

We encouraged Steven's interaction with neighborhood kids. He would always participate in their play and invite them into our backyard. He had a carpentry corner set up with real tools and lumber. They were always building something wonderful and the kids liked to come over finding, as kids do, a way around the language barrier.

Speech was important to us and we found that with continuous private speech therapy in addition to the auditory program, Steven was improving. He participated eagerly in lessons and did not seem to mind being corrected. We did not want a summer to go by without reinforcement in written and spoken speech and language, so we continued his speech and auditory training programs each summer. I also would sit in on many of those classes so that I could get ideas on how to help him at home. The rest of the summer was spent in day camp with hearing children and neighborhood activities.

Steven's lipreading skills also improved yearly. He was very skilled in this area, and we were amazed that he was able to lipread a person from the side. When we would say good night to him in the darkness, he would say, "Turn on the light so I can hear you." Another area that we worked on through the years was to train him to use the telephone. A friend lent us a Tele–e–trainer and showed us how to practice with it. At Steven's request, (age 9), we installed a volume control on the phone. At first he was disappointed that he did not hear more of the conversation. He remarked, "My mind can't think that fast." With years and years of practice, auditory training, and trial and error, he has improved. He uses the phone often and on some days is able to hear better than others.

In junior high school, Steven was the audio-visual aide. He was mainstreamed in religious school, sports, and service clubs. By the ninth grade, he was mainstreamed in all of his subjects in public school. He made extensive use of helpful note-takers. In high school, he was a chemistry lab assistant. He had the support of an outstanding and dedicated resource teacher. She encouraged him to pursue high goals and to have a good image of himself. She provided a link between him and the regular class teachers, monitoring closely all that was expected of him in order that he become an actively participating student. She provided academic reinforcement as well as speech, language, and auditory skills.

We have always felt that the Oral method chose us. The decision made for us at the time of diagnosis was supported by the auditory staff and our families. We believed that the method would work and we worked to make it work. We learned, as parents, to wait—there is no magic, only perseverance, patience, and a true commitment to Oral speech, language, and speech reading. Often success did not happen as quickly as we wanted but waiting and plugging away was worth it. Steven had to work very hard at each level of his schooling but everybody believed in him and he believed in himself. He reached out to others and they responded. Progress in the early years of the Oral method may appear slow, but, like the foundation of a building, it is strong and responsible in its end results.

As a family, we understood the task and were committed to it. Barnett, who is four years older, played a very important role in Steven's growth. He included him in most of his own activities, encouraged him to talk, treated him with pride, and tried to alleviate problems for him. For example, he took Steven on an in-depth tour of the high school, showing him the ropes, suggesting names of teachers who might be easy to lipread. He did this so that Steven would feel right at home on the first day. As a family we were determined to make it work and we feel that we are richer for the experience. It probably brought us closer together as a family. We continue to reach out to others, hoping to make the path easier for them.

Steven never thought of himself as impaired. He said, "If I were not deaf, I would not be Steven. I do not see it as a burden. It is part of me." A touching moment in his life came when he was asked to go to a hospital to interpret the message of a dying man who could not speak to be heard but could only move his lips. It was a great comfort to the family when he could lipread what the dying man was trying to say to his family.

During his college and graduate school years, Steven worked out his own problems and coped with situations that often meant finding alternate solutions. His professors were always willing to work with him. For example, they put lights at the lecterns so that Steven could better speechread them. During these college years, Steven continued to avail himself of the speech services and the hearing and speech department in the college. During the summers, he worked part time at the National Institutes of Health, Georgetown University, and Montgomery College.

Where is Steven now? He has graduated from the University of Maryland Dental School and is a practicing dentist. He has pursued his life's ambition and achieved his goal.

We list these accomplishments not for self–aggrandizement but to show what an otherwise healthy human being can accomplish even with a loss of hearing. The ingredients are: commitment and love from parents and siblings; educational expertise by trained teachers and support staff; understanding of family, friends, and peers; the desire and motivation of the hearing-impaired person; and patience, patience, patience.

Where I Am Today

Steven Rattner, DDS

In May of 1982, I graduated from the University of Maryland Dental School in Baltimore, Maryland. This was a shared honor for my parents, brother, and teachers for their dedication to me over the years. I have pursued my life's ambition and achieved my long–term goals. I have received numerous awards for my efforts and special training in the field of Dentistry. After my graduation, I married Tracey Ballan from Ellenville, New York, who is also deaf and has gone through similar paths with her parents.

My wife and I have two wonderful hearing children, Michelle (8) and Jaclyn (4). Initially, we were concerned about how our children would develop language and speech correctly. From the start, my wife and I made great efforts to speak to our children as clearly as possible. We placed our children in many activities that allowed them to interact with other children and adults. Our oldest daughter, Michelle, learned and understood our disability very quickly and loves to help us, especially with unexpected incoming phone calls. In fact, Michelle's favorite toy is the telephone!

After working full time for a group practice in Greenbelt, Maryland, and part time in a private practice in Montgomery County, which gave me great opportunity and experience, I started my own small dental practice which keeps me hopping. This practice mushroomed into a multi–disciplined dental practice consisting of three general dentists, a periodontist, several dental hygienists, and supporting staff. It is a unique practice and consists of deaf, hard of hearing, and hearing patients. The Practice goal is to create a pleasant setting for all. The cohesive and cheerful staff are mostly fluent in American Sign Language and are familiar with the necessity of facing people who are using their lipreading skills.

The office has a specific telephone line dedicated for TTY users. The biweekly staff meetings consist of discussions that will benefit staff, provide educational growth, and enhance patient satisfaction.

The community has responded very well to a deaf dentist and the communication has not been a barrier. In fact, if anything, it has brought a warm atmosphere to the office. Contact with patients is an utmost priority and their needs and concerns are discussed and met.

I lead a very active life. Over the years, I have devoted time to improving the lives of deaf people. I was chosen to be one of the Ten Outstanding Young Marylanders, awarded by the Maryland Jaycees (one of the other winners was Oprah Winfrey). I was a member of the Advisory Council for TEDI (The Telecommunication Exchange for the Deaf, Inc.). This was an all volunteer organization for the telephone relay service before the major telephone carriers started to provide relay services. I was appointed by then-Governor Harry Hughes of the State of Maryland to be a member on the Advisory Commission for the Hearing Impaired. Additionally, I was on the Board of Directors for an organization called Deaf Reach. Deaf Reach is a large nonprofit organization for deaf people with other disabilities such as learning dysfunctions or mental illness.

I am one of the major investors who started an independent organization whose purpose is to publish an annual directory of TTY numbers in the Greater Suburban Area. This directory links Washington, DC., the Maryland Suburbs, Virginia, and Baltimore and is called the Metropolitan Washington Directory for the Deaf and Hard of Hearing (MWTDD, Inc.) I am also one of the founding charter members for an organization involving other deaf and hard of hearing business owners similar to a Chamber of Commerce.

I have attended dental study groups with fellow dentists whose common goal is to keep up with the latest technology and progress in dentistry. Attending dental conferences also gives me an opportunity to meet other dentists throughout the USA, which allows me a different perspective on how other colleagues operate their dental practices.

I never really stopped taking speech therapy lessons because it is important for me to keep up with clear pronunciation. Being a life member of the Alexander Graham Bell Association has broadened my national and international involvement. As a member of the National Association for the Deaf, I have sponsored Caption Film Theatre Parties for current movies held in movie theatres and have co-sponsored Softball and Racquet Ball Tournaments that benefit deaf causes.

My wife, Tracey, and I have many friends: some hearing, some deaf, and all from different philosophies of education. We are quite social and both love snow and water skiing, bridge, arts, theatre, traveling, community activities, religious involvement, and entertaining. Our children's activities keep us on our toes and we are greatly involved in our children's lives. Obviously, family involvement is very important to us as well: parents, grandparents, cousins, relatives, etc., are included in our lives.

We had a hearing-ear dog named Frostie who was a West Highland White Terrier and was a very important part of our lives. As a supplement to a lighting system that alerts us to doorbells and telephone calls, Frostie did his part to alert us to those sounds and others, especially when our children were small. Sad to say, Frostie passed away at age twelve, and we adopted another dog who is a miniature Yorkshire Terrier named Duke. Duke will eventually be trained as a hearing-ear dog.

My oldest daughter, Michelle, is very outgoing and has to act as my telephone secretary. She assumed this responsibility on her own and handles many incoming calls in a volunteering, fun–loving manner with an adult, business–like response. It seems that this is never an inconvenience for her and something she enjoys doing. Both Tracey and I speak on the phone, although sometimes we hear better than at other times. We use the Maryland Telephone Relay Service to communicate to hearing friends if those people do not have access to a TTY. Our children are very involved with our adult friends and can communicate with them in whatever method our friends prefer (signing, lipreading, or both). Our home is always full of children, guests, neighbors, friends, and relatives.

Life is exciting. My parents, relatives, teachers, patients, staff, friends, and business contacts have made my life wonderful. But above all, the people who have had confidence in me and respected me have given me a great gift. Deafness is something that I have lived with all of my life. It is a part of me and who I am.

A sense of humor helps me keep a positive attitude. Knowledge and interest in world events and progress in medicine all combine to make me an interesting person to be with. A feeling for people is something that I treasure. The people who have encouraged me will always have a special place in my heart. My hands will always be outstretched to others. Silence does not fill my life; people do!

8

Total Communication

A Professional Point of View

Barbara Bodner-Johnson, Ph.D.

For parents of young deaf children confronted with new experiences and decisions, none can be more challenging than the choice of a communication methodology. Key questions that parents often ask are: How can we best communicate with our child? Which communication method is best for him or her and our family? There can be no single answer to these questions. Each child and family is unique and brings individual goals, beliefs, and abilities to the decision table.

The conscientious selection of communication methods based on the communication and educational needs of the child is called Total Communication. This chapter explains what Total Communication is, how it works in practice, and gives you information which will help you in your decision-making process. Reading the information presented here should only be part of this process. It is important for you to also talk with parents of deaf children who are

Special thanks to colleagues Dr. Janice Gatty and Dr. Jan Hafer for their helpful suggestions on updating the information in this chaper.

using a variety of communication methods, to observe children and teachers in school programs that use various methods, and to discuss your options with deaf adults in your community and with professionals such as teachers, speech therapists, and administrators. It will be to your advantage in the long run if you take the extra time to learn as much as possible before making a choice.

What Is Total Communication?

Total Communication is a technical term that is unfamiliar to most people who are not in the field of deafness. When the term was first introduced into our vocabularies in the 1970s, it meant the right of a deaf child to learn to use all communication modalities available to acquire linguistic competence. In other words, Total Communication is a communication philosophy. In practice, Total Communication programs may use signs, speech, gestures, speechreading, amplification, and/or fingerspelling to provide linguistic input to deaf children. In Total Communication programs, children typically are allowed to express themselves in their preferred communication modalities. You might be thinking that this is exactly what you want for your child—she should have the chance to have access to and be free to use whatever she needs to learn language.

Over the years, many school programs have used the Total Communication label to describe their systems. These systems, however, may differ in the value and emphasis they place on each communication modality. For example, each of the following descriptions of Total Communication is commonly used today:

1. Total Communication is the simultaneous use of speech and signs to systematically represent English for the receiver. Often called simultaneous communication, the intent is to provide linguistic input using an English-based sign system (*not* American Sign Language). The assumption is that the child selects or combines information through understanding signs, speechreading, and listening according to her individual abilities.

2. TOTAL COMMUNICATION IS THE CHOICE OR SELECTION OF SIGN *OR* SPEECH AND THE USE OF SPEECHREADING AND RESIDUAL HEARING. The assumption is that, in different situations, some children benefit more from an auditory/oral approach (listening and speaking) and some children benefit more from a visual/gestural approach (watching and signing).

HOW DOES TOTAL COMMUNICATION WORK?

There is a marked difference in how Total Communication would be practiced using these two descriptions. Let's look more closely at how these two perspectives are different.

If we are talking about the first description of Total Communication, we would see an emphasis on the consistent, simultaneous use of oral (speech) and manual (sign) communication modes. The goal is to represent spoken language accurately and consistently in manually coded English. (See Appendix A for a discussion of manually coded English systems.) For your family, this would mean that whenever mother, father, sister, or brother communicates with your deaf child, they would use both speech and sign language (including gestures) at the same time. Often, your child would be expected to communicate using both spoken and manual communication. In school, this means that teachers, administrators, and staff, as well as students, would communicate using manual and oral communication simultaneously both in and out of the classroom.

If you were following the ideas in the second description above, some of the modes of communication might be used alone some of the time. Perhaps one time you might use only sign with your child without using your voice at all. At another time you might use your voice alone with no signs or gestures and expect your child to listen and speechread. This same pattern would also be true in the classroom. When you visit the classroom, you might sometimes see the teacher working with the children using only speech, while at another time, she might be using only signs and gestures.

Both of these views of Total Communication are based on the philosophy that language can be visual and gestural as well as auditory and oral. The belief is that your child's environment should provide access to language by making the full range of communication modalities available to her.

Since the 1970s when Total Communication was "born," new knowledge has been learned about American Sign Language (ASL)—the dominant language of the Deaf community. This has changed how some Total Communication programs work. There is growing agreement that ASL has important educational value for enhancing overall language learning and should be included by programs with both sign and oral components—that is, Total Communication programs. Today, many school programs that call themselves Total Communication may also include some use of American Sign Language. However, because American Sign Language is a different language from English, you cannot sign ASL and speak English simultaneously. Linguists studying ASL over the years have shown that it is a true language with its own vocabulary and grammar.

Programs that offer ASL as the primary language of instruction will likely describe their programs as Bilingual–Bicultural (Bi-Bi). Many school programs for deaf children, both Total Communication and Bilingual-Bicultural (Bi-Bi), offer parents the opportunity to learn American Sign Language.

As a parent, it is important for you to realize that different Total Communication programs give different value and emphasis to different communication modalities. For example, some programs may emphasize speech, while other programs emphasize English-based sign communication. Some programs may include some use of American Sign Language, while others may not. Parents should ask about the program's particular communication emphasis and observe to see if, in practice, it matches the needs of their child.

In the 1970s, "Total Communication" was a liberating philosophy for the field of the education of deaf children. It was a move away from the "either/or" of the manual *or* oral communication controversy that had been going on for centuries. The Total Communication philosophy soon became a movement that was joined by school programs hopeful it would help their students achieve better academically. By 1978, 62 percent of all educational programs for deaf children reported that they were using the Total Communication approach. In 1992, 92 percent of residential schools for deaf children and 72 percent of day schools and local programs reported sign and speech as their primary teaching communication method.

How Does Total Communication Affect the Learning of Language?

The key to language acquisition is the early interaction your child experiences with others using the language. If you decide to use an English-based sign system in your home, it is important that the language (in this case English) is made accessible to your child. This means that the signs must represent English consistently and accurately. Research studies have shown that English signing positively influences English language development.

Parents should request training in sign communication in order to become fluent signers in whatever system is chosen. The goal is to provide a rich language environment for your young child. When this happens, the young deaf child can be expected to use language (first signs and sign combinations) according to the same developmental pattern as hearing children.

One question that comes up time and again with parents who are hearing is the effect of sign language on speech. Using sign language to communicate does *not* have a negative impact on a child's ability to speak. How clearly your child speaks depends, in part, on how much residual hearing she has and on how well she is able to use it.

Your child will need special instruction to develop the speech skills needed to effectively use her speech to transmit language. Your child's success in developing speech skills will be affected by the relative emphasis placed on the oral component in the school's Total Communication system. A Total Communication program which gives significant value to hearing and the use of speech will provide greater opportunities for children to learn to use these modalities for learning and transmitting language.

How Will Total Communication Affect My Relationship with My Child?

Being able to communicate freely with your child is one of the most important ways for you to establish a good relationship. Of course, communication is the major goal all methods are trying to reach. Because the communication between a parent and child is so important for language learning, many people have studied this relationship. The studies have shown that when hearing mothers use speech and sign language with their deaf children and not just speech alone, they spend more time in interactive play and more time on each play activity, and mother and child have more complex communications. They also found that the children who were studied in this group had more spontaneous conversations, were more sociable and cooperative with their mothers, and were able to maintain eye contact longer with their mothers than were deaf children whose mothers depended on Oral/Auditory communication. It was also interesting that when the mothers were asked, those who were using sign and speech said they felt they were effective and confident as parents.

Guidelines for Parents

If you are interested in choosing a Total Communication approach for you and your child, the following summary guidelines will enable you to make an informed choice.

1. It is most important that you observe your child to determine her needs regarding mode of communication for language acquisition.

2. The program you choose should have a clearly defined communication policy available for parents, such as: *English is the primary language of instruction using an English-based sign system with voice, incorporating ASL features* *for language enhancement purposes and to reinforce the language of English.* Discuss the policy with the teachers and administrators; observe communication in the classrooms.

3. The school and teachers must be committed to whatever communication systems are used. Teachers must be knowledgeable in both the sign and oral components, know how and when to use ASL and English-based signing, and be sufficiently proficient to provide consistently accurate language models in the modalities accessible to your child.

4. Each "Total Communication" program will be different in the emphasis it places on the oral and manual components. Find out if the program you are interested in does an equally effective job in promoting sign language acquisition and auditory and speech skill development. Again, the best way to gain this information is to visit the program and talk with the staff.

Conclusion

It is important for you to realize that choosing a program with a Total Communication philosophy does not promise success for your deaf child. There are other factors that you should be looking for when you choose a program for your child. Some of these factors are:

- A strong academic curriculum that emphasizes literacy across the grades;
- Specific program goals to foster social-emotional development;
- Program activities that lead to developing partnerships between teachers and parents;
- Family sign language instruction;
- Regular interaction with deaf adults and other parents;
- Opportunities for group sign language classes;
- Opportunities for activities involving the deaf community.

A very critical element for your child's success is to begin using the communication methods of your choice and her preference as early and as consistently in her life as possible. Even if you feel slow and inadequate with the signs, you can still stay a step ahead of your child while she is young. If you maintain your skills through classes and interacting with deaf adults, you will be able to keep up with your child's language learning. Also, bear in mind that the communication method you choose today may not be the one you use later as your child gets older. Although some children may continue to use Total Communication in adulthood, others may gravitate to ASL or the Oral approach.

If you are able to find all of the factors listed above in a school program that supports Total Communication and if you, as parents, lend your support to your child and her program, I believe the rewards for you, your child, and your family can be great.

References

Bodner-Johnson, B.A. (1986) "The Family Environment and Achievement of Deaf Students: A Discriminant Analysis." *Exceptional Children,* Vol. 52, pp. 443-49.

Commission on Education of the Deaf. (1988) *Toward Equality: Education of the Deaf.* Washington, DC: U.S. Government Printing Office.

Denton, D.M. (1972) "A Rationale for Total Communication." In O'Rourke, T.J. (Ed.) *Psycholinguistics and Total Communication: The State of the Art* (pp. 53-61). Silver Spring, MD: American Annals of the Deaf.

Garretson, M. (Ed.) (1990) *Eyes, Hands, Voices: Communication Issues Among Deaf People.* Silver Spring, MD: National Association of the Deaf.

Greenberg, M.T. (1980) "Social Interaction Between Deaf Preschoolers and Their Mothers: The Effects of Communication Method and Communicative Competence." *Developmental Psychology,* Vol. 16, pp. 465-74.

Greenberg, M.T. (1983) "Family Stress and Child Competence: The Effects of Early Intervention for Families with Deaf Infants." *American Annals of the Deaf,* Vol. 128, pp. 407-17.

Greenberg, M.T., Caldron, R., and Kusche, C. (1983) "Early Intervention Using Simultaneous Communication with Deaf Infants: The Effect on Communication Development." *Child Development,* Vol. 55, pp 607-16.

Jordan, I.K., Gustason, G., and Rosen, R. (1976) "An Update on Communication Trends at Programs for the Deaf." *American Annals of the Deaf,* Vol. 124, pp. 350-57.

Luetke-Stahlman, B. (1988) "Documenting Syntactically and Semantically Incomplete Bimodal Input to Hearing Impaired Subjects." *American Annals of the Deaf,* Vol. 133 (3), pp. 230-34.

Moores, D.F. (1987) *Educating the Deaf: Psychology, Principles, and Practices* (3rd Ed.). Boston: Houghton Mifflin.

Ritter-Brinton, K., & Stewart, D. (1992) "Hearing Parents and Deaf Children." *American Annals of the Deaf,* Vol. 137, No. 2, pp. 85-91.

Schick, B., & Moeller, M. (1992) "What is Learnable in Manually Coded English Sign Systems?" *Applied Psycholinguistics,* Vol. 13, No. 3, pp. 313-40.

Schildroth, A., & Hotto, S. (1994) "Inclusion or Exclusion? Deaf Students and the Inclusion Movement." *American Annals of the Deaf,* Vol. 139, No. 2, pp. 239-43.

Stewart, D. (1993) "Bi-Bi to MCE?" *American Annals of the Deaf,* Vol. 138, No. 4, pp. 331-37.

Stewart, D., Akamatsu, C.T., & Becker, B. (1995) "Aiming for Consistency in the Way Teachers Sign." *American Annals of the Deaf,* Vol. 140, No. 4, pp. 314-23.

Wedell-Monnig, J., & Lumley, J.M. (1980) "Child Deafness and Mother-Child Interaction." *Child Development,* Vol. 51, pp. 766-74.

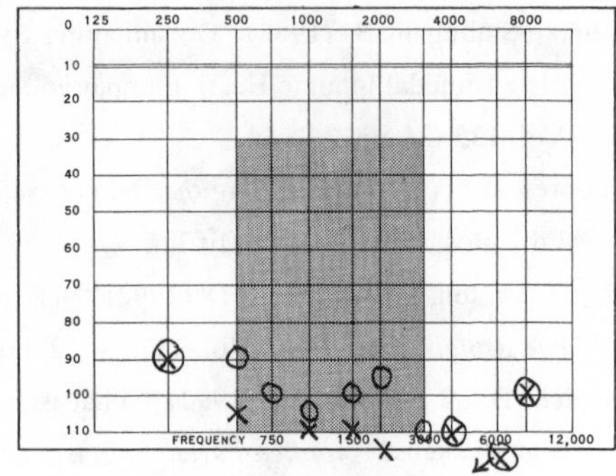

JOSH'S STORY

BARRY AND JACQUELINE Z. MENDELSOHN

Joshua is deaf. We have lived with our deaf child for thirteen years, and we lived with an "undiagnosed" child for three years before learning about deafness. For three long years, we struggled with our highly active, non-responsive, basically "bratty" child.

Our first son, Aaron, was quiet and self-contained, playing for hours in his playpen or on the floor with cars, roads, and building blocks. Joshua, with his shock of red hair, had a completely opposite personality. Two and a half years younger than Aaron, Joshua caused us to doubt our parenting skills, our abilities to be in control, and our patience. He was an extremely physical baby, needing to be held, to be entertained, and to be the focus of all of our attention. He never stayed in a playpen, car seat, or high chair.

When Joshua was nine months old, I asked our pediatrician about the possibility of a hearing loss because he appeared not to respond to our voices or other sounds in the house. The doctor looked at me with great patience and said, "Don't worry—he'll outgrow it." I believed him. Every time I brought Joshua in for an appointment, the doctor, in response to my anxieties would "test" Joshua. He'd slam doors or clap his hands behind Joshua's head. Josh would turn around (from vibrations and air currents, we know now) and I would be placated for the moment, sure that he could hear.

At age two, we took Joshua to an audiologist, who tested him and reported that he had normal hearing. At two years and three months, he was diagnosed by a neurologist as "aphasic," and at two years four months, a psychiatrist diagnosed him as having "early anxious reaction to childhood." We listened to the professionals, but continued to believe that there was something wrong with our child's hearing. We talked to Joshua, read to him, and sang to him. He babbled a little bit, said "mam" and on occasion responded or seemed to respond to the barking of our dog. But most of the time, he ignored us, defied us, had temper tantrums, and remained uncommunicative.

Finally, just before his third birthday, we took him to another audiologist, who diagnosed Joshua as profoundly deaf. Our first reaction was one of relief; we finally had an answer to all our questions and a label for our difficult child. We could find people associated with deafness and learn the right thing to do to raise our deaf son. Our second reaction was sorrow; sorrow for the music we loved so much that he would miss; sorrow for the loss of our dreams for our second son.

Three day after the diagnosis, we learned about a program for parents and deaf children within walking distance of our house. No one had ever told us about it in all our years of questions! We talked to the director and she invited us to attend a parent meeting which included a sign language class and then a parent discussion group. Knowing nothing about methods of communication for deaf children, we decided to try it. We were starving to meet other parents of deaf children. The group was made up of six sets of parents. We were still incredibly raw, whereas the other parents were more experienced in deafness. Their children had been diagnosed as deaf long before. As we talked with other parents, we felt for the first time that we weren't alone, that we weren't crazy for feeling all the grief, impatience, and frustration over Joshua. Other parents felt the same way. They were very supportive. The sign language teacher talked about Total Communication, a new idea in 1972. The idea of being able to communicate with Joshua after three long years was exciting. For three years, we had talked to him and gotten nothing back. For three years, we experienced pushing and pulling, and temper tantrums because he couldn't understand us and we couldn't understand him. We would try anything to communicate.

That first night, we learned how to sign "Twinkle, Twinkle, Little Star," "Bridge Over Troubled Waters," and some basic survival signs such as "no," "yes," "bathroom," "juice," "milk," and "cookie." We madly wrote down descriptions because at that time, there were no books for this new method called "Signing Exact English." We went home with hope and tried some of the signs with Joshua. He looked interested but didn't immediately pick anything up.

The next morning, Joshua, as usual, pulled me out of bed at 6:00 A.M. and pulled me down the stairs. I tried to remember how to sign, "No, mommy tired, sleep"—whatever, but I couldn't bring any signs out at that early hour. He brought me to the refrigerator, and I thought, "I hope I can guess what he wants before he has a temper tantrum." I opened the door and Joshua signed, "juice." It was the first time in his three years of life that he could ask for something and I could understand him and respond. It was like a miracle.

We had a home tutor come to our house three times a week. She was like Mary Poppins with her magic bag of toys, signing everything as she talked to us and to Joshua and Aaron. She modeled behavior for us without "teaching" us. We loved her and needed that kind of warm, loving, listening person in our lives at that time. We studied sign language books and went to sign classes, and Joshua thrived. He learned 100 words during that first month, and with his teacher's help, began responding to sounds and articulating sounds with the use of his new body aids. His behavior and ours calmed down very quickly because we could communicate—haltingly at first, and then with more courage. We always spoke as we signed and asked Joshua to use his voice most of the time.

During these early months, we visited a clinic to observe the Oral method, but came out dissatisfied with the slowness of communication that we saw. We continued signing and were rewarded by Joshua's responsiveness and his behavior, which settled down to the pace of a "normal" three year old.

Three months after Joshua was diagnosed, we moved from San Francisco to Anchorage, Alaska. Joshua entered preschool with other deaf children who were all using Total Communication. We continued sign classes and added a component of Parent Rap Groups so that we could continue our contact with other parents of hearing impaired children.

Now, thirteen years later, we look back with no regrets. Our son has grown to be a regular teenager, still with his red hair. As he enters his senior year in public high school, he worries about college, about his grades, his SAT scores, and his social life. He has twenty other deaf students as his peer group in the high school and is looking at colleges with larger numbers of deaf students. He has been in mainstreamed Honors classes with good academic challenge from his hearing classmates. He communicates freely and easily with both hearing and deaf people. He gets great joy out of life and we get great joy from him. Our days of struggling to learn the language of signs is over, although we continue to pick up new signs every day. All of us sign, including Aaron. Aaron has taught signs to friends in college, and Joshua teaches other students in his mainstream classes. He uses his voice consistently and fairly well for a profoundly deaf person. He loves to sign to music and that is the way that we have found for him to share in the music that is constantly in our home.

More and more people in our society are seeing sign language on television and in shows. More and more schools and colleges are offering sign language to hearing students. The comfort level is growing and people no longer turn away in embarrassment when they see Joshua signing with his friends.

Joshua has grown up to be a complete person. He identifies with his deaf friends with whom he can talk, lipread to some extent, and phone with over his computer. He has become a well-rounded person who strongly identifies himself as a deaf person who will do great things in the hearing world.

WHERE I AM TODAY

JOSHUA MENDELSOHN

Laughing, I let myself be knocked down by a group of young deaf teenagers eager to capture the soccer ball. I leaned back on the grass, watching the group kick the ball back and forth. I felt a tentative tap on my shoulder, and, squinting against the sun, I looked up. A young deaf teenager, with a puzzled expression on his face, stood over me. He signed, "You're going to law school?" I nodded yes.

"I thought Deaf couldn't!"

"Oh, yes, Deaf can," I signed back. "I'm in, and I'm not the first one. I'm not going to be the last one either. You can!" He looked astonished, then relieved.

"Thanks," he signed. He then ran off to join the laughing throng of children.

That was three years ago. Since then, I have graduated from the UCLA School of Law and will be working for the Department of Justice. During the past several years, I have surprised many professors, professionals, parents, and especially deaf children as I tackled and overcame the challenges of the study of the law. I am not the first, fifth, tenth, or even the thirtieth deaf person to survive these much-dreaded years of law school, and I know I will not be the last.

Eight years ago, I graduated from a mainstreamed public high school in Maryland where I had been receiving sign language interpreting services. I moved three thousand miles away to Los Angeles because I wanted a change of culture. I wanted new experiences, new friends, and new independence! I entered California State University at Northridge (CSUN), which had two hundred deaf students intermingled with thirty thousand hearing students; sign language as well as oral interpreting services were provided, as well as note taking and tutoring services.

For all my classes, even for the most technical or the most theatrical ones, I requested and received sign language interpreting services. Being "independent" and wanting a whole new spectrum of experiences, I thought I would go for ASL interpreting; to my surprise, I found that I still preferred the Total Communication method with a mix between ASL and English signs. These were what I had been raised with, and these were how I was able to receive all the information I needed. I refused to use the oral method because I did not have the residual hearing needed to discriminate between the sounds and I could not lipread well enough.

Outside of school, I busily picked up ASL slang and lingo as I room-mated with other deaf people, participated in deafness-related extracurricular activities, and worked in deafness-related jobs. Oh, don't get me wrong—I had no dearth of contacts with hearing people; I steadily dated hearing people as well as deaf people, and my group of friends always included hearing people who could sign.

Law school saw an abrupt change in these patterns. Even though I still received interpreting and note-taking services for my classes, none of my friends in law school could sign. Nor did anybody have time to learn sign language; law is a jealous partner. I went to parties with hearing classmates, danced with them, studied with them, went out to dinner with them, stressed with them, and cried with them. Yet, I felt that some of my needs went unfulfilled. Fortunately, I had my own life outside law school—that, more than anything, helped me keep my sanity throughout law school! I again had a deaf roommate, lived several miles away from school, dated hearing people who signed fluently, and went out regularly with my friends who were either deaf or hearing and knew sign language.

Throughout law school, my sign language hovered around a mix between ASL and English, although I still preferred purer ASL when I went out with deaf friends. My interpreters at UCLA were always among the best, and they could fluently convey the ponderous, complex, and abstract legal thoughts spitting out of my professors' mouths. They also voiced for me as I successfully argued in mock trials. They accompanied me on interviews, and worked with me for sixteen weeks during a UCLA-sponsored externship with a federal judge. To ease communications, my law school installed a TDD pay telephone—which I used voraciously (with curious bystanders peering over my shoulder—which at times became embarrassing!). UCLA also provided a variety of other accommodations—real-time captioning, note taking, and oral interpreting to name a few; I only opted for the sign language interpreters. A sign language interpreter will also be present during my three-day bar exam, and I will likewise have a sign language interpreter on my job.

Some people question the extent of the accommodations I receive. However, I do not question them. With these accommodations, I have shown that I am perfectly as capable as anybody else to survive the rigors of law school; like I said, I surprised many people.

Oh, yes, Deaf can.

photo credit: Cathy Elder

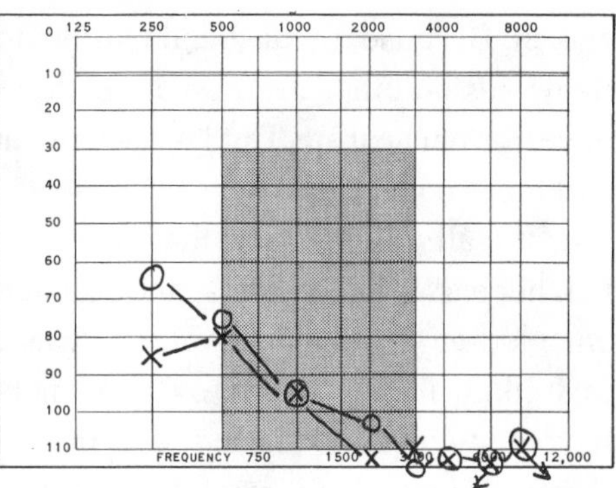

STEFFI'S STORY

ELAINE AIELLO

I knew when I decided to have a child that my baby might be deaf. My husband was deafened at the age of three months by spinal meningitis and I am deaf. My parents and my brother are also deaf. If there had been any other handicap, it would have been a surprise to me, but deafness was something I expected. I knew that because I have been able to accept my own deafness, I would have no problem accepting it in my own child.

And so with a great deal of excitement, I prepared for the birth by gathering all the necessary supplies and attending childbirth classes. An interpreter attended with me so that I understood everything that was said. When the long-anticipated day arrived, I delivered a bouncy little girl. The doctor gave her a clean bill of health, but I knew that deafness was an invisible handicap.

Because I was deaf, I had a baby cry signaler on hand to alert me when Stephanie cried. This was especially important at night when the light flashed to awaken me. I didn't need a flasher during the day because I wore my hearing aid and could hear her crying. In those early months I was curious about her hearing. I would stand next to her where she could not see me and, without touching her in any way, I would vocalize. Sometimes she would open her eyes and other times she would not. I knew that she was a very deep sleeper and did not come to any conclusion. As time went by, I tried a variety of baby noise makers and once again her responses were inconsistent. Because my husband was deafened as a result of illness and there was no other deafness in his family, it was possible for her to have normal hearing. But I grew more and more suspicious and more and more concerned.

Finally, I expressed these concerns to my pediatrician. He said that her ears looked normal and that her delay in spontaneous speech was nothing to worry about. His was a "wait and see" attitude. At this point, following my own instincts, I went to an audiologist. I have had frequent hearing tests myself and so I was familiar with the procedures. However, I had never seen an infant being tested. At this time Stephanie was six months old. The audiologist would create sounds and then watch for facial expressions and eye movement. Since she had responded so inconsistently to my "homemade" tests, I was curious about these results. Finally, after extensive testing, the audiologist confirmed what I had already suspected. Stephanie had a profound hearing loss in both ears.

We knew that we would have to make some choices about her future. With professional advice, our own knowledge of deafness, and personal instinct, we began to lay the cornerstone of her future. The first step was to get a hearing aid and provide her with constant exposure to sound and communication. We were a signing family so she was exposed to Total Communication all the time. Because of my deafness, I knew how important it was to always have eye contact with her. I felt that the most effective way to communicate was to use both signs and speech simultaneously. This way, when she received information, she did not have to rely only on the lip movement and facial expressions but could have the benefit of the visual-gestural movements of signs. Sometimes I would only speak and then if she didn't seem to understand, I would add the sign language. I felt that signing was important too. My mother, father, and I were educated in the Oral method, while my brother went to a residential school where sign language was used. In later years we all used signs.

When Stephanie was first fitted with a hearing aid at around one year of age, she would only keep the aid on for a few minutes at a time. Slowly I was able to increase the time she wore it until finally she was wearing it all day. By using signs and speech, my daughter's language, speech, and lipreading developed informally.

Stephanie was an alert and inquisitive baby. She babbled extensively and by the age of eighteen months was beginning to say a few words such as "ma" for milk and "bye-bye." She also had a very short attention span and seemed to be hyperactive. This made it very difficult to have structured language lessons. It was easier to just continuously talk and sign as I went about doing things all day long. The signs were an added visual clue to what I was saying.

Although signing is the natural language of the deaf, I felt that speech and speechreading were also very important tools and I worked on those areas too. I signed up for a correspondence course and found that she was already doing many of the suggested exercises.

When Stephanie was three years old, she was retested at another center. I was eager to compare the results now that she was a little bit older and the testing would be more reliable. I wanted to make sure that the hearing aid we had was the right one for her. As a result of these new tests, she was diagnosed as having a severe bilateral sensorineural hearing loss and a new hearing aid was recommended.

Then we enrolled her in a preschool class and considerable work was done with her in language training and teaching her to use her residual hearing. I found that her progress was not as good as it could have been and transferred her to another school. Eventually she had four years of preschool education at four different schools. Each time I felt her language development was more advanced than that of her classmates. That is probably because she had had sign language from the beginning. Each of these preschool programs followed the Oral philosophy and she was able to accomplish all that she was asked to do. At the time, these were the only programs that were available to us. Her teachers emphasized lipreading, amplification, reading, and writing, while at home we used signs, fingerspelling, gestures, and speech. Stephanie was able to communicate with people in the way that they communicated with her. If they spoke, she spoke; if they signed with voice, she signed with voice; if they signed without voice, she did the same.

At about the time Stephanie was ready to begin her formal education, we moved to another state and were faced with making an education choice. It was possible for her to attend a residential school with Total Communication or a public day school with either Oral or Total Communication. For the first year we chose a public day school with either Oral or Total Communication. She had classes in a self-contained group or she was mainstreamed depending on the subject and the level of difficulty. By the time she was in fifth grade, she was completely mainstreamed with an interpreter. She also received support from a special auditory teacher.

We felt that Stephanie's oral skills were well-developed. When she was a young child, some people would have difficulty understanding her when they met her for the first time. After a while, however, they would be able to understand her. One day, when she was around seven years old, we were at a fast food restaurant. After she had sat down, she decided that she needed ketchup. I told her to go and get it for herself but she was afraid that the person would not understand her. I insisted that she try anyway. It took two tries but when she came back with the ketchup, she was beaming. "He understands me—I got the ketchup!"

In looking back, our decision to put her into a public school day program for the deaf had its positive and negative points. In the public school she gained a strong academic background in a variety of subjects. She had tremendous support services from trained teachers of the deaf, aids, interpreters, and auditory developmental specialists, as well as support from home. But I don't think that she was able to develop successful social relationships there and I feel now that it would have been easier for her in a residential school.

In an attempt to provide added experiences with deaf friends, I decided to send her to a deaf camp in the summer and encourage other deaf youth-related activities such as the Junior National Association for the Deaf. Through these extracurricular activities, she has become involved with other deaf children and broadened her circle of friends. Her understanding of the deaf community grew as she was exposed to sports events, picnics, captioned movies, and conventions.

When I look back on our choices, I know that Total Communication was right for Stephanie. I am still not sure if the public school was the right choice, but that time is over now. Stephanie now attends a college for the deaf. This is a very different experience for her. Her environment now is all deaf with a handful of hearing teachers and students. There remains a whole future of decision making and choices she will have to make for herself. I know that she has the skills to do this.

WHERE I AM TODAY

STEPHANIE AIELLO SUMMERS

Mr. & Mrs. Mark J. Summers

My future of decision making and choices lay on my lap after my parents had accomplished what choices were best for me early in my life. I graduated from Gallaudet University with a B.S. in Accounting in May, 1989.

As a student, I adapted to the change from the mainstream environment in my high school to the complete deaf environment at Gallaudet very well. Some of the adjustments I had to make were in the classroom setting. I now had teachers who signed for themselves and I needed to take my own notes, whereas in high school there were interpreters and note-takers. I participated in many activities throughout my college years, such as student body government affairs and many committees. I joined Delta Epsilon Sorority. My mom, Elaine, and I are the first mother and daughter members.

My parents often visited me at Gallaudet. With awe, some of my friends would say how fortunate I am to be able to communicate with my parents who are deaf, with ease. There have been several occasions where my mom has joined my friends and me on an outing. One outing was with my rock climbing class when we went to Great Falls, Virginia. My grandmother (my mom's mom) and my mom joined my class and me. Everyone commented to me how nice to have a deaf grandmother and mother to communicate to. My grandmother enjoyed watching us experience the challenge of rock climbing. Having close family members who are also deaf is something I feel fortunate to have and am proud of.

I was fortunate to have a job lined up after graduation with Student Loan Marketing Association (known as Sallie Mae) as a Senior Financial Analyst. Challenges began for my employer and myself in terms of what they needed to provide for me to have equal access. For instance, I needed accommodations such as TTYs for my calls and interpreters for company-wide meetings. My deafness was a new learning experience for everyone who worked with and around me. My first two years with Sallie Mae, I needed to be on top of the human resources department when they failed to provide me with an interpreter. Gradually, it became a checklist item. I had to supply them with information about where to get TTYs, an amplifier phone hand set, and whom to contact for interpreters. I have always stood up to what I was entitled to get and to be treated equally as others.

One incident happened during my first year of employment. At the employee orientation, I received an employee handbook. While reading the handbook, I came across the company's holidays and made a note to myself which holidays we were off. I did not report to work on Columbus Day. My supervisor called home and spoke to my sister. My sister informed me that my supervisor was on the phone wondering why I was not at work. As Ingrid interpreted for me, I informed my supervisor that I had read in the employee handbook that Columbus Day was a holiday.

My supervisor replied, "An announcement was made on Friday reminding employees that Monday was not a holiday."

I answered back, "Well, I was not informed of the announcement and I am not going to work."

When I reported to work the next day, I showed my supervisor the handbook where it had Columbus Day listed as a holiday. The result was that I got paid eight hours regular pay. This was a good lesson to teach co-workers that any time there is an important announcement, they need to inform me. Today, from time to time, I laugh about this incident.

The method of communication I use at work varies and includes talking, writing, E-mail, and signing. Talking is the major mode of communication I use at work, but sometimes I use writing as an aid to a particular word that was said, as well as signing with those who know how to sign. Several of my coworkers have learned how to sign, although it is not very effective because all were spoiled by how well I am able to speak. Yet, I tell them how much I appreciate them learning signs because it certainly helps to get a clearer message across. E-mail, or electronic mail, is another mode of communication I use daily. E-mail is very beneficial to me because I do not have to rely on anyone to relay messages.

With another deaf co-worker, we gave a brown bag presentation called "Learn about Deaf People." We explained different techniques for speaking and getting attention, as well as what obstacles bother a deaf person. Some tips we shared were getting a deaf person's attention by tapping or pounding on the same table because we can feel the vibrations.

For five years I struggled to step upwards in the ladder—whether because of competition in the workplace or my deafness, I am unsure. Finally, I got promoted to my current position, Financial Operations Specialist in a different division of Sallie Mae. Now I need to go through a new wave of teaching my co-workers about me as a deaf person and the culture as a whole. This is something I will always do throughout my career and I do enjoy teaching about my world.

I am currently a part-time Masters of Business Administration student at George Mason University (G.M.U). My core study is finance. I am going through the same experiences I went through in my mainstream years with interpreters and note-takers provided by the Disability Support Services at G.M.U. I anticipate graduating in December, 1997. My ambition is to become a Certified Financial Planner. It is possible that I could become the first deaf woman holding a Certified Financial Planner degree.

Besides working, I am actively involved in deaf community organizations. I became the first deaf woman president and cofounder for the Montgomery County Association for the Deaf. I served a two-year term from 1990-1992. This organization is still going strong today. I am also involved in my college sorority alumni international and local chapters. I served as vice-president of the International Alumnae Delta Epsilon Sorority from 1993 to 1995. This accomplishment for me meant a lot because I have developed the leadership abilities from my parents and my days at Gallaudet.

When I look back at the choices my parents made for me, I am grateful for the opportunities and support they gave me. Now with the decisions and choices I have made, my parents are proud of me.

I am looking forward to a new chapter in my life, following my marriage in October 1995. My husband, Mark Summers, is deaf. I have endured many hours of his studies to be a Certified Public Accountant (CPA). He became a CPA in February 1995.

Speaking of choices we might have to make for our child, we will be prepared to have a deaf child. I'll be delighted to carry the fourth deaf generation. My choices would reflect what my parents did for me.

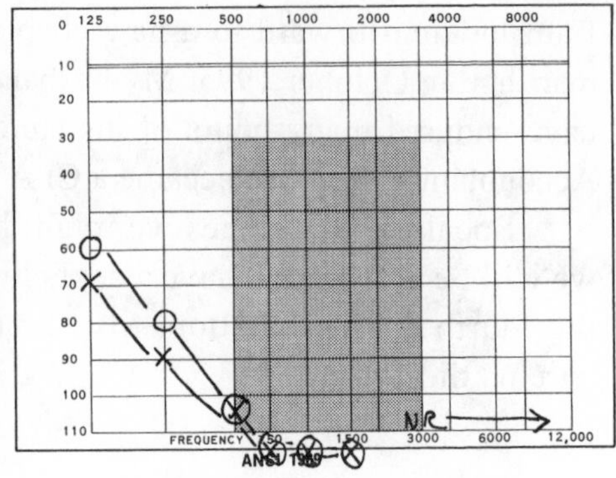

RYAN'S STORY

JOHN AND MARTHA LONG

Ryan spent his second birthday in the hospital with spinal meningitis. As he began to recover from the effects of the disease, we began to suspect that something else was very wrong. Ryan told us that the telephone and the TV in his hospital room were broken. In addition, he did not respond to us when we called him by name. He was recovering in a large teaching hospital, and although he was seen by many residents and interns daily, no one seemed to want to talk to us about our concerns that he was not responding. No one suggested that we have any testing for this problem.

After his long stay at the hospital, we were finally able to take our baby home. We were happy that he was well, but we were still haunted by the fear that he might be deaf. Our doctor advised us that since Ryan had just been through a very traumatic experience, he probably was just choosing to ignore us. He was certain that Ryan would be fine after he been home in his own surroundings for a while.

Finally, after about two weeks of banging pots and pans, hoping for a response, we insisted that our doctor refer us for an evaluation of Ryan's hearing. When tests confirmed our worst fears, we were almost relieved. It had been much worse to live with the hope that he wasn't deaf when we knew deep inside that he really was.

But the finality of the diagnosis that our beautiful boy was profoundly deaf was a terrible blow to our family. We cried a lot and then decided to throw ourselves into doing whatever it was that parents of deaf children needed to do.

Deciding how to help our child and ourselves was no easy task. We got no information from our doctor or from the audiologist who had examined Ryan. As we began to contact anyone and everyone we had ever known who had any association with deafness, it became immediately apparent that people involved with hearing impaired children and their education had adamant ideas on the methods by which these children should be taught. I remember one well-meaning mother who told me that she hoped that I could love my child enough so that I would never use sign language with him! What did love have to do with educating my child? This was a painful and confusing time for us as we struggled to make a decision, confronted with parents and professionals who could not agree among themselves.

We finally decided to trust our own instincts, and we signed up for a crash course in sign language. At this time, Ryan's frustration in trying to communicate with us was building. He seemed to need so many new words at this crucial time in his language development. We felt that we needed to be able to tell him where we were going when the family piled into the car. We needed to be able to tell him what Bert was saying to Ernie on *Sesame Street.* His ideas and his questions were becoming increasing more complex. He needed all the tools that we could give him. In turn, we were gratified that he was able to respond almost at once to our clumsy first efforts at signing. We were careful to always use our voices as we signed and Ryan did the same. Our Total Communication method seemed to be working. We felt all of our needs and Ryan's needs were being met.

At this time, Ryan was enrolled in a program of home study through the State School for the Deaf. Ryan's older brother, Chris, who was only four when all of this happened, understood some of what had happened to his brother, but he began to resent all of the time that was being spent on Ryan. There were lengthy phone calls with well-wishing friends and family. There were hours spent on follow-up lessons when the teacher was not there. There were hours spent on sign language classes and practice. Although the home study program was sensitive to Chris's needs and included him in all of the lessons and sign language classes, this was a difficult time for him. We needed to find special time for him, and this is where Chris's dad stepped in. Slowly, tensions began to ease to within manageable limits.

By the time that Ryan was three years old, we felt that he had outgrown the program that had been offered by the State School. It was at this time that we moved him to the County Parent-Infant Program. Ryan and I spent three mornings a week working under the loving guidance and instruction of a very gifted teacher in a program that was individualized for Ryan's special needs. It was fortunate that I was able to be a "stay-at-home-mom" during this very crucial time since a lot of time was required to maximize this early learning for Ryan. The Total Communication program continued and intensive auditory training was added. Ryan began to be able to respond to some sounds, although he could not learn through listening alone. He learned very quickly and I was always eager to follow up with lessons at home. Through this program, our family received the support and encouragement that was so important to us.

Although Ryan mastered all the age-appropriate educational materials and concepts, his speech remained poor. When he was four and a half, we discussed the possibility of adding Cued Speech to his lessons as a tool for working with his speech. It was felt that this would help him to discriminate sounds that looked the same on the lips. He quickly grasped this new idea and we were able to use both methods, depending on the objective that we needed to accomplish. We had no difficulty moving from one method to the other. We found that Cued Speech was especially helpful for the beginning reading that Ryan was doing. It helped him to discriminate among the families of rhyming words that are often found in early reading exercises.

When Ryan was ready for kindergarten, we enrolled him in the Cued Speech program. He was mainstreamed in a regular kindergarten class and received extra resource help. He continued in this program through the second grade. Ryan had the help of an interpreter in all of his classroom activities. We continued to use sign language at home, supplemented by Cued Speech when needed. Toward the middle of the second grade, Ryan began to ask if he could go to the school where sign language was used. Since all the same services would be provided, we felt that this was a reasonable request. Ryan began third grade in the Total Communication program. Now he is able to move easily between Cued Speech and Total Communication. We were especially pleased to have the tool of Cued Speech when we had to practice his spelling words from his Japanese Social Studies unit! In both programs, Ryan has had hearing and deaf friends. Some of his classmates know or are learning to sign. He seems to be very comfortable in this setting.

We feel that we are fortunate to have the advantages of the dual method experience. We generally use Total Communication at home but if we don't know the sign for something, or if we need to help with a difficult pronunciation of a word, we can cue. If our hands are busy with a task, then Ryan is able to lip-read.

At age ten, Ryan is receiving A's and B's in his regular fourth grade class. He reads with a passion and participates in baseball, gymnastics, and scouting in our community. He went to a sleep-over Boy Scout camp this summer with no interpreter and no one who knew sign language or Cued speech. During this past school year, with the encouragement and support of Ryan's speech teacher, he learned to play a trombone. This instrument has only three keys and is dependent on the ear to play. With a lot of visual cues, an interpreter, and a very willing teacher he is developing skills in this area. It is an invaluable tool for practicing his breath control for speech. We feel that there is nothing that he can't accomplish if he sets his sights on the goal.

Even with all of his successes, it is not easy to be a deaf child of hearing parents in a hearing world. But we feel that signing, speech reading, and cueing have all worked together at our house to create the full communication with our son that is vital to our relationship.

If a parent of a hearing impaired infant were to ask for our advice on selecting a method for communication with their child, I wouldn't necessarily recommend doing what we did. All families and children are different. The advice that we could offer would be the following:

- Observe all of the programs available to you at various age levels.
- Trust your own gut feelings.
- Keep an open mind.
- Know that all methods involve hard work and commitment on your part.
- Know that no one method is perfect for all children, all of the time, in all situations.
- Realize that no decision is set "in granite" and choices can be altered as your child's needs change.

Deafness happened to Ryan and to our family. It was and still is a daily factor in our lives. Our family and our marriage have been strengthened by our shared experience. We are, however, always aware of the extra effort that it takes to have a deaf child in the house and we are careful to always plan time for ourselves and for Ryan to be away. As he grows up, he needs us less and less. This is how it should be. We have had two more children since Ryan became deaf and I have started my own business. Ryan has had a good start, and though we are here to support, encourage, and love him—what he becomes will be up to him.

WHERE I AM TODAY

RYAN LONG

I am glad that I have this opportunity to present my life story. It is very difficult to narrate every single experience that I have encountered in my nineteen years of life. However, some highlights from fifth grade to this day will be expressed. I can only hope that people will take the lessons of my experiences and learn from them as I learn from others' experiences.

Education plays a big role in our lives. Sure enough, I was not an exception. In fifth and sixth grade, I attended a public school in our county with a special support program built in it for deaf people like me. My major means of communication were (and still are to this day) Signed English and spoken English. In the classroom environment, what worked out best for me was to use a sign language interpreter. That way, I could better manage the sometimes chaotic atmosphere that the elementary classroom presents. The interpreter was used mainly (and later exclusively) for communicating with the teacher in both lecture and one–on–one situations. I limited the interpreter to communicating with the teacher because I did not feel it was necessary to have a third party present when I talked with my friends and classmates. In addition to this, interpreters were not available on call. Many times I would find or place myself in a situation that demanded that I do without an interpreter. I did not have much of a problem with this since lipreading and my speech sufficed. In that school, I made many friends, both deaf and hearing. We did the normal things kids do during recess, such as play soccer, tag, and talk, sometimes simultaneously. I also made many more friends as I played football. Basically, I was having a good time.

In seventh and eighth grade, I attended the public middle school that had the same support systems in place for deaf students. Again I used a sign language interpreter for my classes but when it came to communicating with hearing kids such as my friends, I preferred to just talk for myself because that was much, much more efficient. I could catch probably 70-80 percent of what most hearing people said. Only with my very best friends and parents did that number actually go near 100 percent. I took the same classes hearing students took: Math, Social Studies, English, Science, etc. I got average grades. Once during the eighth grade, I got on the Honor Roll. Hooray! Sports played an important role as well. Only by looking back on my life, do I realize that it was these middle school years where I found my passion to study warfare and its history. I continued playing football and started playing lacrosse, which I found to be awesome.

Ninth grade did not go by without hitting a few bumps. Most of those bumps occurred before I even became a freshman. I was expected to attend the High School which had a strong deaf support program in it as my previous schools did. But, I decided not to go there. Instead I wanted to go to my neighborhood school. The reason was simple. Many of the friends that I grew up with were going to attend that school. Most were from my neighborhood, some from sports activities, a few from organizations such as the Cub Scouts. At first, people were reluctant to agree with me but with the help of my parents, some staff from the Deaf program, and the neighborhood high school staff, eventually I went to my neighborhood school. The issue with this school was that no deaf person had ever gone there before. It was a new school, only two years old when I enrolled there as a freshman. There were no established interpreter or resource programs to support me there. Nevertheless, I wanted badly to be with my friends. I had an interpreter for my four academic classes (English, Math, History, Science). For my elective classes, I did not use an interpreter. This was not much of a problem since physical education and photography did not use lectures.

I also had a resource person from the deaf program to come in and check up on me to see if anything was wrong. The result was spectacular! I made twenty times more friends. My grades improved. My passion for studying history and war bloomed to include abstract concepts. I felt comfortable playing JV football and lacrosse. To my surprise, I was elected to be the Freshman Homecoming Prince for the Homecoming Football Game. I had a fun time with my old and new friends. However, my experiences at this high school proved to be too good to last.

My Dad got a job in Indianapolis and we had to move. The move was traumatic for my family, as any move would be. But we adapted very well to the changes. One issue that came up was which school I would go to. I had two choices: the Indiana School for the Deaf or my neighborhood high school. Indiana School for the Deaf is a school that is composed of an all-deaf student body. The neighborhood school was a huge school with about 3400 hearing students. A handful of deaf students had attended this school before me but none of them had used an interpreter. I decided to go to my neighborhood school because it was similar to what I had left in Maryland and the challenges were there. Fortunately, interpretative services were available for me to use. At first, I did not have many friends. I made a few friends playing football for the JV team. I was a new guy in an enormous school who was not accustomed to change. Indeed, I only had a few friends, but through them I gradually acquired more.

In the tenth grade, the issue of communication options had pretty much been settled. Interpreters would only be used for academic subjects. In any other situation, I would speak and listen myself simply because that was what worked for me. Education became much more important for me because I realized that through hard work in the classroom, I would get into a better college and wind up with more career options. I decided to take Latin as a foreign language because many people, including myself felt it would help improve my vocabulary. At first, it was hard to grasp the principles behind the Latin system. Eventually it became easier and indeed, it did help me with my vocabulary. During this time, I volunteered at the Children's Museum and participated in a deaf Big-Little Brother program to help younger deaf children.

Eleventh and twelfth grade can be clumped together because so many events that happened are related to each other and have directly led me to where I am now. I stopped playing football and started focusing on academics more. Consequently, eleventh grade was a turning point in my academic life. I discovered what my true passions were. Deeply rooted in my passion for history and war, international politics turned out to be what I wanted to get involved in. In fact, Karl von Clausewitz, an illustrious military philosopher, claims that war is an extension of politics. This awakening occurred when I took a class called “International Relations” which studied the international scene—past, present, and future. We studied America’s foreign relationships. At some point, a spark was lit. I was fascinated with this stuff. As opportunities came to get involved with activities related to international relations and war, I took every one possible. The first one was to join the high school delegation to the regional Model United Nations at the Indiana University-Purdue University of Indianapolis University. I loved the material and found myself practically obsessed by it. A 100 degree fever and some chills did not stop me from participating in the three-day event. In the end, I came out with some new friends and two awards. One was for the Best Written Resolution and the other one was for the Best Individual Delegate. Those are two accomplishments that I am proud of. After that I was nominated to go to Boys State at Indiana State University. I went and had a blast there. That was the end of my junior year.

In my senior year, I was the chairman of the spirit committee of my school. My grades were much better than before. I had taken all of the social studies classes that I could possibly take at my school. Then Model United Nations occurred again, but this time at the University of Chicago, and this one was not regional but National. Schools from all over the nation sent delegations to the Palmer House Hilton in downtown Chicago to participate in this. I had a good time and made many friends, some of whom attend the same college that I do now. Later on in the year, I accidently wound up on the Academic Super Bowl team for history. For fun, I took the test that all Super Bowl candidates are required to take. I expected to do OK because I didn’t study or prepare in any way. To my surprise, I scored second highest and was invited to join the team. I did join and we competed against other regional high schools and did OK.

Then came the big issue of college. Where should I apply? What major? I was sure I’d be majoring in a field that is closely related to international relations, so I looked at colleges that were known for their international relations programs and had sufficient interpreter services. What popped up was Michigan State University, Colorado University at Boulder, and Miami University of Ohio.

In the fall of 1994, I enrolled at Miami, a medium-sized school that had a reputation of providing an education equivalent to an Ivy League school. Established in 1809, the Miami University of Ohio has proven itself to be the place to be, both academically and socially. I am majoring in Diplomacy and Foreign Affairs. There is a chance I may pick up a second major related to the Diplomacy major. I am currently playing lacrosse for the Miami club and plan to play intermural hockey. I am studying and learning life's little tidbits such as using hot water for washing my white clothes. Basically, I want to get a B.A. in both majors and at the same time have fun as a college kid.

Next year, I plan to take classes that will fulfill more requirements for graduation, including studying Chinese. In the far future, I expect to go on to grad school and acquire an M.A. in the foreign sector, probably specializing in East Asia. In fact, this summer I am going to Shanghai in the People's Republic of China for a six-week political economy study program. I'd like to work for the government for a short time and then change jobs and work for a Multinational Corporation . . . where the money and action is. Hopefully, my future job will be related to my passions and I will be able to fully employ the knowledge and wisdom that I have obtained through my experiences in life.

MICHAEL, GENE, & TAMMY

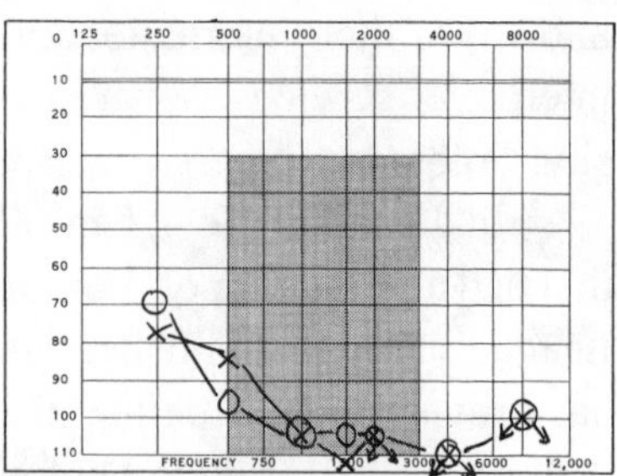

MICHAEL'S AUDIOGRAM

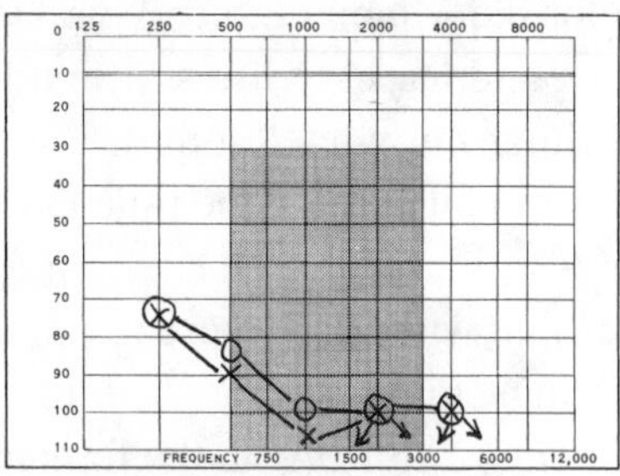

GENE'S AUDIOGRAM

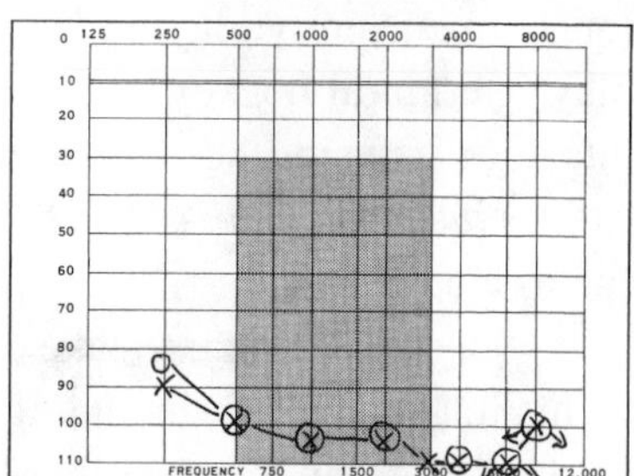

TAMMY'S AUDIOGRAM

TAMMY, GENE, AND MICHAEL'S STORY

JUDY AND GENE MURVIN

We were a very young and happily married couple eagerly waiting for our first child to be born. She certainly took her time because she was two weeks later than we expected. But Tammy was worth waiting for. She was a beautiful and healthy eight-pound baby. All of the grandparents oohed and ahhed as she stole their hearts away. We found many of the days in those early months to be rough because she was a fussy, colicky, and sickly baby. When she was nearly a year old, our mothers began to tell us that they thought something might be wrong with her hearing because she didn't come when she was called and wasn't doing any of the baby talking she was supposed to be doing.

Finally, we talked with our doctor and he sent us to an ear specialist. Because Tammy was so young and wouldn't sit still for the test, he suggested that we take her to an audiological clinic that could test her better. We thought that we would do it just to please our mothers so they would stop thinking there was something wrong with our little girl.

At the testing clinic, we sat in the room with sounds so loud that we couldn't believe that she wasn't turning around. She just kept on playing with the blocks. We didn't know it then but we were both thinking, "This isn't really happening. There is probably something wrong with this place. She's just being stubborn." When the audiologist told us that Tammy had a severe hearing loss, we told her that we thought she was wrong and we wanted a second opinion. She told us about another clinic where we could have her tested again.

As soon as we could, we got an appointment at the new clinic. Again, Tammy sat through sounds loud enough to shake the building. This time we began to see that maybe this was real. We both began to feel guilty, thinking maybe we had done something wrong and maybe we were the ones who were being punished. After all, she was just a little girl. How could this happen to her? This time when the audiologist told us that Tammy had a very severe hearing loss, we listened to what she said. She told us about a program in our County that would work with her even though she was only eighteen months old.

JUDY

This was a very hard time for me because I was pregnant with our second child and I didn't drive. I didn't know how I was going to get Tammy to the school or the clinics for earmolds and hearing aids and all the special things that she needed now. Gene couldn't keep taking off from work or he would lose his job.

GENE

I remember feeling so guilty during this time because I thought it was my fault that the baby had a hearing problem. I had a very bad drinking problem and maybe the drink affected the baby somehow. When I came back from Vietnam, I had a hard time getting a job and the drinking got worse. Now that I finally had a job, I couldn't keep taking time off to take Judy and the baby to all of these appointments. We were really having a rough time.

When we started in the County program, we had problems getting to school all the time. Then the program made arrangements with the Red Cross, and they had a special service that picked us up, took us to school, and brought us back home again. Now we were able to get started helping Tammy. At this time, the program that she was in was Oral-Aural. The teacher worked to help me understand about deafness and to help Tammy with her new hearing aids.

The hearing aids were hard for us to get used to. We felt so sorry that such a little girl had to wear those ugly things. We felt embarrassed for her in public. But we learned in the classes that it was important for her to wear them and we saw that she was learning to listen to some sounds. She didn't seem to be picking up much speech or language, though.

When Tammy was twenty months old, Little Gene was born. We weren't worried about him because we thought it would only be Tammy who had the problem. When he had his first hearing test, he was six months old and he responded as he should. We stopped worrying about him. But the audiologist in the County program said we should keep testing him every six months just to make sure. When we tested him again at one year, his hearing was not normal. We had a second deaf child.

JUDY

I remember thinking, "Well, I guess this is the way it is meant to be. I don't love him any less now that I know that he is deaf." But now I was pregnant again and started wondering about the new baby. Would the third one be deaf also? I guess I felt that it would be okay because I would know what to do.

GENE

When I found out that Little Gene was deaf also, I really got upset. My drinking problem got worse and just to top it all off, I broke my foot and was out of work. Judy was pregnant again, and I thought I just couldn't handle any more. This is really too much.

Little Gene was fitted with his hearing aids, and we did all of the same things with him that we were doing with Tammy. Since he was with me anyway, they both were in the Parent-Infant program. The program was Oral-Aural and they were learning to listen and respond to sounds around them. They were not picking up language or talking very much. I was going to the Parent meetings and was learning about sign language and started thinking about this.

When Little Gene was almost two, Michael was born. Of course we had him tested as soon as we could and he had normal hearing. Now we started to wonder if we would know what to do with a baby who had normal hearing. We wondered how Tammy and Little Gene would feel with a normal hearing brother. Michael was tested again in six months, and his hearing was fine.

By this time, Tammy was ready for preschool. The audiologist talked to me and suggested that maybe she would learn a little faster if she were in the sign language program. She said that if it didn't work out, we could come back into the Oral-Aural program because they had a preschool also. Since I had been learning about sign language in Parent-Infant, I thought maybe we should try it.

We continued to test Michael every six months and when he was two years old, the tests showed that he had a mild to moderate loss. By the time he was four years old, the hearing loss was severe to profound. We now had three deaf kids. How could this be happening to us?

JUDY

I still thought, "Well, I guess this is the way it is meant to be." In a way, it didn't bother me so much because I didn't have to worry about Tammy and Little Gene's feelings now. I knew what to do with deaf children, and now I was learning and using sign language.

GENE

This was really more than I could handle. My drinking only got worse. I was trying to hold down two jobs to pay for the medical bills, hearing aids, batteries, and all of the things the kids needed. I was still feeling guilty and thinking that maybe the kids had hearing problems because of the Agent Orange that I was involved with in Vietnam. So we went to a doctor who could tell us about our genes. He said that he did not think it was because of Agent Orange, but because we each had a recessive gene that was positive for hearing loss. He advised us not to have any more children.

All of the kids were now in the Total Communication program and we were taking sign language classes. They all were wearing their hearing aids and we had learned how to take care of the aids the best that we could so that they were always working. The hearing aids were helping the kids learn how to listen, and they were learning how to talk. The sign language was also helping them learn how to talk. We think if we were starting over, we would probably use sign language earlier than we did.

When we found out that we were going to have another child, we didn't know what to pray for. We weren't sure if we could handle another deaf child, and we didn't know if we would know how to raise a hearing child. Imagine our surprise then when we found out that we were going to have twins. This was probably the worst time in our marriage. We were fighting about these new babies before they were even born.

When Samantha and Jason were born, we really had our hands full. Of course by now, Tammy was seven and she was a big help with the babies. Once again our feelings were confused about their hearing, but we knew that it wasn't anything we could do anything about. Their hearing was tested as early as possible and it was fine for both of them.

Judy

This was the worst part of our married life. We had five kids at home. Gene was still working two jobs to make ends meet. He was still drinking a lot and not coming home after work. I thought maybe that I was going to have a nervous breakdown. A friend of mine told me that I needed to go to church to have some help. So I started going to church and realized that this was the kind of help I needed. I participated as much as I could. I worked with the Sunday School class that Tammy was in so I interpreted for her. I also interpreted as much of the church service as I could.

Gene

I knew that this was a hard time for Judy and I wasn't much help, but I just couldn't take all of the pressure of the jobs and the crying kids without the help of a drink. One night when I was home alone with the kids and I hadn't been drinking at all that day the Pastor of the church came to call on us. It was a cold night and I invited him in. Before I knew it, I was telling him all of our problems and he asked me to pray with him. I did, and I have not had a drink since then. That was more than five years ago. I see now how much help I can be with the kids. I have learned more sign language. I can talk with them and help them learn things. They understand me and mind me when I am taking care of them.

Tammy is in the sixth grade now and is mainstreamed for one-half of the day with an interpreter. She also still spends some of her class time in a special class with other deaf children. With her hearing aids and special speech help, her speech is improving. Her grades in school are fine.

Little Gene is in the fourth grade. He is in a special class with other hearing impaired students and gets very good grades. His speech is improving all of the time. This year he will be mainstreamed for math.

Michael is mainstreamed all day in the second grade with an interpreter and has some resource help from an auditory teacher each day. He also is getting very good grades and enjoys school very much. We think that having sign language earlier has made a big difference in how much language Michael has.

Samantha and Jason will be five years old in November. They have normal hearing and will be going into a regular kindergarten. We are hoping that they will be able to go to the same school as their sister and brothers so they will be able to continue learning sign language and be in a school where there are hearing impaired children. The worries that we had earlier about the feelings of the deaf kids with a hearing brother and sister just do not seem to be a problem. They all get along as well as any other brothers and sisters do. There are the normal amount of fights and the normal amount of playing together. When we look back, we ask, "How could it have been any other way?"

WHERE WE ARE TODAY

TAMMY MURVIN HERRERA
GENE MURVIN
MICHAEL MURVIN

TAMMY

I am the oldest of five children in my family and three of us are deaf. This has made for a very interesting childhood and young adulthood for me. I think I have grown up very quickly. I will tell you about my life since my parents wrote about me in 1987.

At that time, I was just entering middle school and I worked very hard because I dreamed of becoming a lawyer. I was in the school play and won several awards, including one in leadership. I also came in second place in the Optimist Club Oratorical Contest. This was a proud moment for me and my family.

One thing that has never changed in my life is the love and support I received from my parents. When I was in high school, my father was diagnosed with cancer and my life changed drastically. As the oldest child, I had to assume a lot of responsibility for the house and my younger brothers and sister so that my mother could take care of my father. This was a difficult time for me with many questions and lots of anger about the situation. My teachers at school were very supportive of me during this time and I did my best to keep my grades up although I no longer wanted to become a lawyer.

My father and I became very close during his illness and we had a lot of time to be together and talk things over. Still, it was very difficult when he passed away on September 19, 1992. Someday I hope I will understand why he had to get cancer and leave us.

Although I had many responsibilities at home, I was still able to participate in activities at school and outside of school. I joined the Campus Life Youth group, which is a religious and social group of young people. In school, I was a participant in the Montgomery Exceptional Leaders Program, where we went to different elementary schools to tell youngsters about our different challenges that we faced having different handicapping conditions. I was on the volleyball team and was the vice-president and secretary of the Deaf Culture Club. I was very busy between school and home responsibilities.

During Christmas of 1992, my friend, Robert, proposed to me with an engagement ring and we planned to get married after I finished high school. During my senior year, I had a lot of fun going to the Banquet and Prom with Robert. At the same time, I had sad feelings about graduating and leaving high school and a life I had known for so many years. I graduated in June, 1993, and went to a junior college in Rockville, Maryland.

On June 11, 1994, I married Robert and I am still attending the junior college. I am very happy and plan to have children in a few more years.

My life has been full of many experiences and many memories and I will always be glad that I made my mother and father very proud with all that I have accomplished.

GENE

In 1987, I was in elementary school and participated in the patrol squad and the Fabulous Flying Fingers. I got awards for both of these activities. The Fabulous Flying Fingers is a group of deaf and hearing students who sing and sign songs and give performances all around our area. It is led by our school's music teacher and the group has won several awards. It even performed at the White House when President Reagan was the President.

After elementary school, I went to middle school. I participated in many activities there such as the teen club and the yearbook staff. I worked very hard in all of my classes and enjoyed the time that I was in middle school.

When I got to high school, I wanted to play lots of sports but the only team I got on was the wrestling team. Then my Dad got sick with cancer and I had to quit the wrestling team so that I could get a job and help with the family. This was a hard time for me because when my father died, I had to be the man of the house and help everybody else.

It helped me a lot during this time to belong to the Campus Life Youth program because I had understanding people that could help me deal with my father's death.

In my senior year, I participated in some activities at school, but I also had to work to help bring some money into the house. I went to the Senior Banquet and the Prom with one of my long-time deaf friends. I graduated in June, 1994 with a high school diploma.

I was very lucky to win a scholarship award and that helped me to go to college at National Technical Institute for the Deaf in Rochester, NY. I did not stay in college for very long because I needed to come home and help the family by getting a job. I work as a shift manager at a pizza shop and am now planning to take more classes to learn how to be a good shift manager.

I am thankful to my parents for helping me get a good education and for always giving me love and support.

MICHAEL

Since I was little, I have always enjoyed performing. I have been in many plays and joined a group in elementary school called the Fabulous Flying Fingers where we sang songs in sign language. I just loved performing in all of the shows.

While I was in elementary school, I was in puppy love with a girl and then I liked a lot of girls. By the time I got to middle school, I had a serious relationship with one girl and we went out on dates. This was a fun time.

In middle school, we wrote speeches for the Optimist Club Oratorical Contest. The first year that I tried, I was really nervous and didn't get picked as a finalist. But the next year, I practiced harder and tried to win. I was picked as a finalist and was able to present my speech at the contest. I won second place and got a silver medal and a $200 bond. I was so happy and excited. After the contest, my parents took me out for dinner.

One thing I am not very good at is math. When I was in seventh grade, I had to go to summer school because I failed math during the school year. In summer school, I worked hard and got an A so was able to go on to eighth grade.

After eighth grade, I went to high school and had a very exciting year. A deaf teacher came to our school and taught us how to perform in plays. I went to the tryouts and made it! I was so excited!! When we had a matinee performance, I was in the play but by the evening performance I was sick and couldn't make it to the performance. I was very disappointed! Later we did the same play at a school in Virginia and I was able to perform.

For two years since my father passed away, I have not been in any performances because it has been too hard for me to do. I feel bad about my father's death and I have to work to help with the family so I have no time for performances.

During the summer, I went to a program that showed me how different jobs are, and since then I have had jobs as a stock boy, cashier, and sales associate in a clothing store.

In 1995, I am a senior in high school and am looking forward to graduation. After graduation, I want to go to Gallaudet University for four years and study acting and then go to California and become a movie star! All of my experiences since childhood have made me sure that I want to be a movie star.

9

A Cultural Identity: Peace & Grace in Being What You Are

Jack R. Gannon, Ph.D.

As a young boy I would often stop by the barbershop on the corner of the Square in the small southern Missouri town where I grew up to visit Willie. Willie was a tall, skinny, elderly black man. He had salt-and-pepper fuzzy hair, gold-capped teeth, and a broad, happy smile. He was the bootblack in the barbershop and, like me, he was deaf. That formed a common bond between the two of us.

Willie considered himself a businessman—which he was—and he was very proud of his shoeshine business. He always wore a tie and suit to work. The way he dressed was important to him because it reflected how he felt about himself and his work. That was one of the first lessons I learned from him: be proud of the work you do.

Willie had received very little education during his youth and he was quite illiterate. While our conversations were not always enlightening or stimulating, I liked to visit Willie because we were able to carry on a relaxing, easy to understand, and stress-free conversation in sign language.

The sign language Willie and I used once traced its recorded history back to Spain around the sixteenth century where some historians credit its origin to a group of Spanish monks who had taken a vow of silence. In order to communicate their basic needs, the account went, they had developed a sign system. Later this sign system found its way to France, where it was used to teach deaf children at the world's first free school for deaf children in Paris. The National Royal Institution for the Deaf was founded sometime between 1755 and 1760 and still exists today as the St. Jacques School. It was this school that gave America Laurent Clerc, our first deaf teacher, and laid the foundation for education of deaf children in our country.

Today's linguists, however, believe there is a strong possibility that sign originated simultaneously with the spoken word if it did not come before. Many of us Deaf people now believe that wherever there is a group of deaf people, sign language will evolve naturally, as it is a natural language. Sign language most likely existed among deaf people in America from the earliest times. A good book on this subject is Nora Ellen Groce's book, *Everyone Here Spoke Sign Language: Hereditary Deafness on Martha's Vineyard.*

The world in which we live today is a very diverse one. America, which long prided itself as a melting pot, is now coming to recognize the strengths of its diversity. No matter who we are, where we live, what we do, or which language we use, each of us is part of that diversity and has an identity. Some of these identities are reflected by the language we use, the customs and traditions we observe, how we dress, the way we cut—or don't cut—our hair. These identities are important to us because they tell the world—and ourselves—that we are somebody.

To appreciate Deaf Culture it helps to understand what deaf people need to do in order to cope with a world of sound. As deaf persons, we are family members, neighbors, co-workers, friends; yet because of our deafness in many ways we come across as "foreigners" in the "hearing world."

The degree of hearing among deaf people—if there is any—varies from individual to individual. As for many other profoundly deaf persons, sound has no value to my wife or me. Those of us born deaf or deafened early in childhood learn about or are re-introduced to sound at different stages throughout our lives, often under embarrassing encounters. We learn or are reminded, for instance, that we make noises which sometimes irritate hearing people. We burp (excuse me) and our bodies make different kinds of noises. We shuffle our feet when we walk, make strange, throaty sounds when we use our voices, and some of us, I am told, laugh "funny." Some of us even make noise the way we breathe, or when we pick up a piece of paper. These are some of the lessons we should have learned in Deaf Kindergarten!

In order to function "normally," we deaf people must be very observant. For example, early in the morning many hearing passersby will greet us pleasantly with a cheerful "good morning." Unless we pay close attention and watch their lips and faces we won't be aware they greeted us and by not acknowledging their greeting with a smile or a nod of the head or a good morning of our own, we will appear to be rude, cold, uncaring, or a snob.

At the airport we must always be on visual alert and pay attention and not only keep an eye on the clock, but watch the information board and the behavior of other travellers, because should our flight be re-routed, delayed, or moved to another gate, the ticket agent who makes the vocal announcement will most likely have forgotten we are deaf. On the plane we inform the airline host or hostess we are deaf and two minutes later he/she is back to ask if we would like to use the headsets to listen to a movie or the radio.

Out of courtesy we inform our seatmate we are deaf and the first question we always get is, "Can you lipread?" When we shake our head (sometimes on purpose!) a look of panic usually streaks across his or her face. Too often the burden of carrying on a successful conversation with a hearing person is almost always placed on the deaf person.

Those of us who successfully develop or retain our speech skills spend a lifetime trying to figure out our quirky national language,

English, one of the world's most confusing spoken and written languages. We attempt to pronounce sounds we have never heard and have no idea how they come out until we read the answers on the listener's face or by his/her behavior.

Receiving information by reading lips for most of us is seldom quick, easy, or reliable. At the very best, only a small percentage of the spoken words or sounds appear on the lips. McCay Vernon and Jean Andrews estimate it to be around one-third of the spoken words (1990). That plus the shape of the speaker's mouth and teeth and their facial expressions and how they pronounce words, all contribute to make lipreading difficult and challenging. Family members, hearing friends, and strangers quite often assume we deaf people are following what is being spoken because of the way we react and nod our heads and not let on. After years and years of frustration trying to lipread a spoken conversation, many of us have more or less given up and developed a skill at "hoodwinking" hearing people into believing we are following what they are saying, when, in truth, we don't understand what is being said or, at best, are only getting bits and pieces.

While hearing children grow up learning the proper usage of the English language and effortlessly hearing the spoken word, many deaf children grow up learning and using *two* separate and different languages simultaneously—American Sign Language and English. Then some of us wonder why deaf kids have such a difficult time mastering English. That's where the "bilingual" concept that we are hearing more and more about these days enters the picture. There are a growing number of schools that believe that teaching deaf children English should first begin with their native and natural language, American Sign Language.

If learning/using two languages was not enough, the subject of speech is added as another communication mode. Speech is a funny game. More deaf people have speech skills than many hearing people realize, but may choose for one reason or another not to use them or to use them only sparingly. As speakers, we deaf people spend our lives stumbling over words that are spelled one way and pronounced another, often to the confusion or amusement of our listeners. We must constantly remind ourselves, for example, that a word like antique, is pronounced "an-*têk*" not "an-*ti-que*," the way it is written, and that the international automobile race is "Grand-*pre*" <u>NOT</u> "Grand *Prix*." And, personally, I try very hard to remember not to use my infamous "sh-" lisp when inviting people to sit.

In spite of all this, some deaf people are very successful in developing or retaining the use of their voices. Some become such skilled lipreaders you wonder if they can actually hear. Others master English and become great writers and, yes, we have some very beautiful poetry written by deaf poets!

This background information may help the reader better understand what follows.

The inability to hear makes us deaf people a visually oriented people. We "listen" with our eyes, as we are visual communicators. How much information we receive visually determines to what extent and whether or not we are part of the world of sound around us.

Today that sign language which Willie and I used in the barbershop long ago and which critics have tried to discredit as "just a collection of wild gestures" has earned respect as a legitimate, national language. American Sign Language (ASL), as its name indicates, is the sign language used in America. Today ASL is a recognized, legitimate and ranking national language in the United States used by Deaf Americans, their families, friends, co-workers, neighbors.

ASL has its own grammar, structure, and unique expressions. One of those popular expressions, "Pah!" (a word mouthed while signing, "finally," "at last," or "success") captured people's attention, as did the "Deaf applause" gesture (waving hands above the head for visual impact instead of clapping them for sound) during the Deaf President Now protest at Gallaudet University in 1988.

There are other sign languages throughout the world—French Sign Language, German Sign Language, Chinese Sign Language, etc. And, no, sign language is not the same everywhere. Every nation has its own form of sign language. Deaf signers can in most cases, however, strike up a conversation with a deaf foreigner quicker in sign language than can the speakers of two different spoken languages.

Those individuals who take the time to learn ASL will discover a rich, beautiful, and expressive language. It is an effective form of communication and it is the roots of a unique culture in which many of us live, thrive, and make positive contributions to the larger society in which we live.

As a group, we d/Deaf[1] people may have some unusual traits in the eyes of hearing beholders who do not know or understand us and our needs. We are a touching/contact group of people. Tapping each other on the shoulder or touching one another is as natural to us as calling a person's name is to hearing people. That is the way we get each other's attention. (Wouldn't *we* know that it doesn't make any sense to yell to get a deaf person's attention?!) We wave our hands, blink the lights, pound on the table, stomp our feet on the floor to get each other's attention. Hugging one another is another cultural element. We think nothing of hugging a person we've just met if we like the individual. While it may seem a bit strange, we seldom address each other by first names.

Our facial expressions and our body language represent our "voice volume" and "tone" and visually communicate our emotions as well as hearing people do by voice.

Technology is also opening up our world. The national telephone relay system, television and movie film captioning, the computer, and professional interpreters are making the hearing world more accessible to us and changing our lives.

We have our share of success stories. Success stories are important to all of us because they tell us that deafness need not stop us from pursing our dreams. A few examples:

During President George Bush's administration, he appointed Dr. Robert R. Davila Assistant Secretary of the Office of Special Education and Rehabilitative Services, the highest position in the

---

1. The use of the small "d" in "deaf" identifies deaf people in general from an audiological perspective. The use of the big "D" as in "Deaf" identifies those individuals who consider themselves culturally deaf. *Deaf in America: Voices from a Culture* by Carol Padden and Tom Humphries explains the composition and culture of the Deaf Community. This is the book that gave us the big "D" identity. Another good book on the subject is *American Deaf Culture: An Anthropology*, which is a collection of articles by Deaf and hearing writers.

federal government ever held by a Deaf person. And, the reigning Miss America, Heather Whitestone, is deaf, and Kenny Walker, the deaf All-American football player at the University of Nebraska, went on to play for the Denver Broncos professional football team.

In the summer of 1995 a poet's park was dedicated in Glyndon, Minnesota, to the memory of Laura Searing, a Deaf journalist and poet. The park honors a graduate of the Missouri School for the Deaf who was a newspaper reporter, author, and poet. She wrote under the pen name of Howard Glyndon, for whom the town is named. Her biographer, Judy Yeager Jones, believes Searing was the first woman writer in the United States to be so honored by having a community named for her during her lifetime.

1994 saw the publication of the book, *Douglas Tilden: The Man and His Legacy,* by Mildred Albronda. It is one of the most beautiful books my wife and I have ever come across about a Deaf artist. Tilden (1860-1935) earned the distinction of being called the "Father of Sculpture on the West Coast."

Our history, likewise, is very important to us. Knowledge about our history has grown drastically in recent years and has become such an important area of interest that there are a growing number of national Deaf history organizations and an international organization, Deaf History International, was established in Hamburg, Germany in the fall of 1994. This world organization is devoted to research, preservation, and dissemination of historical information about d/Deaf people.

In Faribault, Minnesota, three private residences and one commercial building designed by Deaf architect Olof Hanson are listed in the national registry of historic places. Hanson, incidentally, is the architect of one of the buildings on the Gallaudet University campus.

How many of us know that Deaf people claim credit for the football huddle, which Paul Hubbard started using at Gallaudet in the 1890s? And that the baseball hand count originated with William "Dummy" Hoy, one of our Deaf professional baseball players?

How many of us are aware that at least twenty-five schools for deaf children in the United States were started by deaf persons, or that Andrew Foster, the first Black Deaf person to graduate from

Gallaudet University, founded more than twenty-two schools for deaf children in West Africa? Or, that Thomas Marr, another prominent Deaf architect, designed, among other things, the plant of the Tennessee School for the Deaf and the state Supreme Court building? Or, that Cadwallader Washburn, for whom Gallaudet's industrial arts building is named, was an internationally recognized dry point etcher? The Washburn building, incidentally, is just one of over a hundred permanent structures and memorials recognizing the significant contributions of d/Deaf persons throughout America.

As we make note of the accomplishments of d/Deaf people in America, we note that Glenn Shelton, a Deaf man in Tennessee, was recently elected to his eighth term as a constable. There are a growing number of deaf persons with earned doctorates (in 1970 there were only 22 on record). Today there are approximately two dozen superintendents of schools for the deaf who are either d/Deaf or hard of hearing themselves, and a few years ago, state special education programs in Hawaii and North Carolina were led by Deaf administrators.

We are seeing more books, videotapes, television ads, and episodes with deaf characters and more plays written by and about deaf people than we have ever had. There are even a growing number of small community theaters of the deaf and in 1987 McGraw-Hill, Inc., published a three-volume *Gallaudet Encyclopedia of Deaf People and Deafness.*

Throughout the United States we find clubs and organizations devoted to the interests of d/Deaf people.[2] Nearly every state has a state association of the deaf and most of these organizations are affiliated with the National Association of the Deaf, a voluntary, national membership organization founded in 1880.

The National Association of the Deaf is one of 112 members of the World Federation of the Deaf, which was established in Rome in 1951. The WFD is an international organization recognized by the United Nations and supported by membership dues, contribu-

---

2. The National Information Center on Deafness (NICD) at Gallaudet University (800 Florida Avenue, N.E., Washington, DC 20002) published a directory of such clubs and organizations in the United States a few years ago.

tions, and government grants. The WFD and its national members are committed to advocating for the rights and improving educational, employment, and social opportunities for deaf people worldwide. If it were not for these organizations, deaf people in the United States and throughout the world would not have many of the benefits and opportunities we enjoy today.

The "Deaf President Now" protest which took place at Gallaudet University in the spring of 1988 and captured the world's attention went far beyond just giving Gallaudet University its first deaf president and a 51 percent deaf majority on its Board of Trustees. It provided the push that led to the passage of landmark legislation, the Americans with Disabilities Act, that is benefitting some 49 million Americans. DPN opened the eyes of much of the world to deaf people and deafness. The protest, in all likelihood, was the world's largest sign language class, as countless television viewers learned those three signs of the students' signed chant, "Deaf President Now! Deaf President Now!" shown repeatedly on television.

Today at Gallaudet University, our current president, chief academic vice president, the vice president of Pre-College Programs, and two deans are deaf. The current chairman of the Board of Trustees holds the distinction of being one of the first Deaf African Americans to earn a doctorate.

This awareness has been crucial to the forward movement of deaf people. I remember as a youth trying to persuade my mother to get the local newspaper to do a story about my deafness so everyone would know I was deaf and *stop talking to me behind my back!* It didn't actually happen, but the concept of creating more awareness about deafness was good and what DPN did and all the Deaf Awareness programs around the nation are doing keeps this awareness current. As more people better understand deafness, the communication barriers that isolate us are further reduced and we are better able to become more a part of and contribute to the society in which we live.

What does this historical information and all these success stories tell us and young deaf children? They tell us that it is alright to be deaf. That if young deaf people have the ambition, the foresight, and the desire, they too can become whatever they want to be. This is a knowledge, a heritage, and a culture we pass on to them.

That's why Deaf people do not see the term "hearing impaired" as describing us correctly because we do not see ourselves as "broken." Ours is a communication barrier that can be overcome with awareness, sensitivity, and the necessary tools. Reduce or remove that communication barrier and we are no different than anyone else.

A cultural identity is knowing who we are and how we see and feel about ourselves. It is an attitude "thing" that has a tremendous impact on our lives. Any person with a disability has the choice of spending a lifetime dwelling on the negativity of that disability or accepting it as a challenge to overcome. Those of us who have accepted our deafness see it more as a challenge and are determined not to let it hold us back. Deaf people have the choice of shunning Deaf Culture and being only a member of the hearing world to the fullest extent it is possible for a deaf person to be. We have the choice of not being a member of either world. And we have the choice of being a member of both—which most of us are. As individuals, we can embrace Deaf Culture, become part of it, share its richness, be proud of the accomplishments of d/Deaf people. The choice is ours and ours alone. Parents, teachers, professionals, friends can advise or tell us what to do, but in the end, we deaf people must make the decision. Our lives are ours. Those decisions must be ours. Accepting one's identity as a deaf or Deaf or hard of hearing person, learning about, becoming involved in and contributing to the richness of Deaf Culture is one of the choices.

The words from a poem by Dr. Mervin D. Garretson, a Gallaudet colleague and close friend, now retired, ring especially true here. These lines are excerpted from the poem, "Words from a deaf child," which is also the title of his collection of poetry:

> *"LET ME CHOOSE IF I WILL*
> *TO BE DIFFERENT FROM THE MASS*
> *LEARN THAT THERE IS BEAUTY IN A SINGLE STAR*
> *PEACE AND GRACE IN BEING WHAT YOU ARE."*

Effective communication within any family—whether or not that family has a deaf member—is crucial to the success of the family as a whole. We all know that. With a deaf member it is even more critical that effective communication take place, because it will have an impact on the future of that deaf individual, on his/her education, information input, knowledge, social awareness, development, and ties to the family. Effective communication within the family will determine whether or not the deaf member is truly a member of the family or just an observer hanging on to the fringes or, worse still, isolated from his/her own family.

Today there are few excuses for family members not to learn American Sign Language. There are sign language classes almost everywhere. There are more books and videotapes on the subject than there have ever been. ASL can now even be learned by CD-ROM on a personal computer.[3]

One day, in the barbershop on the Square, I complained to my friend, Willie, about my deafness and the frustrations of being deaf. Willie listened with a look of surprise on his face. Then, he slowly stood up, got down from his high shoeshine chair, and came over to where I sat. He slowly shook his head sideways, crooked his left arm and rested his closed fist on his hip, and with his other hand pointed and shook his long, bony finger at me in an admonishing, scolding manner. "You," he pointed at me, and signed: "Proud yourself always!"

It may seem a bit strange considering all the many wonderful deaf and hearing teachers I have had, but that advice I got from my illiterate, deaf bootblack friend turned out to be one of the best pieces of advice I have ever received.

---

3. For information on American Sign Language classes in your area contact your local library, local community college or adult education program, or the American Sign Language Teachers' Association. Another source is the National Information Center on Deafness at Gallaudet University.

References

Garretson, Merv. (1993) *Words from a Deaf Child*. Bethany Beach: Fragonard Press (P.O. Box 398, Cotton Patch Hills, Bethany Beach, Delaware).

Groce, Nora Ellen. (1985) *Everyone Here Spoke Sign Language: Hereditary Deafness on Martha's Vineyard*. Cambridge, MA: Harvard University Press.

Padden, Carol and Tom Humphries. (1988) *Deaf in America: Voices from a Culture*. Cambridge, MA: Harvard University Press.

Van Cleve, John, ed. (1987) *Gallaudet Deaf Encyclopedia of Deaf People and Deafness*. New York: McGraw-Hill, Inc.

Vernon, McCay and Jean F. Andrews. (1990) *The Psychology of Deafness: Understanding Deaf and Hard-of-Hearing People*. New York: Longman.

Wilcox, Sherman, ed. (1989) *American Deaf Culture: An Anthology*. Burtonsville, MD: Linstok Press.

A Communication Fairy Tale

Sue Schwartz, Ph.D.

Once, a very long time ago in the Forest of Language, there lived two communication tribes: the Oralists and the Manualists. They lived at opposite ends of the forest, usually at peace and content with their lives. Every so often one member would wander too far into the center of the forest and would be snatched away by the other tribe, but that didn't happen very often. By and large each tribe stayed in its own corner of the forest, happily procreating its own members and cultivating its own tribe pride.

Many generations later, a new tribe wandered into the Language Forest and occupied one of the unused corners. They sent out scouts to each of the other tribes to see what was going on. Both groups came back very enthusiastic about what they saw in the corners they visited. The new tribe took some of what each of the others were doing and made a new system and called it Cued Speech.

As the young children of each tribe grew, they ventured further and further into the center of the forest to explore and play. Gradually members of each tribe began to meet. Of course, the first obstacle to overcome was communication. Being children, and therefore somewhat naive and innocent, this posed no problem at all. They played and talked and cued and signed to one another. The children frolicked in the Language Forest, grew older, and, naturally, in the course of time, fell in love.

There was still one unoccupied corner of the Forest and there arose a great debate as to how and when they should occupy this last corner. Being young, idealistic, and full of hope for the future, they decided: Why should we hide in our corner, never to visit our brothers, sisters, and parents in the other three corners? Why should we limit our vision to such a small space of this beautiful and vast Forest of Language? Let's join together with all of our families and live peacefully together throughout the Forest. In that way, we can share and give the best of what we each have.

And so they did. They drew a circle of love and peace which enclosed them all and lived happily ever after in the spacious Forest of Language.

Contributors

Elaine Aiello, deaf since birth, is a graduate of Gallaudet University and also holds a Master's in Deaf Education from Western Maryland College. She has two married daughters, Stephanie and Ingrid. Elaine is teaching American Sign Language at Eleanor Roosevelt High School in Prince Georges County, MD. In the evenings she teaches ASL at the University of Maryland and Montgomery College. In 1995, she received a community service award for her work in teaching sign language and Deaf culture to high school students.

Andy and Linda Balderson are the parents of three children. Both are graduates of Michigan State University. Andy, a landscape architect, is a principal in a private landscape architectural firm in Gaithersburg, MD. Linda holds a Master's degree in Deaf Education and has worked in the Montgomery County Public Schools Program for Students Who are Deaf and Hard of Hearing since 1978. She coordinates interpreters and transliterators who work in the program.

Barbara A. Bodner–Johnson received a bachelor's degree from Creighton University, a Master's degree in Education of the Deaf from the University of Iowa, and a Ph.D. in Instructional Design, Development and Evaluation from Syracuse University in 1973. She has received numerous awards and grants to further work in the area of deaf education. She has written many articles about early intervention with the deaf, teacher training needs, and family needs regarding their deaf child. She has traveled extensively, giving presentations on many aspects of deafness. Her most recent travel was to the International Congress on Education of the Deaf in Tel Aviv, Israel. She is currently the Chair of the Department of Education at Gallaudet University, as well as Professor in the same department.

AUDREY BYRNE is a stay–at–home mom of four children. She actively volunteers with the local Parents of Twins and Triplets Club. She has worked in the field of supporting families of children with disabilities and her previous volunteer positions include: board member of the American Society for Deaf Children, President of Deaf Children's Society of British Columbia, and member of the Special Needs Daycare Committee lobbying for change on behalf of preschool Deaf children.

LEWIS AND DEBBIE COHN are the parents of three children. Lewis is a graduate of the University of Maryland and attended law school. He is the president of Automobile Dealerships. Debbie attended college in Boston and is presently a homemaker.

KATHRYN S. COPMANN received her Master's degree in Audiology and her Ph.D. in Special Education with emphases in Education of the Deaf and Hard of Hearing and Audiology from Kent State University. Dr. Copmann is currently the Director of Audiology and an Assistant Professor in the Department of Speech-Language Pathology and Audiology at Loyola College in Baltimore, MD. Prior to accepting this position, she taught deaf and hard of hearing children in the Howard County Public School System in Maryland.

SHEILA DOCTORS is the Supervisor of a nationally recognized public school program for over three hundred deaf and hard of hearing students, birth through high school graduation. She has been a teacher of deaf, hard of hearing, and hearing students in a variety of school settings in Maryland and New York. She is the co-founder of the Maryland State Steering Committee for Programs for the Hearing Impaired. She is the recipient of the Outstanding Administrator/

Supervisor Award from the Convention of American Instructors of the Deaf. In addition, she is a member of the congressionally mandated National Advisory Panel on Education of the Deaf, advising Dr. I. King Jordan, President, Gallaudet University.

Stephen Epstein, M.D., F.A.C.S., hearing impaired since birth, is an ear, nose and throat specialist and a Fellow of the American Academy of Otolaryngology - Head and Neck Surgery and the American College of Surgeons. Dr. Epstein is an Associate Clinical Professor of Otolaryngology - Head and Neck Surgery and Pediatrics at George Washington University School of Medicine. Dr. Epstein's area of expertise is in the diagnosis and management of hearing loss, especially in children. He is in private practice in Wheaton and Rockville, MD.

Warren Estabrooks, B.A., M.Ed., Dipl. Education of the Deaf, Certified Auditory Verbal Therapist, is the Clinical Director of the Auditory Verbal Therapy Programme at North York General Hospital in Toronto, Ontario, Canada. He is a Charter Director of the Board of Auditory Verbal International, Inc. In addition, he is on the advisory staff of several universities and has lectured internationally about the Auditory Verbal approach. He has received several awards in connection with his work with students who are deaf. Mr. Estabrooks is the author of *Auditory Verbal Therapy for Parents and Professionals* (1994) and co-author of *Do You Hear That?* (1992), *Hear and Listen! Talk and Sing!* (1994), and *The ABCs of AVT* (1995).

Carin and Paul Feldman are the parents of two teenagers, Shane and Mimi. Carin is the Supervisor of the Speech and Language Department at a local hospital in Rockville, MD. She has worked with deaf children and adults in the areas of speech, language, and auditory training. Paul is a physician specializing in adult and adolescent gynecology and infertility. He has published numerous articles related to adolescent health and infertility primarily for the consumer. He enjoys outdoor sports.

HARRIET SUSAN AND ODED FRIED are busy and proud parents of four children. Golda is working on her Master's degree in creative writing. Ari is working on his bachelor of science degree in physiology. Shawn is finishing high school and Sol has just begun seventh grade. Harriet Susan is a registered nurse and Oded is a family physician. They live in Toronto, Ontario, Canada.

BOB AND SHERYL FORREST live on a farm near Hensall in rural Southwestern Ontario, Canada. Bob is an agrologist and Sheryl is a dietician. They are proud parents of Kim, age 14, Ben, age 13, and Kathryn, age 5.

LAURENE E. GALLIMORE is a graduate of the Indiana School for the Deaf. She received a bachelor's degree in Elementary Education from the University of Nebraska, a Master's in Deaf Education from Western Maryland College, and is currently a Ph.D. candidate at the University of Arizona. She was the Assistant Superintendent of Education of the Indiana School for the Deaf, where she was instrumental in the movement to convert the program to a bilingual-bicultural model. An acknowledged expert on the topic of using American Sign Language as the language of instruction for children who are deaf, she is currently an Assistant Professor at the Western Oregon State College in teacher preparation in Deaf Education.

JACK R. GANNON, deaf since the age of eight, was educated at the Missouri School for the Deaf and at Gallaudet University. He and his wife, Rosalyn, who is a graduate of the North Carolina School for the Deaf and Gallaudet University, are former teachers. They are the parents of two hearing children. Dr. Gannon is the Special Assistant to the President for Advocacy at Gallaudet University. He has traveled and spoken widely on the subject of Deaf Culture. He is the author of *Deaf Heritage: A Narrative History of Deaf America* and *The Week the World Heard Gallaudet.*

JANICE GATTY received her Bachelor's degree from Mills College, two Master's degrees in Deaf Education from Smith College, and her

Doctorate in Education from the University of Massachusetts in 1990. She has written extensively about early intervention using the oral approach and has lectured internationally in Australia, Japan, and Taiwan. She is currently the Director of the Comprehensive Education Evaluation and Cochlear Implant Assessment Program, as well as the Director of the Preschool Center for Evaluation and Early Intervention at the Clarke School for the Deaf in Northampton, Massachusetts.

LOIS HUROWITZ is the mother of three young adults. She has a Master's degree in Deaf Education and is a Master teacher in a therapeutic school for emotionally disturbed and learning disabled youngsters in an inner city school system.

SHIRLEY AND JULIAN KELLER live in Thornhill, Ontario, Canada, and are the parents of three children: Jeremy, Josh, and Dara. Shirley is a pharmacist and Julian is a lawyer. Both have been involved in volunteer work for a variety of causes and they enjoy going on summer holidays and ski vacations with their children.

ELIZABETH L. KIPILA received a Master's of Linguistics of American Sign Language degree from Gallaudet University in 1984. She learned both cueing and signing in 1972 and later served as the Coordinator of the Cued Speech Team at Gallaudet University from 1985-1995. Ms. Kipila is certified as both a Cued Speech Instructor and a Cued Speech Transliterator, and is currently working as a freelance Cued Speech Transliterator and a Sign Language Interpreter.

JOHN AND MARTHA LONG reside in Indianapolis, Indiana, where John manages a television station and Martha works in an Early Childhood Program in their church. Their oldest son, Chris, will graduate from college in May of 1996. Twins Justin and Rob are in high school and Ryan is in college at Miami University of Ohio. Ryan continues to be a great source of pleasure and inspiration for us all.

JACQUELINE Z. MENDELSOHN is the parent of Aaron and Josh. She is a psychotherapist with a general private practice in Santa Fe and Los Alamos, NM. Formerly the Executive Director of the American Society for Deaf Children (ASDC), she continues to work with families of disabled children and remains actively involved with issues affecting deaf individuals and their families.

JUDY AND THE LATE GENE MURVIN are the parents of five children. The three oldest, Tammy, Gene, and Michael, are deaf. The twins, Samantha and Jason, are hearing. Judy works for the Giant Food Corporation in Maryland.

ADRIAN AND THE LATE LULA NELSON are the parents of two children. Adrian II is married and practicing law in Silver Spring, MD. Kellye received her bachelor's degree from Spelman College and will receive a master's degree in Public Health from the University of Michigan in the spring of 1996. Adrian, Sr. works for the International Monetary Fund in Washington, DC.

GLENN PRANSKY, M.D., works as a physician and teacher at the University of Massachusetts Medical School. His research focuses on the relationship between health and ability to work, and health care for persons with disabilities. He is on the Board of Directors of The Learning Center for Deaf Children, in Framingham, MA. **TERRY SNYDER, M.A.**, is an engineer and consultant. They have two children, Jackie and Lena (who is hearing), and live in Sudbury, MA.

JOHN AND SALLIE PRIDE are both originally from Ohio and have lived in Silver Spring, MD, for the past 25 years. They are parents of four children, Jackie, Curt, Christie, and Leonda. John is the Deputy Executive Director of the President's Committee on Mental Retardation. Sallie is a registered nurse and is currently a homemaker involved in many community activities.

BARBARA RAIMONDO, J.D., is on the board of directors of the American Society for Deaf Children and is legislative consultant to the Consumer Action Network, a coalition of national organizations of, by, and for deaf and hard of hearing Americans. Her husband, Dennis Kirschbaum, executive director of a national professional organization, helped establish the *Simon Tov* program, a Jewish education program for deaf children taught in ASL at Tifereth Israel Congregation in Washington, D.C.

SYDNEY AND LUCILLE RATTNER are the parents of two sons. Lucille is co-founder and past president of the Montgomery County (Maryland) Association for Hearing Impaired Children. She was instrumental in founding and organizing the MCAHIC library as a resource for parents and professionals interested in deafness. She is recently retired from the McKeldin Library at the University of Maryland. Sydney served as the first president of MCAHIC and has retired as an engineer at the Harry Diamond Laboratories.

SARINA ROFFÉ is the mother of three children, the oldest of whom is deaf. She is the founder of the newly established Cued Speech Center in Brooklyn, New York. The center will hold its first CueCamp in the summer of 1996. She received a Bachelor's degree in Journalism, which has resulted in a variety of writing and editing career opportunities. She has worked as a Cued Speech Transliterator and currently is employed by the New York City Department of Juvenile Justice. In this position, she directs all public information for the agency. She has spoken widely on the use of Cued Speech and has received several community awards for her contributions.

ARIELLA AND JULES SAMSON live in Toronto, Ontario, Canada, and are the parents of three children. Jonathan is a graduate of the University of Western Ontario and is working in the financial industry. Noam is studying mechanical engineering and Alana is a senior in high school. Ariella is a lecturer, teacher, and writer. She co-authored *Learning to Listen* and authored *A Letter from My Father.* Since Jonathan's diagnosis, she has worked in hearing health care with geriatric and pediatric patients, and is completing her studies in oral interpreting.

BARBARA WILLIAMS–SCOTT has a Master's Degree in Deaf Education. She taught deaf children in Oral and Cued Speech classes for eight years in a public school setting. In 1984, Ms. Williams-Scott became a Cued Speech Instructor and Materials Specialist with the Cued Speech Team in the Department of Audiology and Speech-Language Pathology at Gallaudet University, where she also edited the *Cued Speech News.* She coordinated the summer Cued Speech Transliterator Training Program, which she initiated. Currently she is a full-time mother of two, teaches Cued Speech Adult classes, and does some private consultant work.

SUSAN WOODRUFF has a Bachelor's degree from State University of New York at Albany, a Master's degree from Western Maryland College, and has done postgraduate work at Hood College, Clarke School for the Deaf, and the University of Maryland. She has worked for more than twenty years in the field of deafness. She has taught children from preschool to high school. She has been an educational interpreter for the last eight years.

APPENDIX A

SYSTEMS OF MANUAL COMMUNICATION

Many of the educational options described in this book use some system of manual communication (signing). This appendix provides a brief overview of the systems of manual communication most commonly found in the United States. (Every country has its own sign language system, although many of the sign systems of different countries have similar components.)

AMERICAN SIGN LANGUAGE (ASL)

American Sign Language (ASL) is used by many members of the Deaf community. It is a visual language, not a spoken language. One or both hands are used to make signs, and meaning depends on visual components such as shape of the hands, the space in which the sign is displayed, orientation of the hand when signing, and the movement of the hands. Because ASL is a visual language, ASL users do not use speech and amplification is discouraged.

ASL is a language distinct from English. Therefore, it has its own grammar and syntax (rules for arranging words to form meaningful sentences and phrases). In ASL, words are not represented in

English word order. Just as English has rules for which part of speech goes where in the sentence, so does ASL. Generally, "ASL tends to set the stage, put in the characters, and then describe the action" (Jensema, 1996).

Like all living languages, ASL is continually evolving. New signs representing new vocabulary are added, while outdated signs fall by the wayside. This makes it possible to express anything in ASL that can be expressed in English.

Manually Coded English (MCE)

As the name implies, the purpose of Manually Coded English (MCE) systems is to "translate" spoken English into manual signs. That is, these systems are not distinct languages as ASL is. Instead, the signs for words are presented in the same order as in English, and invented signs are used in some systems to convey tenses, plurals, possessives, and other syntactical aspects of English. The conceptual base of ASL, however, is maintained in most of these sign systems.

The most commonly used systems of Manually Coded English are Signed English, Seeing Essential English (SEE I), Signing Exact English (SEE II), and Contact Signing. These sign systems are only used in a Total Communication approach. (As Chapter 8 explains, Total Communication refers to the use of a communication system that involves a form of sign language, use of residual hearing through amplification, speechreading, and speech production.) There are many similarities between the different systems of Manually Coded English; someone who uses one system can often communicate fairly easily with someone who uses another.

Signed English

Signed English is an educational tool meant to be used with speech and amplification. It is designed to represent English as closely as possible. It uses sign words based on American Sign Language, with one sign used to represent each word. Signed English also uses fourteen special signs (markers) to indicate past tense of verbs, plural nouns, pronouns, possessives, comparatives, superlatives, and other elements of grammar. With these markers and signs, language can be conveyed visually in English word order.

Seeing Essential English (SEE I)

This system was created by a deaf teacher of the deaf and further developed by a committee which included linguists. The signs in this system were based on the root of the word and not on the meaning of the word. This was a radical departure from systems based on ASL signs. For example, the word "gene" was considered to be the root for both the words "general" and "generous," and signs were developed that incorporated the root for "gene" in both of these words. Of course, there is no relationship between the words "general" and "generous," and this system has become generally disregarded by educators of the deaf and the deaf community.

Signing Exact English (SEE II)

Signing Exact English (SEE II) was a spinoff from SEE I. The difference is that the system is based on the "two out of three" rule: Is the word spelled the same? Does the word sound the same? Does the word mean the same thing? If any two of these are the same, then the same sign is used to represent different words. If only one of these is true, different signs are used. For example, "right," "rite," and "write" are signed differently because the spelling and meaning are different. On the other hand, only one sign is used for "bear" in the phrases "to bear a burden," "to bear a child," and "to meet a bear," because only the meaning is different.

Another feature of this system is that it retains the ASL sign whenever it is clear and unambiguous. However, when an ASL sign can be interpreted several different ways, a letter or initial is added to the sign to make it more clear. For example, the base sign for "face" is used with the addition of an "L" handshape to indicate "lovely" or a "p" handshape to indicate "pretty."

CONTACT SIGNING (PIDGIN SIGN ENGLISH)

Contact Signing (formerly known as Pidgin Sign English) uses a combination of vocabulary and grammar from both English and ASL. Signs are presented in English word order but retain the literal meaning of the ASL signs. For example, "He ran out of paper" would be signed using the ASL sign for "used up," rather than the sign for "ran." No sign markers are used to indicate grammatical elements.

FINGERSPELLING

It is possible to have an entire conversation using only the hand configurations for the twenty-six letters of the English alphabet. However, this is quite tiresome for a lengthy conversation and is difficult to follow.

Most individuals who use sign language (both ASL and Manually Coded English systems) use fingerspelling for parts of their conversation. For example, a person might spell the name of someone they are talking about, followed by the first initial of that person's name. Thereafter, that person is referred to by the initial and it is not necessary to spell the name each time. Fingerspelling may also be used for a technical word for which a sign is not available.

It is relatively simple to learn the twenty-six hand configurations necessary to be able to fingerspell. At one time, there was a method known as the Rochester Method which relied totally on fingerspelling. This is rarely used today.

REFERENCES

Bernstein, Harry, ed. (1990) *Manual Communication: Implications for Education.* Washington, DC: Gallaudet University Press.

National Information Center on Deafness. (1987) *Communicating with Deaf People: An Introduction.* Washington, DC: Galluadet University Press.

Jensema, Carl. (1996) Personal Communication.

APPENDIX B

READING LIST

Adam, Arlie, Pam Fortier, Gail Sclel, Margaret Smith, and Christine Soland. (1990) *Listening to Learn: A Handbook for Parents with Hearing Impaired Children.* Washington, DC: Alexander Graham Bell Association.

Allen, Peter. (1993) *Understanding Ear Infections.* Self-published by Peter Allen, Australia.

Altman, Ellyn. (1988) *Talk with Me.* Washington, DC: Alexander Graham Bell Association.

Anderson, Winifred, Stephen Chitwood, and Deidre Hayden. 1990. *Negotiating The Special Education Maze: A Guide for Parents and Teachers.* Bethesda, MD: Woodbine House.

Barnes, Judith, Darla Franz, and Wallace Bruce, eds. (1994) *Pediatric Cochlear Implants: An Overview of Options and Alternatives in Education and Rehabilitation.* Washington, DC: AG Bell.

Benderly, Beryl Leiff. (1980) *Dancing without Music: Deafness in America.* New York: Anchor/Doubleday.

Bornstein, Harry. (1987) *The Signed English School Book.* Washington, DC: Kendall Green Publications.

Bradford, Tom. (1991) *Say That Again, Please.* Dallas, TX: Tom Bradford.

Bragg, Bernard. (1981) *Tales from a Clubroom.* Washington, DC: Gallaudet College Press.

Calvert, Donald R. (1986) *Physicians' Guide to the Education of Hearing-Impaired Children.* Washington, DC: AG Bell.

Cline, Foster and Jim Fay. (1990) *Parenting with Love and Logic: Teaching Children Responsibility.* Golden, CO: Love & Logic Press.

Cochlear Implants: Audiological Foundations. (1993) San Diego, CA: Singular Pub. Group.

Cochlear Implants in Young Deaf Children. (1989) Boston: College Hill Press.

Cohen, Leah Hager. (1994) *Train Go Sorry: Inside a Deaf World.* New York: Houghton Mifflin.

Cole, Elizabeth B. (1992) *Listening and Talking: A Guide to Promoting Spoken Language in Young Hearing Impaired Children.* Washington, DC: AG Bell.

Cornett, R. Orin and Mary Elsie Daisey. (1992) *Cued Speech Resource Book for Parents of Deaf Children.* Raleigh, NC: National Cued Speech Association.

Davis, Dorinne S. (1994) *A Parent's Guide to Middle Ear Infections.* Stanhope, NJ: Hear You Are.

Deafness in Perspective. (1986) San Diego, CA: College-Hill Press.

Deafness and Communication: Assessment and Training. (1982) Baltimore, MD: Williams & Wilkins.

Dockery, Karen. (1993) *When a Hug Won't Fix the Hurt.* Washington, DC: AG Bell.

Estabrooks, Warren. (1994) *Auditory Verbal Therapy for Parents and Professionals.* Washington, DC: AG Bell.

Estabrooks, Warren and Lois Birkenshaw-Fleming. (1994) *Hear and Listen! Talk and Sing!* Washington, DC: AG Bell.

Family Resource Center on Disabilities. (1993) *How To Get Services By Being Assertive: For Parents of Children with Disabilities and Their Helpers.* Chicago: Family Resource Center on Disabilities.

Family Resource Center on Disabilities. (1993) *How to Organize an Effective Parent/Advocacy Group and Move Bureaucracies.* Chicago: Family Resource Center on Disabilities.

Fay, Jim and Foster Cline. (1994) *Grandparenting with Love and Logic: Practical Solutions to Today's Grandparenting Challenges.* Boulder, CO: Nav Press.

Flexer, Carol. (1994) *Facilitating Hearing and Listening in Young Children.* San Diego, CA: Singular Publishing Group.

Forecki, Marcia Calhoun. (1985) *Speak to Me.* Washington, DC: Gallaudet College Press.

Gallaudet Encyclopedia of Deaf People and Deafness. (1987) New York, NY: McGraw-Hill.

Gannon, Jack. (1981) *Deaf Heritage: A Narrative History of Deaf America.* Silver Spring, MD: National Association of the Deaf.

Garretson, Merv. (1984) *Words from a Deaf Child and Other Verses.* Silver Spring, MD: Fragonard Press.

Geers, Ann E. and Jean S. Moog. (1994) *Effectiveness of Cochlear Implants and Tactile Aids for Deaf Children: Sensory Aids Study at Central Institute.* Washington, DC: AG Bell.

Golan, Lew. (1995) *Reading Between the Lips: A Totally Deaf Man Makes It in the Mainstream.* Washington, DC: AG Bell.

Gray, Daphne. (1995) *Yes, You Can, Heather: The Story of Heather Whitestone, Miss America 1995.* Grand Rapids, MI: Zondervan Publishers.

Greenberg, Judith. (1985) *What is the Sign for Friend?* New York: Franklin Watts.

Groce, Nora Ellen. (1985) *Everyone Here Spoke Sign Language: Hereditary Deafness on Martha's Vineyard.* Cambridge, MA: Harvard University Press.

Hairston, Ernest and Linwood Smith. (1983) *Black and Deaf in America.* Washington, DC: TJ Publishers.

Haspiel, George S. (1987) *Lipreading for Children.* Mill Valley, CA: Dragon Press.

Higgins, Paul C. (1980) *Outsiders in a Hearing World: A Sociology of Deafness.* Beverly Hills, CA: Sage Publications.

Holcomb, Roy. (1985) *Silence Is Golden, Sometimes.* Washington, DC: Dawn Sign Press.

International Organization for Education of the Hearing Impaired (IOEHI). (1993) *Guidelines for Evaluating Auditory Oral Programs for Children Who Are Hearing Impaired.* Washington, DC: AG Bell.

Jacobs, Leo M. (1989) *A Deaf Adult Speaks Out.* Washington, DC: Gallaudet University Press.

Kisor, Henry. (1990) *What's That Pig Outdoors?* New York: Hill and Wang.

Klein, Stanley and Maxwell Schleifer, eds. (1994) *It's Not Fair: Siblings of Children with Disabilities.* Reston, Va: Exceptional Parent.

Lane, Harlan L. (1993) *The Mask of Benevolence: Disabling the Deaf Community.* New York, NY: Vintage Books.

Ling, Daniel. (1984) *Early Intervention for Hearing Impaired Children: Oral Options.* Washington, DC: AG Bell.

Ling, Daniel. (1984) *Early Intervention for Hearing Impaired Children: Total Communication Options.* Washington, DC: AG Bell.

Luterman, David M. and Mark Ross. (1991) *When Your Child Is Deaf: A Guide for Parents.* Timonium, MD: York Press.

Luterman, David. (1979) *Counseling the Communicatively Disordered and their Families.* Boston: Little Brown and Co.

Luterman, David. (1987) *Deafness in the Family.* Boston: College Hill Press.

Lyons, Kenneth. (1995) *Understanding Hearing Loss.* London; Bristol, PA: J. Kingsley Publishers.

Mangiardi, Amanda. (1995) *Twenty-Five Ways to Promote Spoken Lanugage in Your Child with a Hearing Loss.* Washington, DC: AG Bell.

Marschark, Marc. (1993) *Psychological Development of Deaf Children.* New York, NY: Oxford University Press.

Maxon, Antonia and Diane Brackett. (1992) *The Hearing Impaired Child: Infancy through High School Years.* Boston: Butterworth Andover Medical Publications.

McArthur, Shirley. (1982) *Raising Your Hearing Impaired Child: A Guide for Parents.* Washington, DC: AG Bell.

McCormick, Barry. (1993) *Pediatric Audiology 0 to 5 years,* 2nd edition. San Diego, CA: Singular Publishing Group.

McCracken, Wendy. (1991) *Deaf-ability—Not Disability: A Guide for the Parents of Hearing Impaired Children.* Philadelphia, PA: Multilingual Matters.

Meadow, Kathryn. (1980) *Deafness and Child Development.* Berkeley, CA: University of California Press.

Mendelsohn, Jacqueline and Bonnie Fairchild. (1983) *Years of Challenge: A Guide for Parents of Deaf Adolescents.* Washington, DC: American Society for Deaf Children.

Moore, Matthew S. (1992) *For Hearing People Only: Answers to Some of the Most Commonly Asked Question about the Deaf Community, Its Culture, and the "Deaf Reality."* Rochester, NY: Deaf Life Press.

Moores, Donald F. (1987) *Educating the Deaf: Psychology, Principles, and Practices.* Boston: Houghton Mifflin.

Multicultural Issues in Deafness. (1993) White Plains, NY: Longman.

Oberkotter, Mildred L. (1990) *The Possible Dream: Mainstream Experiences of Hearing-Impaired Students.* Washington, DC: AG Bell.

Oral Interpreting: Principles and Practices. (1984) Baltimore, MD: University Park Press.

Paul, Peter V. (1990) *Education and Deafness.* New York: Longman.

Pluznik, Nehama and Rochelle Sobel. (1986) *Messy Monsters, Jungle Joggers and Bubble Baths.* Potomac, MD: Elan Publishing House.

Riski, Maureen Cassidy and Nikolas Klalow. (1995) *Patrick Gets Hearing Aids*. Naperville, IL: Phonak (850 E. Diehl Rd., P.O. Box 3017, Naperville, IL 60566).

Ross, Mark, ed. (1990) *Hearing Impaired Children in the Mainstream*. Timonium, MD: York Press.

Schein, Jerome Daniel. (1989) *At Home Among Strangers*. Washington, DC: Gallaudet University Press.

Schwartz, Sue and Joan E. Heller Miller. (1996) *The New Language of Toys*. Bethesda, MD: Woodbine House.

Schwartz, Sue. (n/d) *Communication, Consistency and Caring: A Parents' Guide to Raising a Hearing Impaired Child* (brochure). Washington, DC: AG Bell.

Scouten, Edward L. (1984) *Turning Points in the Education of Deaf People*. Danville, IL: Interstate Printers and Publishers.

Simmons-Martin, Audrey and Karen Glover Rossi. (1990) *Partners in Language Development*. Washington, DC: AG Bell.

Star, Robin Rognoff. (1980) *We Can*. Vol. 1 and 2. Washington, DC: AG Bell.

They Grow in Silence: Understanding Deaf Children and Adults. (1991) Austin, TX: PRO-ED.

Tucker, Bonnie Poitras. (1994) *Federal Disability Law in a Nutshell*. St. Paul, MN: West Publishing.

Tucker, Bonnie Pointrus. (1995) *The Feel of Silence*. Philadelphia: Temple University Press.

Turkington, Carol. (1992) *The Encyclopedia of Deafness and Hearing Disorders*. New York: Facts on File.

Tye-Murray, Nancy. (1982) *Cochlear Implants and Children: A Handbook for Parents, Teachers, and Speech and Hearing Professionals*. Washington, DC: AG Bell.

Vernon, McCay. (1995) *The Psychology of Deafness: Understanding Deaf and Hard-of-Hearing People*. Washington, DC: Gallaudet University Press.

Vodehnal, Susan K. (1981) *They Do Belong: Mainstreaming the Hearing Impaired*. Englewood, CO: Listen Foundation.

Wilcox, Sherman. (1991) *Learning to See: American Sign Language as a Second Language*. Englewood Cliffs, NJ: Prentice Hall Regents.

Zazove, Philip. (1994) *When the Phone Rings, My Bed Shakes*. Washington, DC: Gallaudet University Press.

Appendix **C**

National Organizations Serving Individuals Who Are Deaf or Hard of Hearing

Listed below are many of the national organizations that provide services for individuals who are deaf or hard of hearing. If you are looking for local organizations that can assist you, the audiological center where your child was diagnosed as deaf or hard of hearing should be able to refer you to the proper services in your area. For educational information, call the special education division of your local school system and ask for the program for students who are deaf or hard of hearing.

Academy of Rehabilitative Audiology

P.O. Box 26532
Minneapolis, MN 55426
Voice: 612-920-6098

Alexander Graham Bell Association for the Deaf

3417 Volta Place, NW
Washington, DC 20007
Voice/TTY: 202-337-5220
Toll Free: 800-HEAR-KID

A nonprofit membership organization that supports the availability of all communication options and promotes the opportunity for children who are deaf to learn to speak for themselves. The Association provides financial aid programs, publications, educational programs, advocacy services, and free first-year membership for parents. Three association sections serve different populations:

- **International Organization for the Education of the Hearing Impaired (IOEHI)** consists of professionals in the field and works to improve oral/auditory programs.
- **Parents' Section (PS)** consists of community-based support groups which promote early diagnosis, appropriate amplification, and development of speech and listening skills in children who are deaf or hard of hearing.
- **Oral Hearing-Impaired Section (OHIS)** is an active service group of deaf adults which meets with parents and youth to provide guidance, serve as role models, and sponsor conferences, workshops, and family outings.

American Academy of Otolaryngology

Head and Neck Surgery
One Prince St.
Alexandria, VA 22314
Voice: 703-836-4444
TTY: 703-519-1585

Provides information about medicine relating to otolaryngology or head and neck surgery. Provides pamphlets about ear problems and makes referrals to physicians.

AMERICAN ATHLETIC ASSOCIATION OF THE DEAF, INC.

3607 Washington Blvd., #4
Ogden, UT 84403-1737
Voice: 801-393-8710
TTY: 801-393-7916

Sanctions and promotes state, regional, and national basketball, softball, and volleyball tournaments. Coordinates international participation of United States athletes who are deaf in the World Games for the Deaf, and Sponsors A.A.A.D. Hall of Fame and Deaf Athlete of the Year.

AMERICAN DEAFNESS AND REHABILITATION ASSOCIATION (ADARA)

P.O. Box 251554
Little Rock, AR 72225
Voice/TTY: 501-868-8850

Focuses primarily on professional development, continuing education, and practical research dissemination to and for professionals in deafness-related human service fields.

AMERICAN HEARING RESEARCH FOUNDATION

55 E. Washington St., Suite 2022
Chicago, IL 60602
Voice: 312-726-9670

Keeps physicians and laymen informed of latest developments in hearing research and education.

AMERICAN LARYNGOLOGICAL, RHINOLOGICAL AND OTOLOGICAL SOCIETY, INC.

10 S. Broadway, Suite 1401
St. Louis, MO 63102
Voice: 314-621-6550

Publishes articles about assistive listening devices and hearing aids.

AMERICAN SOCIETY FOR DEAF CHILDREN

2848 Arden Way, Suite 210
Sacramento, CA 95825-1373
Voice/TTY/Toll Free: 800-942-2732

Provides information and support to parents and families with children who are deaf or hard of hearing. Supports the use of sign language in families with a deaf member.

AMERICAN SPEECH-LANGUAGE-HEARING ASSOCIATION

10801 Rockville Pike
Rockville, MD 20852
Voice/TTY: 301-897-5700
Toll Free: 800-638-8255

Professional organization for speech and language pathologists and audiologists. Can provide information about where to obtain services in your area.

ASSOCIATION FOR PERSONS WITH SEVERE HANDICAPS (TASH)

29 W. Susquehanna Ave., Suite 210
Baltimore, MD 21204
Voice: 410-828-8274

An organization for parents and professionals which advocates for a dignified lifestyle for individuals with severe and multiple disabilities. Publishes a newsletter and other publications.

AUDITORY/VERBAL INTERNATIONAL, INC.

2121 Eisenhower Ave., Suite 402
Alexandria, VA 22314
Voice: 703-739-1049
TTY: 703-739-0874

Professional and parent organization which promotes the use of Auditory Verbal Therapy with individuals who are deaf or hard of hearing.

BEGINNINGS FOR PARENTS OF HEARING IMPAIRED CHILDREN, INC.

3900 Barrett Drive, Suite 100
Raleigh, NC 27609
Toll Free: 1-800-541-4327
Voice/TDD: 919-571-4843
FAX: 919-571-4846

In an unbiased, family-centered atmosphere, provides emotional support and information and referrals about all methodologies and different educational programs for families with children who are deaf or hard of hearing.

BETTER HEARING INSTITUTE

5021B Backlick Road
Annandale, VA 22003

Voice/TTY: 703-642-0580
Toll Free: 800-EAR-WELL
A private, nonprofit, educational organization dedicated to informing the public about hearing loss. Provides written information on hearing loss and the different kinds of help that is available, including lists of places to go for help with hearing loss.

CALIFORNIA STATE UNIVERSITY AT NORTHRIDGE
Northridge, CA 91033
V/TDD 818-885-2611
First university program to fully integrate deaf students on a large scale into the mainstream of university life. Provides full support services and access to 4600 courses in 52 academic majors leading to Bachelor's and Master's degrees.

CAPTIONED FILMS/VIDEOS
Modern Talking Picture Services, Inc.
5000 Park St. N
St. Petersburg, FL 33709
Voice/TTY/Toll Free: 800-237-6213
Loans educational and entertainment captioned films.

CAPTIONS, INC.
2619 Hyperion Ave.
Los Angeles, CA 90027
Toll Free: 1-800-CAPTION
Provides closed and open captions for major Hollywood studios as well as corporations and other individuals interested in captioning videos or films.

COMPUTER PROMPTING AND CAPTIONING CO.
1010 Rockville Pike, Suite 306
Rockville, MD 20852
Voice: 301-738-8487
TTY: 301-738-8489
Toll Free: 800-977-6678
Provides closed captioning in English, Spanish, and French as well as subtitling in over 20 additional languages for schools, colleges, corporations, and television. Also develops and sells captioning software.

CONFERENCE OF EDUCATIONAL ADMINISTRATORS SERVING THE DEAF

c/o Lexington School for the Deaf
75th St. and 30th Ave.
Jackson Heights, NY 11370
Voice: 718-899-8800
TTY: 718-899-3030

Promotes professional development through annual conventions, special workshops, and conferences, certification activities, advocacy for legislation and services, and information and referral regarding education of the deaf.

CONVENTION OF AMERICAN INSTRUCTORS OF THE DEAF

c/o Helen Lovato
PO Box 377
Bedford, TX 76095-0377
Voice: 817-354-8414
TTY: 510-794-2409

Promotes professional development through biennial conventions, special workshops and conferences; advocacy for legislation and services to benefit education of the deaf; information services on the education and services for the deaf; evaluating and captioning educational materials.

COUNCIL FOR EXCEPTIONAL CHILDREN

1920 Association Dr.
Reston, VA 22091
Voice/TTY: 703-620-3660

Promotes the education of all exceptional children, both disabled and gifted, through legislation and other government action, and the development of standards for professional personnel. Provides educational information and materials such as the ERIC Clearinghouse to teachers, administrators, other related professionals, and parents. Offers computer research services and sponsors conferences, technical training sessions, and special projects.

CENTER FOR BICULTURAL STUDIES, INC.

5506 Kenilworth Ave., Suite 105
Riverdale, MD 20737
Voice: 301-277-3945

TTY:301-277-3944
FAX: 301-699-5226
Provides classes and workshops on Deaf culture and American Sign Language.

CUED SPEECH CENTER, INC.
304 E. Jones St.
P.O. Box 31345
Raleigh, NC 27622
Voice/TTY: 919-828-1218
FAX: 919-828-1862
A resource center which provides information, instruction, and support services regarding Cued Speech, for deaf and hard-of-hearing people of all ages, their families, and professionals who work with them.

DEAFPRIDE, INC.
1350 Potomac Ave., SE
Washington, DC 20005
Voice/TTY: 202-675-6700
Educates both deaf and hearing people about the rights of deaf people, specifically for access, via classes, conferences, and, workshops. Deafpride Interpreting Services provides interpreters under contract and works for the provision of accessible services for deaf consumers and the development of access policies where they are not established.

EAR FOUNDATION
2000 Church St., Box 111
Nashville, TN 37236
Voice/TTY: 615-329-7807
Toll Free: 800-545- HEAR
Provides college scholarships for deaf individuals. Provides continuing medical education program for physicians on a variety of ear disorders. Has a network and support group for those with Meniere's Disease.

GALLAUDET UNIVERSITY
800 Florida Ave, NE
Washington, DC 20002-3695

Voice/TTY: 202-651-5000
Toll Free: 800-672-6720
Gallaudet is a liberal arts university for deaf students with a commitment to education, public service, and research in the area of deafness. In addition to an undergraduate and graduate program, Gallaudet has two tuition-free federally funded model schools: Kendall Demonstration Elementary School and the Model Secondary School for the Deaf. Other services at Gallaudet include:

- **GALLAUDET UNIVERSITY LIBRARY** (202-651-5566)—The library has the world's leading collection on deafness and deaf people. Gallaudet Media Distribution Center distributes videos and films on deafness and sign language to the general public, as well as to parent groups, educators and others interested in deafness.
- **NATIONAL INFORMATION CENTER ON DEAFNESS** (voice: 202-651-5051; TTY: 202-651-5052; FAX: 202-651-5054)—NICD provides information related to deafness, hearing loss and Gallaudet University. Has access to a multitude of resources and experts on and off the campus and collects information from around the country.

HOUSE EAR INSTITUTE

2100 W. Third St., 5th Floor
Los Angeles, CA 90057
Voice: 213-485-4431
TTY: 213-483-0112
A private nonprofit organization which has become a world center for basic and applied research into disorders of the ear, and for advanced training of ear specialists. Has been involved with cochlear implants. Has a Parent to Parent Talkline available at the voice number above.

INTERNATIONAL HEARING SOCIETY

20361 Middlebelt Rd.
Livonia, MI 48152
Voice: 810-478-2610
Toll Free: 800-521-5247
Professional association of specialists who test for hearing loss and dispense hearing aids. This organization is responsible for the qualifications, competencies,

and accreditation of professionals in this area. There is a Hearing Aid Hotline, which provides free information for deaf individuals and their families about hearing loss and assistive listening devices.

JOHN TRACY CLINIC
806 West Adams Blvd.
Los Angeles, CA 90007
Voice: 213-748-5481
TTY: 213-747-2924
Toll Free: 800-522-4582
Offers free correspondence course and summer programs for parents of deaf and hard of hearing children.

NATIONAL ASSOCIATION OF THE DEAF
814 Thayer Ave.
Silver Spring, MD 20910-4500
Voice/TTY: 301-587-1788
Provides information and nationwide referrals and evaluation of media for captioning recommendations. Publishes and sells books in the Halex House store. Does research funded by government research and demonstration grants. Operates National Association of the Deaf Law Center (301-587-7732), which develops and provides a variety of legal services and programs to the deaf community. The NAD Legal Defense Fund (LDF) handles lawsuits which affect the deaf community.

NATIONAL CAPTIONING INSTITUTE, INC.
1900 Gallows Road, Suite 3000
Vienna, VA 22182
Voice/TTY: 703-917-7600
Toll Free: 800-374-3986
Advocates closed captioning and provides television access to deaf people by captioning prerecorded and live television programs for all broadcast networks, cable channels, home videos, and commercials.

NATIONAL CUED SPEECH ASSOCIATION
P.O. Box 31345

Raleigh, NC 27622-1345

Voice/TTY: 919-828-1218

Membership organization which provides advocacy and support on using cued speech. Information and services provided to deaf people of all ages, their families and friends, and professionals who work with them.

NATIONAL FRATERNAL SOCIETY OF THE DEAF

1300 W. Northwest Highway

Mt. Prospect, IL 60056

Voice: 708-392-9282

TTY: 708-392-1409

Sells life insurance to deaf people, their relatives, and hearing people who work in the field of deafness. Scholarships are given annually to Society members entering college. Outstanding graduates of U.S. and Canadian schools for the deaf are given U.S. Savings Bonds.

NATIONAL INFORMATION CENTER FOR CHILDREN AND YOUTH WITH DISABILITIES (NICHCY)

P.O. Box 1492

Washington, DC 20013

Voice: 202-884-8200

Toll Free: 800-695-0285

Provides information about children and adolescents with disabilities to parents, professionals, students, advocates, and adults with disabilities. Answers questions, researches, develops and shares information, provides advice to groups of people, publishes newsletters and other publications, and connects people nationwide who are working on similar problems.

NATIONAL INSTITUTES ON DEAFNESS AND OTHER COMMUNICATIVE DISORDERS

National Institutes of Health

9000 Rockville Pike

Bldg. 31

Room 3C-35

Bethesda, MD 20892

Voice: 301-496-7243

TTY: 301-402-0252

Conducts research and symposiums on deafness and other communicative disorders.

NATIONAL TECHNICAL INSTITUTE FOR THE DEAF

Rochester Institute of Technology
52 Lomb Memorial Dr.
Rochester, NY 14623-5604
Voice: 716-475-6834
TTY: 716-475-6205

The only technical college in the world exclusively for deaf students. Has cross registration with Rochester Institute of Technology. Degrees offered are Certificate, Diploma, Associate, Bachelor's, Master's. Study in business and computer careers; science and health education. Academic support services available. Interpreters, tutors, and note-takers provided for students at RIT who request them. Has "Vestibule Summer," which invites eleventh-grade deaf students to explore career and college options.

NIDCD HEREDITARY HEARING IMPAIRMENT

Resource Registry
Boys Town National Research Hospital
555 N. 30th St.
Omaha, NE 68131
Voice/TTY/Toll Free: 800-320-1171
FAX: 402-498-6331

Publishes educational materials related to deafness. Has a newsletter and bulletin. Provides Fact Sheets on subjects such as Genetics, Syndromes, Balance disorders. Maintains a registry of individuals who are deaf who are interested in participating in research on deafness.

REGISTRY OF INTERPETERS FOR THE DEAF

8630 Fenton St., Suite 324
Silver Spring, MD 20910-3919
Voice: 301-608-0050
TTY: 301-608-0562
FAX: 301-608-0508

Acts as certifying body for sign language and oral interpreters. Provides lists of certified interpreters by state, and confirms certification of specific interpreters. Furnishes general information on interpreting and offers publications on interpretation to interpreter training programs.

SELF HELP FOR HARD OF HEARING PEOPLE, INC.

7910 Woodmont Ave., Suite 1200
Bethesda, MD 20814
Voice: 301-657-2248
TTY: 301-657-2249

Provides information, education, referral, and advisory services to deaf and hard of hearing people and interested hearing people. Promotes awareness about hearing loss, assistive devices, and alternative communication access through publications, exhibits, and presentations.

TELECOMMUNICATIONS FOR THE DEAF, INC.

8719 Colesville Rd. Suite 300
Silver Spring, MD 20910
Voice: 301-589-3786
TTY: 301-589-3006

A TDD/PC consumer-oriented organization that installs TDDs and TV decoders for deaf people. Supports legislation and advocates the use of TDDs in the public, private, and government sectors.

TRIPOD

2901 North Keystone St.
Burbank, CA 91504-1620
Voice/TTY 818-972-2080
FAX: 818-972-2090

Provides packets of information for parents who have a child who is deaf. Has videos for sale and for rent in the area of deafness. Also has an educational program for children who are deaf.

VOICE FOR HEARING IMPAIRED CHILDREN

124 Eglington Ave. West, Suite 420
Toronto, Ontario, Canada M4R 2G8
Voice/TTY: 416-487-7719

Nonprofit organization for families with a deaf member and professionals. Particularly focuses on the Auditory Verbal philosophy.

Index

About the Editor:

Sue Schwartz received her master's degree in Speech and Hearing from Central Institute for the Deaf in St. Louis, MO, and her Ph.D. in Curriculum and Instruction with an emphasis in Family Counseling from the University of Maryland. She developed the Parent Infant Program in the Programs for Deaf and Hard of Hearing Students in the Montgomery County, Maryland Public Schools, where she currently works as Provider of Family Services. Dr. Schwartz is also the co-author of *The New Language of Toys* (Woodbine House, 1996).